OUTSMARTING THE SAT

OUTSMARTING
the SAT

An Expert Tutor Reveals Her
Proven Techniques, Strategies,
and Confidence-Building Exercises
That Will Maximize Your Score

ELIZABETH KING

TEN SPEED PRESS
Berkeley | Toronto

Ten Speed Press and the Ten Speed Press colophon are registered trademarks of Random House, Inc.

Author photo by Tommy Manuel.
Excerpt on page 28 reprinted from Fodor Dostoyevsky, Notes from the Underground, 1864.
Excerpt on page 30 reprinted from Jerome K. Jerome, Three Men in a Boat, 1889.
Text on pages 89–90 from Leigh Esposito.

The SAT® is a registered trademark of the College Entrance Examination Board, which neither
sponsors nor endorses this product.

Library of Congress Cataloging-in-Publication Data

King, Elizabeth.
    Outsmarting the SAT : an expert tutor reveals her proven techniques, strategies, and confidence-
building exercises that will maximize your score /
Elizabeth King.
        p. cm.
    Includes index.
    Summary: "One of the country's top test-prep tutors presents her innovative core strategies for
optimal results on the SAT in a book designed for students of all levels, featuring detailed explanations and practice problems"—Provided by publisher.
    1. SAT (Educational test)—Study guides. I. Title.
    LB2353.57.K56 2008
    378.1'662--dc22
                        2008021113

ISBN 978-1-58008-927-2

Printed in the United States of America

Cover design by Katy Brown
Text design by Jeff Brandenburg

11 10 9 8 7 6 5 4 3 2

First edition

CONTENTS

ACKNOWLEDGMENTS

When I was sitting in my little New York apartment two years ago and I thought "I've got to write a book," it's safe to say that I didn't have the foggiest idea what I was getting myself into. Without the following folks (and a legion of others, who know who they are), *Outsmarting the SAT* would still be only a twinkle in my eye.

Thanks to:

Jeff Herman, my agent; I'm grateful for our serendipitous meeting and for your extraordinary knowledge of the business. Designers Jeff Brandenburg and Katy Brown, copyeditor Kristi Hein, and proofreader Elisabeth Beller: each of you has gone above and beyond the call of duty on this project. Thank you so much for your patience, fortitude, and incredible willingness to deal with 342 hand drawn illustrations. Melissa Moore, my editor at Ten Speed, you were the one who envisioned what this book really could be and gloriously dragged me through the process. The product is as much yours as it is mine. You're a champion.

My students, my guinea pigs: thanks for your insight, enthusiasm, and patience while I experimented with different test-taking tactics. It is your flexibility that allowed for the development of these tried-and-true ideas.

Leigh Esposito, thanks for your contribution of the fantastically tedious and boring passage about the Netherlands. It's truly an achievement in ennui. Nikki Geula, my colleague and friend, you so often see more capability in me than I even see in myself. Dan Klein, you're a model of what reaching for personal excellence can truly be—thanks for continually inspiring it in me. Heather Forgione, you've been my tutoring go-to girl since day one; thank you for your endless encouragement and empathy. Mark Syben, thank you for modeling true bravery—you make writing a book look like child's play. Tommy Manuel and Claudette Ramos, you've been my cheerleaders and anchors: you've read, typed, and contributed in my most overwhelmed moments and generally tolerated and applauded me while I ate, slept, and dreamt the SAT. You make my life bright in so many ways.

Karl and Lee Syben, my parents, whose love for the dictionary, wild creativity, and general excellence convinced me that I could create and achieve anything. This book is for you, of course.

INTRODUCTION

What will it really take for you to improve your score on the SAT? Look, you're a teenager, you're busy, and you probably have what feels like way too much on your plate already. You've got sports, clubs, a job, community service, stacks of schoolwork, friends, and family, and you don't have a minute to waste on anything, let alone SAT prep that isn't going to pay off. Maybe you even have college applications on your mind.

I know you. I talk to and teach students like you every day. Of course you want a higher SAT score, but not at the expense of what feels like your last few hours of freedom during the week. Believe me, we're on the same page.

So here's the truth: maximizing your score on the SAT takes effort, no matter what your score already is. Fortunately for us, the SAT is not a test of everything you were ever taught in high school. In fact, the SAT tests a relatively short list of specific skills. Even the questions themselves are fairly predictable. You will see incredible score gains if you master these specific skills and become familiar with the test's different types of questions. If you're an average student, I can help you brush up on skills that may always have been tough for you, show you what this test is really all about, and bump your total score a good 200 to 300 points. If you're one of those naturally good standardized test takers, I can help you get well into the 700s on each section. (Perfection? I leave that to you.)

We'll go through the process together. Here's the plan: This book is written as though I were sitting right next to you during a series of private tutoring sessions. Since my end of the bargain is to show you everything you need to know and expect on the test, I've tried to make sure the book directly reflects what I would teach you and the sort of notes we would generate if we were to meet and work together. Just like I would if we were hanging out at your kitchen table, I've broken up the material into smaller lessons and taken the time to explain the most important details of each topic. Looking at each topic individually can completely change how you see, understand, and answer its questions.

Still, for your score to increase, you need to hold up your end of the bargain. Merely owning this book or sleeping with it under your pillow the night before test day isn't going to cut it. But don't worry: most likely you won't have to read the book cover to cover, either. Since this book is written for students from all sorts of different schools and backgrounds, you're bound to find topics with which you're already comfortable. I do not expect you to pore over things you already know. Instead, your best bet is to grab a highlighter and mark the stuff that *is* new to you (even those concepts that are explained differently than you originally learned them)—then follow through and review! I want you to treat this book like it's a personal notebook, not the Holy Grail of standardized test prep. Make it your own. Scribble. Highlight. Circle. After all, this is *your* SAT.

You may use this book either by itself or concurrently with the sample tests in *The Official SAT Study Guide*. What's most important is that you *believe* you can do this. This process and these ideas *will work*. They always do. Be patient. Keep going. Good luck.

Fast Facts on All Things SAT

○ **Fact:** You should prepare for this test the way you're going to take it. Before we even begin, I should warn you not to hang out in your room watching TV with your cat and talking on the phone while you try to study. You can be flexible while you start to learn new math concepts or study vocabulary, but be sure you take at least one full, timed practice SAT before test day.

○ **Fact:** Every question on the SAT is worth 1 raw point, regardless of how difficult it is. On the Critical Reading section, it's possible to earn 67 raw points; on the Math section, you can earn a possible 54 raw points; and the Writing section contains a possible 49 raw points. These raw points are then weighted based on the difficulty of the question, then converted to a score between 200 and 800 for each section (with your essay score influencing your final Writing score).

○ **Fact:** Each correct answer earns you 1 point, each incorrect answer deducts ¼ point, and omitting an answer does nothing to your score. It's like making a $1 deposit in the bank every time you're correct, keeping all your money if you omit, and losing a quarter if you make a mistake.

○ **Fact:** SAT scoring is calibrated so that, overall, 500 is generally the average score on each section of the test. A 500 is earned by having a raw score that is half of the total raw points available on that section. This means if you answer half of the questions on each section and get each of them correct, you'll get at least a 500 on each section, or a 1,500 total.

○ **Fact:** Each question is assigned a level of difficulty between 1 and 5. I'll refer to difficulty levels throughout the book so you can easily see which problems are particularly challenging and focus on working your way up to them.

○ **Fact:** You are permitted to write in your test booklet, but only answers that appear on your bubble sheet are reviewed and scored.

○ **Fact:** You may want to practice using the bubble sheets that the College Board provides with their sample tests. If and when you skip a question—any question—you always run the risk of improperly filling out your answer sheet—a frustrating and heartbreaking scenario for any well-prepared test taker. I once had a student who consistently scored nearly perfectly on each practice SAT, but when he actually took the test he noticed in the last two minutes that he had 26 questions bubbled in a section with only 24 questions. Needless to say, he cancelled his scores. Pay careful attention when you choose to skip questions.

○ **Fact:** You have 72 hours after the SAT to cancel your scores.

○ **Fact:** I have an unusual guessing strategy. Statistically, randomly guessing when you can eliminate some answer choices should increase your score. However, those statistics are based on *completely random* guesses. On the SAT, I find that my students don't guess randomly; instead they develop a hunch about an answer, usually because it "sounds like" some other word, and frequently find that they guess incorrectly. Personally, I guess incorrectly nearly *every time*, so my rule for myself is always to omit. This philosophy is unorthodox, I know, but I'm just telling you what I tell the kids I work with. In short: if you're a lucky guesser, by all means, don't let me hold you back. If you're like me, you might want to consider leaving the answer bubble blank instead of guessing incorrectly and being penalized.

○ **Fact:** The SAT is extremely long. It breaks down like this:

One 25-minute Essay portion
Six 25-minute sections (two Math, two Critical Reading, one Writing, one Experimental)
Two 20-minute sections (one Math, one Critical Reading)
One 10-minute Writing portion

Additionally, the folks who proctor the SAT are not people sent out by the College Board; they're hired especially for the occasion. That means that your proctors may be proctoring for the first time, and it may take them a little time to get going. This comes with the territory. The latest I've ever gotten out of the test is around 1 P.M.

○ **Fact:** The already tedious SAT is made even longer by the inclusion of what is lovingly known as *the Experimental Section of Despair*. OK, no—it's only known as the "Experimental section," but I consider it cause for despair. Here's the scoop: because you've already agreed to sit through an entire SAT test, the College Board takes advantage of your commitment by including an extra, unscored section on the test. Do they tell you which section is unscored beforehand? No. You're expected to do an extra, full 25-minute section giving 100 percent effort so that the College Board can measure the fairness of potential test questions (for example, if you're an average scorer and you ace the experimental section, they'll know something's up). Even if you think you can tell which section is experimental, don't be so sure you're right and cop out. If you just happen to have an unusual set of math problems or a difficult reading passage and you blow it off, you could destroy your score.

○ **Fact:** You must bring something to eat during each of the lightning-fast 5-minute breaks. By this I do not mean a donut and a cola. In all seriousness, your brain needs food to function, so you'll need some protein and some carbohydrates. A banana, some peanut butter crackers, and a bottle of water will do. Oh, you're also not allowed to have any beverages on your desk while you're working and all your snacks need to be in your bag, hidden from sight.

○ **Fact:** It's new policy that you're not even allowed to *bring* a cell phone with you on test day. I once had a proctor who made everyone drop his or her cell into a shopping bag to be held during the test. Unless you want to—at best—put your cell into a giant grab bag and pray you get it back or—at worst—be turned away from the test center, you really should leave it at home.

○ **Fact:** If you write your essay in pen it will not be graded because the machine supposedly can't scan it. Why, in the twenty-first century, is this the case? I have *no* idea. Nevertheless, for the entire SAT, old-school #2 pencils are the only way to go. The rules also say that you're not supposed to use mechanical pencils. I know, "They are just like #2 pencils," you'll say; well, the risk is yours, but I wouldn't do it. You never know.

○ **Fact:** If a licensed psychologist has diagnosed you with a learning disability, you likely qualify for extra time on the test. You'll need a *Student Eligibility Form* that should be available in your local high school guidance counselor's office. Please be aware that you need to apply several months in advance to allow time for processing; you can find more information at www.collegeboard.com/ssd/student/index.html.

One last thought: It's really pretty difficult to get an 800 on any of the sections, if only because we're all human, which means we have a tendency to make mistakes. Imagine my anguish last October when I earned a score of 790 on the Critical Reading because *I forgot to turn the page and accidentally omitted the last two questions in the final section*! The lesson? If it can happen to me, it can happen to anyone. Make sure you've at least *seen* all the questions—don't get robbed!

Now, let's get going!

CRITICAL READING

CRITICAL READING OVERVIEW

The Critical Reading section contains two types of questions: Sentence Completion and Passage-Based Reading. The idea behind a Sentence Completion question is straightforward: you choose an appropriate vocabulary word that most effectively completes a given sentence from a selection of choices. The same thing goes for Passage-Based Reading questions: you read a passage and answer some multiple-choice questions about what you've read.

Overall, you'll see a total of 67 Critical Reading questions, which are usually made up of about 19 Sentence Completions and 48 Passage-Based Reading questions. These 67 questions are broken up into three timed sections, all of which include a few Sentence Completions and at least a dozen Passage-Based Reading questions. Two of these sections will be 25 minutes long, and the third will be 20 minutes long.

Each Critical Reading section starts with a set of Sentence Completion questions. The first 5 to 8 questions increase in difficulty predictably: the first question will be the easiest; the last will be the most difficult. The same is not true for the Passage-Based Reading questions. It is very important that you understand that the difficulty of reading questions is not incremental: questions of varying level of difficulty are all mixed up because questions are asked in the order of their line references (questions about the first paragraph will be first and questions about the concluding paragraph will be asked last). It's entirely possible for the last question in the section to be a level 2 and the first to be a level 5. That's why you really want to make sure you at least see each question in the Passage-Based Reading sections.

The Critical Reading section often ends up becoming the section in which students feel they need to buy themselves the most time to complete as many questions as possible. If this is you, this is what you need to know about how many questions you need to answer correctly to reach your goal score.

Shooting for Your Goal Score

I'm going to assume that if you're all college-bound students, you're all shooting for at least a 500 on every section of the test.

To score at least 500:

Answer 46 questions (36 correct/10 errors), for a raw score of 34.

To score at least 600:

Answer 62 questions (52 correct/10 errors), for a raw score of 50.

To score at least 700:

Answer 67 questions (64 correct/3 errors), for a raw score of 63.

Critical Reading Fast Facts

○ **Fact:** While I'll explain this idea in more detail later in the section, I'd like you to go into the Critical Reading section with an understanding that this is not a passage analysis test, where you read and respond to a passage like you might in your English class. Instead, this is a test of your critical-thinking skills—it measures how well you can arrive at the same conclusion (answer choice) as someone who has already read the passage—namely, the test maker.

○ **Fact:** The strength of your vocabulary affects your ability to answer both Sentence Completion and Passage-Based Reading questions. While it's obvious why not knowing a vocabulary word can trip you up on the Sentence Completions (you could get stuck if you need to know the difference between *metastasize* and *metamorphosis*, for example), it may be less intuitive in the reading passages. As you'll see, on the SAT the questions themselves aren't always challenging, so simple statements about a passage may be made to seem more complex by using tougher vocabulary. The most important thing to remember is that *an answer isn't necessarily incorrect just because you are not familiar with a vocabulary word it contains*.

○ **Fact:** There will be only one scored double reading passage per SAT. Sometimes an extra double reading appears as an experimental section (the top-secret unscored section I told you about earlier), but only one of them will be graded.

○ **Fact:** The Passage-Based Reading questions pose an extra danger for misbubbling—sometimes the first question is tucked at the foot of the page below the passage rather than starting on the next page. Be on the lookout so that you don't skew all of your answers!

sentence
completion

There are two major elements of outsmarting the Sentence Completions: a robust vocabulary and solid understanding of the ways these questions are constructed. In this section we'll discuss the importance of a great vocabulary, then we'll learn a step-by-step process that guides you through the basics, followed up by an insider's look at how the questions are made to seem more difficult.

Vocabulary

There is plenty to consider when preparing for the Sentence Completion section of the SAT. For starters, the size of your vocabulary absolutely matters. There is no better way to prepare for both the Sentence Completion and the Passage-Based Reading sections than to spend time learning new words. I'll show you a few good ways to do this in a moment, but for now I want to mention a couple of other ideas that are important when you're trying to motivate yourself to study vocabulary.

Now: The more vocabulary you know, the more familiar you will be with the answer choices on each Sentence Completion question and the more likely you will be to be able to eliminate your way to the correct choice. Basically, more vocabulary = more right answers = higher score.

Later: If you want to go to a top school, building your vocabulary is an absolutely worthwhile investment in your college education. Think about it: if the whole point of excelling on the SAT is to help you get into the best school for you, doesn't it make sense for you to be ready to perform at your best once you arrive on campus? That means you'll want to be able to communicate with your professors and fellow students as best you can, and the bigger your bank of words, the more successful you'll be.

The Long Run: Communicating effectively is extremely important in today's job market, especially when so much of modern business involves representing yourself, your product, and your ideas. The better you are at representing yourself, I guarantee, the further you'll go.

Techniques to Learn Vocabulary

There are all sorts of ways to increase the sheer size of your vocabulary, and though everyone works differently, these are the methods my students and I agree work the best.

The Classic Flashcard

Rest assured that you'll be making at least a few of these while studying for the SAT. There are always going to be stray words here and there that demand flashcards, and I'll admit that I still use them when I come across something new to memorize. The process of creating the classic flashcard is pretty straightforward: the new word goes on the front of the card, and the simplest definition you can find goes on the back. You don't need to bother copying and memorizing the full definition from the dictionary. On the SAT you'll find that each Sentence Completion question includes five distinct answer choices, all of which mean *entirely* different things. The test is so fast-paced that questions can't include answer choices that require you to take your time and really pick apart the deep, nuanced meanings of words; every answer choice must either be completely correct or dead wrong. Therefore, insofar as the SAT goes, as long as you know what words basically mean, you'll be in good shape.

If you want to upgrade your flashcard, you could put a little mnemonic device or sketch on the back of the card.

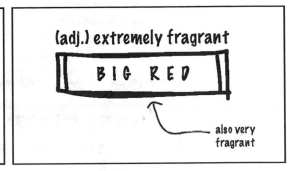

Word Roots Diagrams

Mastering word roots can be a little labor intensive but absolutely rewarding. For those of you who may not already know, the English language is an amalgam (a big mixture) of words taken from other languages—primarily the Romance languages (French, Spanish, Portuguese, and Italian) and German. Studying the *etymology* of a word (more or less the history of its existence) will help you not only remember more words but also figure out the meaning of words you come across that you've never seen before. Whenever you look up a word in the dictionary, take the time to look at all those italicized bits written before the actual definition. You'll eventually start to recognize and make connections between root meanings and the words into which they've evolved, thereby enhancing your ability to really remember new words and—even better—use them.

Plus, there's good news: you already have a huge number of these little guys buried in the language you use every day, so learning them and applying them to SAT words is actually pretty simple and makes learning new words easy. We're going to use your existing vocabulary more or less as a spider web in your brain to "catch" new words with stuff you already know.

Let's look at the root *mal* as an example:

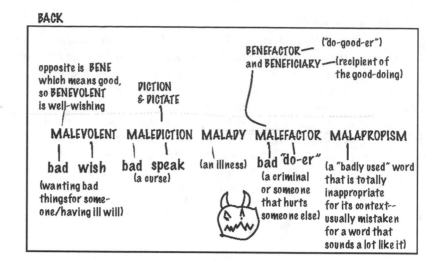

FRONT

root: **mal**
meaning: bad OR ill

BACK

opposite is BENE
which means good,
so BENEVOLENT
is well-wishing

DICTION
& DICTATE

BENEFACTOR— ("do-good-er")
and BENEFICIARY —(recipient of
the good-doing)

MALEVOLENT   MALEDICTION   MALADY   MALEFACTOR   MALAPROPISM

bad wish   bad speak   (an illness)   bad "do-er"   (a "badly used" word
                                                              that is totally
(wanting bad   (a curse)   (a criminal   inappropriate
things for some-   or someone   for its context--
one/having ill will)   that hurts   usually mistaken
                                             someone else)   for a word that
                                                             sounds a lot like it)

See? Just by learning one root, you learn five new vocabulary words and can find relationships to another seven—that's twelve words for the price of one! I recommend putting these roots together on bigger cards; the 5" by 8" ones usually work best, especially if you have big handwriting. Plus, when they're not so small, you always have room to add something new!

It's important that you always include everything you can think of on your root card—the idea is to use what you know to remember what you don't know, so the more familiar stuff you put on your card, the easier it will be for you to remember the new stuff.

Store-Bought Flashcards

It's true, your local bookstore offers all sorts of mass-produced preprinted flashcards, and plenty of students use them with varying degrees of success. Particularly if you're really busy, I say find a set that you like and start studying them every day. But I would encourage you to not kid yourself—many people, including me, find that memorized information is reinforced most effectively when we write and study the info ourselves. If you have time, skip the glossy commercial cards and pick up a pen. However, commercial cards are better than nothing.

Read in Your Free Time

There is one trump card that some students hold over others—they're avid readers. I have to be totally honest here: the students who are most successful on the Reading Comprehension section are those students who enjoy reading and generally do so for fun. If you're spending four hours a night in front of the television or playing video games, you're at a disadvantage because you're not putting yourself in a position to see and learn new words. "But that's what makes playing *Halo 3* so relaxing," you say. I know. But we both know that the student who reads for pleasure is likely to be a high scorer on the SAT. If you really want to learn, you have to read.

Sentence Completion, Step by Step

Let's take a look at the process I'd like you to use while you're working through the Sentence Completion questions. Many tutors use a process somewhat like this, which is a testament to its effectiveness. Make sure you take the time to read the explanations of *why* I recommend you follow these steps. When you really understand why you're doing what you're doing, you're likely to use the ideas more effectively and, of course, score higher.

Step 1: Read the Sentence

Please notice that I don't say: "Glance at the answer choices, get really overwhelmed, and then read the sentence." Simply read the sentence. Reading the sentence is especially important on more difficult questions, as the context of the sentence contributes to the difficulty level.

DON'T LOOK AT THE ANSWERS YET.

Looking at the answers at this stage of the game is the worst move you can make and precisely what the test maker is most hoping you'll do. Why? You're vulnerable when you're under pressure, at which point you're very likely to fall victim to the "I'm never going to get into college!" freak-out.

What could very well happen is that you'll see a word in the list of answer choices that "sounds good" (a classic student comment) or a word that you know really well, and you'll choose it without thinking it through and making sure it's an appropriate option.

Step 2: Choose a Guideword

A *guideword* is a simple word from your own vocabulary that could work in the sentence. When I say a simple vocabulary word, I mean *really* simple; sometimes it can be more an emotion or idea than a specific word; sometimes it's a phrase. What is most important is that you be as specific yet as flexible as you can be. If it helps you to write the simple word you come up with in the blank before you check out the choices, I say go for it—just jot it down quickly so that you don't waste time. More than anything, I just don't want you to get sucked in by a word that's fancy and "sounds good" but ultimately isn't the correct choice.

If you're struggling to find the right word, try out the following hints.

Look for Definitions Hidden within the Sentence

Within the first three-quarters of the sentence completions, you will usually be able to find a minidefinition or a couple of synonyms that will help you pick an appropriate word for the blank (or at least one of the blanks if there are two) right there in the sentence. And although high school students generally loathe grammar and punctuation, in this case, commas and semicolons can be your friends.

In each of the following examples, I've added italic emphasis to identify the hidden definition:

Procrastination can promote ongoing _____, *lethargy and disinterest in work.* [Possible answer: indolence.]

Architect Rem Koolhaas is best known for his *extraordinary* structural theory; his innovations as a writer and publisher are equally _____. [Possible answer: distinguishing.]

The president always appears in public *accompanied*: Secret Service officers _____ him everywhere he goes. [Possible answer: escort.]

In each of these examples a definition that expresses the answer choice is embedded right in the sentence. Although the definition usually comes right after the punctuation, it can appear before it, with the punctuation acting as a sentence divider. Before you start making up your own definitions from thin air, use what you've been given in the sentence to direct you.

Can't Come Up with a Perfect Word? Feel One

Because of the pressure you'll likely feel when taking the SAT, even the ability to access your everyday bank of language can be on the fritz. It's stress. It happens. If you are struggling to fill in a blank with your own vocabulary word and you're starting to panic, it's perfectly acceptable to put a doodle that represents an attitude or feeling into the blank. Some students like writing + or − for answer choices that must be positive or negative; others draw smiles or frowns; others circle synonyms and draw arrows. Whatever helps you focus on moving forward and finding the correct answer choice is fine.

Look for "Changeup" Words—They Denote a Shift in Mood, Tone, or Meaning

Just as a pitcher throws a changeup pitch in baseball, the test maker can throw the same sort of confusion at you by including words that change the speed or direction of the sentence. Basically, any word that makes you think the sentence is going one way but causes it to go another is a changeup. Be on the lookout for the following changeups:

However	Even so
In spite of	Although
Even though	Nevertheless
Yet	Despite
	Nonetheless

Here are some examples of changeups in action, with italic emphasis:

Claudette wanted to eat ice cream for breakfast; *however,* she ate oatmeal.

Although Claudette wanted to eat ice cream for breakfast, she ate oatmeal.

Despite wanting to eat ice cream for breakfast, Claudette ate oatmeal.

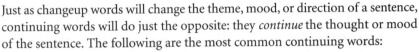 Also, be on the lookout for *still* and *while*, both of which act as changeups in more difficult sentences. I don't mean you should look for "Incredibly, Susan stood *still* for three hours" or "Jack is an expert at singing *while* biking." What you may come across, though, are the following:

> *While* Claudette wanted to eat ice cream for breakfast, she ate oatmeal.

> Claudette wanted to eat ice cream for breakfast; *still*, she ate oatmeal.

Look for "Continuing" Words—they Tell You that the Mood, Tone, or Meaning Stays the Same

Just as changeup words will change the theme, mood, or direction of a sentence, continuing words will do just the opposite: they *continue* the thought or mood of the sentence. The following are the most common continuing words:

Moreover	Additionally
Furthermore	Likewise

Using these strategies to identify a guideword will help you find the correct answer more consistently—and quickly!

Double Blanks

Sentence completions that involve two blanks have been known to strike fear in the hearts of students; they can be overwhelming as their answer choices include ten vocabulary words.

Eliminate a Pair by Ruling out One Word or the Other

When we're faced with double blanks, we can usually zero in on individual blanks, strategically eliminating complete answer pairs, often without even having to acknowledge several of the listed words. Keep in mind that the easiest blank to fill is often not the first, but the second—just one more way the test maker throws a curve ball. Consider the following:

EXAMPLE 1: LEVEL 3

Local deer have a _____ to appear in the most unlikely places: one recently wandered into a neighborhood elementary school to _____ for food.

- (A) passion . . assess
- (B) propensity . . forage
- (C) drive . . dispense
- (D) predilection . . peddle
- (E) remedy . . raid

Before we even attempt to answer this, let me start by saying: do not try to answer the question by simply reading the answer choices as one long list of words. I have had students sit in front of me and actually read aloud, "passion, assess, propensity, forage, drive, dispense, predilection. . . ." Doing this is going to waste your time and confuse you.

Here's how to single out a blank effectively: Let's start with what we know—the deer most likely show up at the elementary school to look for food (rather than to cook food or become food). Since this is a pretty safe assumption, we'll focus on eliminating words from the second column of answer choices first.

Immediately we can get rid of *assess* and *dispense*, as these are not remotely like our word *look*. That gets rid of A and C, which is great, even though we probably know what *passion* and *drive* mean, anyway. We can also get rid of the word *peddle* (choice D), which basically means to sell, just like a peddler would do in a fairytale. By eliminating *peddle* we're off the hook if we're not familiar with the word *predilection*. By knowing three words we've eliminated six as possibilities.

Here's the list as it would appear in your test booklet:

(A)   passion . . assess
(B)   propensity . . forage
(C)   drive . . dispense
(D)   predilection . . peddle
(E)   remedy . . raid

This is your SAT. Do what works for you.

Now we're down to B and E. Both second choices—*forage* and *raid*—could be what the deer do at the school. If you know what *remedy* or *propensity* means, you're in great shape. You'll most likely know *remedy* as part of the term *cold remedy*—it's something that makes you feel better. Deer don't have a *remedy* to appear in unlikely places. That leaves *propensity*, a natural inclination, so answer B is correct. And if you don't know what either *propensity* or *remedy* means, you could guess, depending on your personal guessing reliability.

Let's look at another example of a double-blank sentence completion.

EXAMPLE 2: LEVEL 4
Some airport concourses are so heavily laden with people and luggage that even the most _____ travelers find them virtually _____.

(A)   cumbersome . . cluttered
(B)   spry . . unnavigable
(C)   weary . . byzantine
(D)   seasoned . . unsullied
(E)   active . . passable

You should get an overall negative impression from this sentence right off the bat—it's a crowded airport full of people and luggage. These two blanks must be related to each other, but it's likely that they'll be opposites of some sort, like "even the most *tough* travelers find them virtually *impossible to get through.*" I know, that's not full of finesse, but we're not looking for perfection here; we just want to make sure we have an understanding of the sentence before considering the answer list.

Because these concourses are so full of people and stuff, let's focus on eliminating words that would describe them in a positive manner. Right away, I want to eliminate *passable*, because that means they're easy to travel through. Strike E. Now, let's assume that you, like many students, are unfamiliar with the words *unsullied, unnavigable,* and *byzantine*. If you're not familiar with them you *can't* eliminate them. You may also feel like *cluttered* is a decent possibility just because we're talking about airports full of stuff. So we'll leave the other choices as they are.

(A)   cumbersome . . cluttered
(B)   spry . . unnavigable
(C)   weary . . byzantine
(D)   seasoned . . unsullied
(E)   active . . ~~passable~~

Rather than throwing in the towel because you don't know what the other words in the second column mean, let's go back and look at the options for the first blank and see if we can eliminate some words from the first column of answer choices. While we initially chose the word *tough* as our guideword for the first blank, any word that means *good, strong traveler* will do. Now, the word *weary* in C might pop right out at you as a word that definitely doesn't mean *good, strong traveler*. Let's also look at that word *cumbersome*. The tricky thing is that *cumbersome* could be a possibility for the second blank because it means *hard to handle,* so it's somewhat confusing to have it available in the first blank. However, does it mean *good, strong traveler*? No. So we strike it.

Now your list should look like this:

(A)   ~~cumbersome~~ . . cluttered
(B)   spry . . unnavigable
(C)   ~~weary~~ . . byzantine
(D)   seasoned . . unsullied
(E)   active . . ~~passable~~

There's something cool that's happened here: either *spry* or *seasoned* could be acceptable answers, and *unnavigable* and *unsullied* mean entirely different things. Even if you're unsure of the meanings of *unnavigable* and *unsullied,* you'll probably guess because both of the first words would work in the sentence. Now, just like ships *navigate* the ocean, something that is *unnavigable* is something that can't be traveled through. On the other hand, something that is *unsullied* is spotless, totally clean, and unblemished (not a very good description of the airport concourses). So we strike *unsullied,* and we end up with *spry* and *unnavigable,* which work perfectly in the sentence.

What I most want you to understand is that by focusing on one column of answer choices, you may be able to avoid challenging vocabulary. This is not a sales pitch for ignoring vocab so much as it's a timesaver and a great way to eliminate incorrect answer choices when you're feeling stumped.

Identify the Relationship Between the Pair

Sometimes you may not be able to zero in on an individual blank's meaning in a double-blank question; instead, the definition of one blank is completely reliant on the definition of the other. For example, you could find a sentence in which, if the first blank is positive, the second blank must also be positive, but if the first blank is negative, the second blank must be negative, too. Use the relationship between the two blanks to guide your choices; thinking about relationships like "they must both be positive words" or "they can be either good or bad, but they have to mean the same thing" will help you find the correct answer.

Take the following example:

EXAMPLE 1: LEVEL 4
The screenwriters, whose contracts included only payment on television and DVD sales of their work, were predictably _____ when they learned that payment on online sales of their work had been purposely _____.

(A) fulfilled . . annulled
(B) stymied . . comprehensive
(C) unconvinced . . sustained
(D) displeased . . integrated
(E) dissatisfied . . excluded

In this case, our screenwriters could have responded in one of two ways: they could have been *happy* that payment *had* been included in their contract or they could have been *unhappy* that the service had *not* been included. Here, whatever we choose for the *first* blank dictates what we can choose for the second. The relationship between the words matters just as much as the vocabulary words themselves matter.

This time, because the relationship between the words is most important, we address each pair individually. Again, we don't just read the whole list of answer choices and hope something jumps out at us. Instead, we calmly work our way down the list, subbing each pair of words back into the given sentence.

First of all, would our scriptwriters be *fulfilled* if their payment was *annulled*? If payment were annulled, someone would have declared that the payment service had never happened. Not getting paid is not usually fulfilling. These folks aren't Red Cross volunteers. So we ditch A.

Would the screenwriters be *stymied* that the payment has been *comprehensive*? Well, perhaps. When something is *stymied*, something has gotten in the way of its success, so to speak—like a lineman could stymie a quarterback's ability to pass the ball. In this context, *stymie* is not a very good choice, but we can leave B as a possibility—many students would simply because it's not entirely clear what exactly the sentence is saying.

Would screenwriters be *unconvinced* when their payment was *sustained*? This doesn't make any sense, so we strike C.

Would screenwriters be *displeased* if payment on online sales was *integrated*? Absolutely not. If the payment was *integrated*, it would be *included*. If anything, additional pay would be very pleasing, so we ditch choice D as well.

We still have choice B as an option, but E turns out to be a pretty good choice: Would screenwriters be *dissatisfied* if they learn payment on online sales was *excluded*? Yes. And E is certainly a better answer than B, so E is the answer we want to go with.

Now, I know that process looks really laborious and extremely repetitive, but it's the repetition itself that allows you to size up possible answer choices without confusing yourself. Did you notice how I repeated the same question to myself every time I looked at an answer choice? This repetition is designed to be uptight—it is the only way to make sure you're comparing answer choices accurately. Don't get bored with the pattern around answer C and just start reading pairs of words. You will eventually make a mistake. Take the time to repeat each new version of the sentence and plug-and-play your way to the correct choice.

It's incredibly important to remember that your not knowing a vocabulary word does not necessarily mean it's the wrong choice for the given sentence. If, while you're eliminating answer choices, you come upon a word you've never seen before, *do not automatically cross it out*! I've seen students do this a million times, but frankly, your vocabluary and the test maker's vocabulary are two entirely different things. If you use the techniques I'm walking you through here, you can eliminate down to a vocabulary word that you're convinced has never before been uttered by human lips but is still the correct answer.

With this type of question it's really important to consider the answer choices methodically—try to repeat the same question as you think about each answer choice.

Making Sentence Completions More Difficult

Just like in the rest of the SAT, the test maker uses several methods of increasing the level of difficulty of Sentence Completion questions.

It's Not Just the Words That Get More Challenging

Although initially you may be responsible for finding a definition and knowing a selection of challenging vocabulary, the last question or two involves reading the sentence, understanding the motivations of the subjects or circumstances described, and then choosing an appropriate word for the blank (which may not be defined in the sentence, anyway). Here's an example:

EXAMPLE 1: LEVEL 5

Members of the planning committee that hopes to stage a three-day music festival in the wilderness preserve argued that, environmentally, the consequences of previous festivals in comparable parks have been _____.

(A) insurmountable
(B) negligible
(C) myopic
(D) haphazard
(E) supercilious

It is impossible to answer this level 5 question if you don't consider what's going on in the sentence—there is no definition or little catch phrase to safely steer you. In the midst of your SAT "I'm never going to get into college!" freak-out, you'll need to identify the perspective from which the planning committee in the sentence is working; they're a "selfish big business" that wants to use land for profit and doesn't necessarily care about wildlife and the wilderness eco-system. Then you'll need to see that they are making a claim about the effects of holding what sounds like the Coachella Music Festival in a national park. Finally, you need to think, "Well, if I were a selfish music production company that wanted to hold a huge concert in a national park, I'd have to say that these types of events have never affected any natural habitats before (whether or not that's true), and say that environmentally, the consequences of previous festivals in comparable parks have been *not that bad.*" The process does take a minute, but it's not impossible.

After you've come up with *not that bad*, you can begin eliminating answer choices. If you get that far and you're unable to eliminate answer choices due to the sheer difficulty of the vocabulary words, just move on. Don't waste time hemming and hawing and wishing you'd done more flashcards. Remember, this question isn't worth any more than any other question on the test.

While we're here, let's take the time to look through those vocabulary words in the answer choices and, if you need to, you can make flashcards for them! (Convenient, no?)

(A) insurmountable: unbeatable or unable to be overcome (like an insurmountable task)
(B) negligible: able to be ignored, unimportant (also look up the word *negligence*)
(C) myopic: looking at something from only one perspective; being narrow-minded
(D) haphazard: all over the place; random (like a road hazard would be out in the middle of the street)
(E) supercilious: acting *superior* and snobby; haughty

By now you should see that the only option that's vaguely close is choice B. *Members of the planning committee that hopes to stage a three-day music festival in the wilderness preserve argued that, environmentally, the consequences of previous festivals in comparable parks have been* <u>negligible</u>.

Let's look at another example that requires you to pay attention to what's happening in the sentence.

EXAMPLE 2: LEVEL 4

Hoping to reverse the final call in the game, advocates for the defeated champions submitted a statement claiming that the game had been run by _____ referees.

(A) venal

(B) incorruptible

(C) illustrious

(D) prodigious

(E) veracious

While there is no hidden definition in this example, it's probably a bit easier than the first because it's a situation you need to think less about. Anyone who is trying to get a play reversed is going to say that the referees did a bad job; good guideword choices for this blank would be *lousy* or *bad*. Nevertheless, the vocabulary in this example is pretty challenging; again, maybe you should stop and make some flashcards for the words you don't know!

(A) venal: able to be bribed or bought; corrupt; like a mercenary (soldiers for hire)

(B) incorruptible: not able to be corrupted ("in-" = "not"; "-ible" = "able"); the opposite of corrupt cops

(C) illustrious: wonderful and honored; glorified (like lustrous or luster, which means having beauty and depth and shine, like polished wood or shiny hair)

(D) prodigious: like a child *prodigy* is someone who performs exceptionally at something; something that is *prodigious* is something exceptionally large and fantastic

(E) veracious: truthful; when we *verify* something we find it to be truthful; related to *veracity*, which means *truthfulness*

As you can see, the only option that could possibly mean *lousy* or *bad* is *venal*, and that option makes sense; the referees could easily have been bribed to rule against the team that lost no matter how well they played.

The main point here is that these level 5 problems can be really challenging, particularly when you're feeling pressured. My opinion is this: if you are a student aiming for a score of 650 or above in the Critical Reading portion of the test, read the last Sentence Completion question, assess it carefully, and do the best you can. I don't generally recommend guessing, so if you have no idea what's going on, forget about it. If you are not shooting for higher than a 650, ignore the last question and go on to the reading passages. There will be plenty of easier points for you to earn there!

passage-based
reading

Let's face it: the Passage-Based Reading freaks students out. Even the most adept advanced placement and international baccalaureate English students loathe this part. Why? Because the passages are pretty dry, generally not on topics one would find in the latest issues of *Vanity Fair* or *Sports Illustrated*, and it often feels like we've only got seventeen seconds to read them. Nevertheless, Passage-Based Reading questions are a huge part of scoring well on the SAT and cannot be ignored.

You'll be glad to hear that you already possess most of the skills necessary to be successful on this portion of the test. This is particularly true if you're one of those avid readers I mentioned earlier. Let's get real about what you need to know to do well on the Passage-Based Reading.

Imagine yourself sitting in the doctor's office waiting to get some immunization shots for school. You've been sitting in the waiting room for, say, two hours; you've read both copies of *AARP* magazine in the rack and you've watched all the *Judge Judy* you can take. There's a sticky label on the television that reads DO NOT CHANGE THE CHANNEL. Bored out of your mind, you reach for one of the brochures that a sales rep has left on the table by your chair. It's entitled "Pink Eye: Prevention and Treatment." Granted, you don't have pink eye and you don't know anyone who does, but like I said, you're truly bored.

So you read it. You don't read it like you care; you just read it. The funny thing is, though, when the nurse comes to take you back to an exam room, you'd be able to tell her some really basic stuff about pink eye: it's also known as conjunctivitis, it makes eyes swell and get pink, antibiotics help it go away, and if you'd like to avoid catching it, you're better off not picking your nose and scratching at your eyes. Simple and gross, but you got that information from reading the brochure in a state of utter boredom and disinterest. And exactly how does this relate to the SAT, you may ask? The amount of information you would get from the pink eye brochure is about as much as you'll need to get out of any reading passage on the SAT.

Basically not a lot

Sound crazy and impossible? It's not.

Because choosing a correct answer is the only way to earn more points and increase your score, this section focuses on specific ways to approach reading and responding to the questions to be more systematic, more confident—and more frequently correct.

In high school we are taught that when we take a multiple choice test, we read a given question and circle the correct answer. On the SAT reading passages this method can become a huge problem. Commonly a student will read the passage, read a question, come up with an answer in her head (which could very well be correct), and panic when her expected answer choice doesn't appear as an option. It's a scary moment, especially when the student is feeling like "My Whole Life Depends on This."

How to Read the Passages

Listen, the SAT Reading Comprehension is not a test of how well you read or what you think about things you've read—it's a test of how quickly and easily you can arrive at the same answer as the test maker. After all, that's the person who wrote the questions and decided which answer is correct. Who cares what you or I think about the correct answer? We need to find the test maker's answer, because it's the only answer that will earn us another point.

If you think about it, this sounds like a pretty unfair situation: someone else chooses the passage, makes up questions about the passage, and then chooses the correct answer to those questions. Your impressions of the passage are totally left out of this process, and it's extremely important that you come to terms with that. Surprisingly, the College Board does not care about what we, the test takers, think of the reading passages. It's all about *them*: their passage, their question, and their answer. Our entire method of approaching the reading is going to totally ignore what we think and feel after reading the passage; from here on out, we care about *only* what the test maker thinks.

Because we're only interested in things the test maker is interested in, we need to treat these passages differently than we would treat material read for school. It's likely that when you're reading books for school, no matter the class, one of the basics of studying history or analyzing literature is underlining as you read through the material. We underline key points and main ideas and often write notes or questions in the margins to make our learning more efficient later. If you're not already doing this when you study, I highly recommend it.

However, with the SAT reading passages you should underline only what the test makers say is important, *not* what *you* think is important. Fortunately, the test makers flat-out tell us what they think is important and where to find it. Before you read a passage, skim the questions for line references; they'll look like this: "(lines 23 through 26)." As soon as you find specific line numbers, mark those lines in the passage with an arrow, bracket, or whatever you prefer. This step should take you no more than forty-five seconds once you're really good at it.

There is no sense in actually trying to memorize the questions before reading the passage—there are far too many of them, and you'll never remember what they asked while you're reading. However, by marking the line numbers that relate to questions beforehand, you set up a guided tour for your reading: every time something is underlined or bracketed you'll take that as a sign to pay extra attention because you know the test maker wrote a question about it.

Remember, all we care about on the SAT Reading Comprehension are ideas that are important to the College Board. Don't distract yourself and make things more complex by underlining and highlighting things that are important to *you*.

[handwritten margin note: Mark specific Line As in the passage]

After you've underlined, pay careful attention to the italicized portion that appears at the start of each of the longer passages. These sentences are not part of the instructions! In fact, they are full of information you can use while you read. In the italics you'll find answers to a few, if not all, of the "5 W" questions that you probably learned in elementary school: they contain the Who, What, Where, When, and Why information that will lead you to form commonsense preconceptions of what you're about to read.

Frankly, the College Board is in no hurry to be sued by angry students and their families, and the content of the test reflects that. For example, if you find a passage written by a Native American woman, you can rest assured that you are not going to be reading a passage about how wonderful it is that Europeans came to the New World and stole land from innocent people. Expect a fair commentary by a woman whose people have experienced displacement and all sorts of negative repercussions from that experience. This applies to any group of people that has been historically marginalized: African Americans, women, immigrants, and most any other minority. Use your common sense when considering main ideas and themes, keeping in mind that the College Board doesn't want to end up in court for saying the wrong thing.

Moreover, in a double-passage section, it's easier to understand the actual comparison being made between the two passages when you read the italics. Passages are often written on the same topic but from two different perspectives. You may find a piece by a social historian talking about the 1940s in tandem with some travel writings by a woman who lived at that time. The first passage will be analytical, written by an expert who has scientifically studied the lives of middle-class women in a specific time period; the other passage may be written by someone who is interested in the joys of travel. The travel writer's account will be far more personal and less likely to make grand sweeping social statements. If you find yourself struggling to understand the main idea, considering who wrote it can be really helpful.

You will notice that italicized portions do not appear before the short passages. That's generally because the Who, What, Where, When, and Why of those paragraphs are often the topics of the questions. Other than that difference, you should follow the same procedure for both short and long passages.

After reading the italics, read the passage. Don't overdo it: think "nothing more than the pink eye brochure." You'll be referring to the passage as you answer the questions, anyway. Still, it's a good idea to read the passage to understand it as a whole piece of writing; that way it will be easier to assess the primary purpose of the passage or the author's particular stance on an issue. It's likely that you'll get those few key pieces of information out of the passage, provided you pay attention and think logically about what you're reading.

If you lose track of what you're reading and you're running low on time, read the first and last sentence of each paragraph. These main idea and transition sentences will help you get a basic, filtered view of what the author is discussing. Sometimes stress or sheer boredom can also make retaining information really difficult—if you're struggling to pay attention, invest five seconds at the end of each paragraph of the passage to stop and remind yourself what you just read. Although this could add an extra minute or two to your reading time, it may make answering the questions quickly much simpler.

How They Ask (and How You'll Answer) the Questions

Consider this: if any of the "correct" answers to the Reading Comprehension questions were at all debatable, the College Board would have a huge problem on its hands. Students would receive their score reports, find a way to argue that their chosen answers were correct, and the College Board's mailbox in New York City would be flooded with letters from angry students demanding score changes and furious parents threatening to sue. Just as they don't want to meet your folks in court for including culturally offensive subject matter, the College Board does not want to go head to head with you about why the answer to question 19 could be A when they say the correct answer is D. This would be an expensive and tedious process that the College Board does not want to risk. In avoiding this scenario, they give us something we can bet on: all of the incorrect answers in the Reading Comprehension have to be absolutely, provably *wrong*—court-of-law wrong. How does that help us? We're going to use the process of elimination to get rid of wrong answers instead of looking for correct answers.

Methodically Eliminate Incorrect Answers

I want you to focus on crossing out the precise word that makes each answer choice incorrect. On the SAT, you can and should eliminate every incorrect answer choice by drawing a line through the specific word that makes that option incorrect right in your test booklet.

There are a lot of great arguments for employing this strategy. For starters, it's going to help you think more clearly. Instead of going with your gut reaction, you're going to make a specific decision about the content of the question that goes beyond saying to yourself, "That can't be right." Instead, you'll more specifically say, "OK, I know the word *decline* is incorrect." As you eliminate, you'll notice it becomes easier for you to choose between two answer choices by looking for what's wrong rather than what's right. Additionally, by crossing out each word you'll be leaving yourself a paper trail so that when you go back to check your work, instead of having to totally rethink and reconsider each element of each question, you'll have left yourself a little note about why you eliminated the answer the first time. Ultimately, this process enables you to choose the correct answer more systematically without bringing too much of your own opinion into the process.

When you've finished working through a question, it should look like this on your paper:

- (A) angry yet ~~understanding~~
- (B) quiet and ~~serene~~
- (C) cautious yet brave
- (D) ~~happy~~ and exhilarated
- (E) ~~wild~~ and terrified

or

(A)   eliciting an emotional response
(B)   reminding the reader of a ~~moral imperative~~
(C)   eliminating the need for ~~scientific~~ thought
(D)   causing the reader to respond with ~~anger~~
(E)   bringing about a ~~historical~~ reference

Now that you're all set to focus on finding and eliminating *incorrect* choices rather than seeking out the *correct* choice, let's learn what we should be looking for specifically.

First, look for specific, incorrect details in the answer choices. If a passage is about art, you may find an answer choice pertains only to *modern* art; if a passage is about politics during wartime, you may find an answer choice that refers only to the goals of pacifists. Sometimes the details you'll find in an answer choice are exactly the opposite of what are in the passage; sometimes they're erroneous but "sound good" (so students like to choose them because they sound fancy). Because of this, it's imperative that you know when a detail is wrong or when it has been added to an answer choice to distract you from the correct answer.

Spot the Exaggeration That Makes an Answer Wrong

Sometimes answer choices don't contain details that are necessarily wrong; instead, they are exaggerated or overstated, which can be extremely distracting and confusing. You may come across two choices that have the same general meaning, but one is far more extreme and specific than the other. For example, if we compare (C) *offering lodging to politicians* and (E) *providing extraordinary accommodations for heads of state*, at first glance they mean more or less the same thing: having hotel rooms for government officials. But answer E is far more specific; it refers only to extraordinary accommodations (not just any hotel room) and reserving those for heads of state (not just anyone associated with the government). Nine times out of ten the less-specific answer, like answer C, will be correct.

To make sure you understand this test maker's tactic, let's look at the comparison between (B) *relative nervousness* and (C) *debilitating fear*. Again, we have two answer choices that basically characterize the same thing: being scared. However, relative nervousness is, well, relative. You may be relatively nervous if you're presenting a history project in front of your class or skiing a black diamond mountain trail for the first time. Debilitating fear is experienced in only the most terrifying circumstances, like a hostage situation. That level of fear and emotion is not often seen in the SAT.

This sort of tactic also frequently appears in questions related to an author's opinion: most passages are chosen specifically because they are not offensive, so it makes sense that an author's opinion about most everything would be just as inoffensive. Generally, that means that answer choices that suggest that an author is being extremely negative (for example, *cynical* or *resentful*) or incredibly positive (for example, *undeniably confident* or *in awe and wonder*) should be avoided. Usually an author's tone or perspective will be qualified with a word like *somewhat* or *usually*. These noncommittal words keep the College Board out of trouble.

The fact of the matter is that the correct answers to Passage-Based Reading questions are designed to be really vague—so vague, in fact, that you might not want to choose them because it sounds like they don't say anything profound about the passage. Then again, because we're only supposed to be able to get a few key ideas from the passage, it makes sense that the answer choices would be really nonspecific—we can't know a whole lot from a two-minute reading. You'll often find that the phrases that sound as though they say nothing (such as *certain types of emotions* or *parallel a current issue*) turn out to be the only viable correct answer; the alternatives will often be more specific (but specifically wrong) versions of the vague answer you select.

Be on the lookout for words like *relative, somewhat,* or *generally;* they modify emotions. These are "safety words" that make answer choices broader—and better.

Base Your Answer on the Passage

One thing that may haunt you while you take the SAT is that, believe it or not, you already know an awful lot about many different topics. You've been reading about astronauts and dolphins and the invention of the light bulb for as long as you have been in school. You have most likely read about sound waves and the Industrial Revolution and Dr. Marin Luther King Jr.'s "I have a dream . . ." speech. Knowing a bit about the topic of a passage on the SAT, though, can make things a little trickier, because some of the wrong answer choices will be accurate facts or common opinions that don't actually appear in the passage. This sort of pitfall is likely in a question that asks about a "generalization that is supported" by a passage. Be extra sure that you choose the generalization that you *read* in the passage (say, "apes have a distinct social order") rather than something you already know (say, that apes are intelligent or that some apes have learned to communicate with humans).

Deconstructing Question Types

Now that you're familiar with how the test makers create incorrect answers, let's get into the nitty-gritty about the questions themselves and how they're designed to trip you up.

For starters, always read a little more than the line reference in the question directs you to read. If a question asks about a phrase within a sentence, read at least the entire sentence. If a question refers to an entire sentence, read the sentences that come before and after it. Because most of the questions must be answered using context clues, it makes a lot of sense to stop and read the context. Remember, this reading is in addition to your having already read the passage—never attempt to answer a question without at least quickly refreshing your memory by referring back to the passage.

Pronoun Reference Questions

Because the test maker makes things more confusing than they already are, many of the questions refer to phrases or sentences that begin with pronouns (those little representative words that stand in for real people or places or ideas). In the SAT reading passages, these pronouns and the nouns they represent are really important. If a quote from a passage begins with a word like *they, it,* or *those,* you must go back into the passage and find out that *they* are *Europeans* or *it* is *the belief in aliens,* or whatever. Even if you have to dig three sentences back in the passage, it's worth the time to go look it up—and you will likely struggle to answer the questions if you don't. Generally, the more difficult the question, the farther back in the passage the answer lies. In fact, many questions are pointedly designed to be misleading and confusing if you fail to correctly identify the pronoun.

Definition Questions

A few of the questions in the Passage-Based Reading section are simply definition questions that will cite a word in the passage and ask you to select a word that it is most nearly related to. The answer will sometimes be a fairly direct synonym that can be gleaned from context clues; more often you'll need to use parallel structure within the sentence to find the word's meaning. In fact, the way to answer this kind of question is like finding the definition in the sentence when you're doing sentence completions. In the sentence completions the test maker restates or defines the blank within the sentence; in the Reading Comprehension, the blank is merely the word you're asked to define.

Let's look at the structure of the following example:

EXAMPLE 1: LEVEL 3

"High school students tend to regard winning the homecoming game as the most important football game of the year, signifying their hard work and dedication, denoting a presumed collective superiority."

Which of the following words is closest to the meaning of the word *denoting* in the above sentence?

(A) mastering
(B) indicating
(C) collecting
(D) amortizing
(E) harboring

We can analyze the sentence carefully and find that *denoting* is related to the verb *signifying* because of the parallel structure in the sentence. To dig out that parallel structure you can read the sentence like this:

Students . . . regard winning . . . as (1) *signifying* their hard work . . . (2) *denoting* a presumed collective superiority.

The parallel structure shows us that winning the homecoming game *signifies* collective superiority to the high school students. When we set out to eliminate answers, we should eliminate all words that are entirely unrelated to the word *signifies* and work from there. As usual, there will be only one choice that will work; in this case, B, *indicating*.

Be Aware of Themes

Look for patterns in the questions: often the same question or same concept is addressed more than once. Use the fact that you're supposed to be able to gather only so much information from the passage to your advantage by looking for paired questions. In the "pink eye" story in the introduction, I listed a few key facts that you would conceivably remember from reading a brochure just once. As there are sometimes twelve questions after a hefty reading passage, the test maker must be up to something. How can he ask so many questions when we are expected to get so little out of our reading? Often questions about the same concept are asked twice, sometimes one question right after the other. The challenge for the test maker to create and for you to uncover is how the same concept has been hidden in two questions.

Let's look at questions based on the following sample paragraph:

> I was chewing on antacid even before we arrived, in fact. It was an unseasonably cold and rainy morning when we woke up in Hartford. We chose to stop in Hartford technically because Amy's sister lives there but really because it provided a last-minute
> (5)   escape route. We had come this far the night before, but we felt as though we hadn't truly committed to reuniting until we sailed past the *Welcome to Massachusetts* highway sign. It was a technicality, but a comforting technicality nonetheless.

EXAMPLE 1: LEVEL 3
Line 4 ("but really . . . escape route") suggests that the narrator

(A)   has committed a crime on the trip
(B)   has always dreamed of visiting Hartford
(C)   is still considering not attending the reunion
(D)   struggles to plan in advance
(E)   is as excited about staying in Hartford as she is about attending her reunion

After the phrase "escape route," the narrator goes on to suggest that she and her friend felt like they had not committed to attending the reunion until they had crossed the state line. We eliminate everything that is not along those lines:

(A)   has committed a ~~crime~~ on the trip

This is obviously the literal association with *escape route*, but there's no evidence of this in the passage.

Many students shy away from broad, generalized answer choices because they sound too obvious or fundamental. Don't over-complicate the SAT: if a broad, generalized answer choice makes sense, it's likely correct.

(B)   has ~~always dreamed~~ of visiting Hartford

This is also out of left field and even less related to "escaping" something.

(C)   is still considering not attending the reunion

I like this one, particularly because she says she finds the existence of the escape route to be "comforting" later in the passage.

(D)   struggles to plan in ~~advance~~

The word *advance* here is particularly wrong, as they have clearly not chosen on a whim.

(E)   is as excited about staying in Hartford ~~as she is about attending her reunion~~

Particularly because the author makes little mention of being excited about the reunion at all, we strike that.

Just like that, we're left with answer C.

EXAMPLE 2: LEVEL 4

The "comforting technicality" in lines 7 and 8 most directly underscores

(A)   a degree of discomfort
(B)   a physical stressor
(C)   an illegitimate complaint
(D)   an instantaneous emotion
(E)   a broken resolution

First we have to define the *comforting technicality*, which takes a little digging. If we look back in the passage we see that the *comforting technicality* sentence begins with *It*, so we need to go back and dig further to figure out what *It* refers to. It turns out that not having crossed over to Massachusetts—specifically, again, *staying in Hartford*, is the *comforting technicality*. Now, we can rephrase the question for ourselves as "staying in Hartford most directly underscores":

Keep in mind that to *underscore* is to *emphasize* something, so staying in Hartford really emphasizes what?

(A)   a degree of discomfort

Yes, she is uncomfortable about attending her reunion. Moreover, a *degree* broadens the statement and makes it a very safe choice.

(B)   a ~~physical~~ stressor

Nope, there doesn't seem to be anything wrong with her body.

(C)   an ~~illegitimate~~ complaint

Nor is there anything that would lead us to believe that it's an illegitimate concern.

(D)   an ~~instantaneous~~ emotion

To be instantaneous, it would have to be something that she experiences spontaneously, and there doesn't seem to be an isolated moment of panic.

(E)   a broken ~~resolution~~

If she had promised to go to Massachusetts and finally decided not to, this would work. But nothing in the passage would lead us to believe that's the case.

Again, easy as pie, we're left with A.

Both of these questions refer to the central theme of the narrator's nervousness about attending the reunion and simply find two different ways of asking about it. You'll start to pick up that the test maker does this a lot; so when you're answering questions, you should start to pick up on themes. While this is not a cut-and-dried tactic, if you're really struggling between two answer choices, it's generally a good idea to choose the one that is most in keeping with the themes of the other answer choices you've selected.

How They Turn Up the Difficulty

Here are a few ways ordinary sentences are made more complicated on the SAT.

The Appositive: Making a Question Harder Than It Really Is

One of the great ways the test makers confuse you is to ask you about an appositive. The term *appositive* may be new to you, but don't feel intimidated—you don't have to learn the word; you just need to know how to identify one. An appositive is basically any noun phrase that renames another noun in the sentence. Now let's take a second to make sure we can recognize one. Check out the following example sentence:

> Mr. Clark, our local pie-eating champion, is running for mayor.

In this sentence *our local pie-eating champion* renames Mr. Clark. That's the appositive. If you look carefully at tougher questions on the SAT (or questions that just seem more confusing), the quote in the question will ask you about the appositive (the *pie-eating champ*) and your answer will be in reference to the original noun (*Mr. Clark*). They turn up the difficulty by asking you about an appositive for a pronoun, like this:

EXAMPLE 1: LEVEL 4

It's a classic joke, a real zinger, but my grandmother was not amused.

The phrase "a real zinger" refers to which of the following?

(A)   a political manifesto
(B)   a slur with cultural implications
(C)   a modest attempt at reconciliation
(D)   an amusing jab
(E)   a tart comment

OK, so the real zinger is what? Oh, it's the joke she told her grandmother. Again, the appositive in the sentence is *a real zinger*, renaming the *classic joke*. OK, so my answer is going to be something that characterizes or describes the joke. Using what you know about SAT questions and without even seeing the passage, you should be able to guess that the answer to this question is D. As passages are never offensive on this test, it would be very hard to argue that a joke within it could be anything other than *an amusing jab*.

How Vocabulary Upgrades Simple Questions

Here's the test maker's final difficulty-enhancer: the answer choices use revved-up vocabulary to say something fundamentally simple. We're not talking arcane vocabulary here so much as language that is extremely formal. Some of my students who are not as well-read as others struggle through the options, not because they didn't understand the passage but because of the words used in the answer choices. Because formal language may not be familiar or reflexive for you, the test may seem even more challenging than it actually is, particularly because you're stressed while you're taking the test. Let me show you what I mean.

EXAMPLE 1: LEVEL 4
The author mentions Sonia's surprise at Nemo's sudden greed in order to highlight the

(A) way that Sonia's disposition lightened when Nemo was nearby
(B) contrast between Sonia's reserve and Nemo's exuberance
(C) fervor with which Sonia regarded Nemo
(D) unpredictability of Sonia's everyday chores
(E) duality of Nemo's personality

Don't get intimidated by these choices: just stop and think carefully, rephrasing the answers into downgraded, simpler vocabulary. Let's pop out the formal vocab and look at the real meanings here:

(A) way that Sonia's disposition lightened when Nemo was nearby
Translation: how Sonia perked up when Nemo showed up

(B) contrast between Sonia's reserve and Nemo's exuberance
Translation: difference between Sonia being quiet and Nemo being loud

(C) fervor with which Sonia regarded Nemo
Translation: how much Sonia really liked Nemo

(D) unpredictability of Sonia's everyday chores
Translation: how Sonia had no idea what chores she'd be doing on any given day

(E) duality of Nemo's personality
Translation: how Nemo seems to have two sides to his personality

It will benefit you to start reading for pleasure at least a half an hour a night (yes, in addition to your school-assigned reading). If you want a break from books, I recommend reading the articles in *Vanity Fair* or *GQ*. Contributors to these magazines are serious writers, and you will learn a lot of vocabulary and idiomatic language just from reading them. For more tips on learning vocabulary, check out the Sentence Completion section.

Whenever possible, try to rephrase formal answer choices using normal vocabulary.

Questions That Characterize the Purpose or Direction of Passages

Sometimes it's easy to get caught up in the heat of the moment when taking the SAT. The pressure is on, you're all wound up about college and competitive scores, and your brain may be working faster than it needs to. Suddenly, no matter how much eliminating you may do, everything sounds like it could be right. This is especially common when we're asked to characterize an author's attitude or main point or a passage's style or tone. When this happens, it can be helpful to take an answer choice out of context and ask yourself, "What would I expect to have read in the passage if this answer were true?" Then compare your natural expectation to what actually appears in the passage.

Specifically, if you were deciding if the "primary purpose" of a passage is to "profile the various personalities of twentieth-century poets," the passage would be exactly that: an essay about a variety of poets from the twentieth century and all of their different personalities. You'd find depressed poets, poets who were known for being comical, and those who were extremely romantic. Use this natural expectation and compare it to the passage on the whole, asking yourself if the passage and your expectation match. If those poets only appear in one paragraph, or if the passage is about a different kind of poetry, you can easily eliminate the answer choice. Removing an answer choice's concept from its passage's context can often clarify its meaning.

Mix-and-Match Questions

If you're usually pressed for time during the reading section, do the questions that involve mixing and matching choices I, II, III, and (heaven forbid) IV last. Fortunately, these only pop up now and then, anyway; your test may not include a single example. Nevertheless, these questions don't require that you decide whether just one particular idea is wrong, but frequently you have to decide whether three or four ideas are wrong. Frankly, they're time-wasters and tedious, but they're still worth only the single point that any other correct answer would earn you. So come back to them.

When you do approach the I, II, III questions, you need to find evidence in the passage for including or excluding each of the options, treating each option as though it were part of a multiple choice question. The only sticky thing is that just because you've eliminated one element of the question doesn't mean that the others are automatically correct.

Double Reading Passages

When faced with a double reading passage, it's commonly advised that you read passage 1, answer its corresponding questions, read passage 2, answer its corresponding questions, and then finally answer the questions that refer to both passages. Some students find this to be an immense help; others find it confusing, but you can decide what works for you. I read them both together and answer the questions. If you do decide to break it up and do each passage's questions separately, please keep careful track of how you bubble your answers in. Remember that jumping around a reading passage is a prime opportunity to lose track of the question you're on, particularly when you're nervous or tired at the end of the test.

Contextual Examples of Reading-Passage Issues

Let's take a look at two sample passages.

PASSAGE 1

In the following excerpt, a man observes how moral consciousness impacts his everyday life.

I want now to tell you, gentlemen, whether you care to hear it or not, why I could not even become an insect. I tell you solemnly, that I have many times tried to become an insect. But I was not equal even to that. I swear, gentlemen, that to be too conscious is
(5)   an illness—a real thorough-going illness. For man's everyday needs, it would have been quite enough to have the ordinary human consciousness, that is, half or a quarter of the amount which falls to the lot of a cultivated man of our unhappy nineteenth century, especially one who has the fatal ill-luck to inhabit Petersburg, the most
(10) theoretical and intentional town on the whole terrestrial globe. (There are intentional and unintentional towns.) It would have been quite enough, for instance, to have the consciousness by which all so-called direct persons and men of action live. I bet you think I am writing all this from affectation, to be witty at the expense of
(15) men of action; and what is more, that from ill-bred affectation, I am clanking a sword like my officer. But, gentlemen, whoever can pride himself on his diseases and even swagger over them?

Though, after all, everyone does do that; people do pride themselves on their diseases, and I do, maybe, more than anyone. We
(20) will not dispute it; my contention was absurd. But yet I am firmly persuaded that a great deal of consciousness, every sort of consciousness, in fact, is a disease. I stick to that. Let us leave that, too, for a minute. Tell me this: why does it happen that at the very, yes, at the very moments when I am most capable of feeling every
(25) refinement of all that is "sublime and beautiful," as they used to say at one time, it would, as though of design, happen to me not only to feel but to do such ugly things, that . . . well, actions that all, perhaps, commit; but which, as though purposely, occurred to me at the very time when I was most conscious that they ought
(30) not to be committed. The more conscious I was of goodness and of all that was "sublime and beautiful," the more deeply I sank into my mire and the more ready I was to sink in it altogether. But the chief point is that all this was not accidental, but as though it had

been planned. It was as though it were my most normal condition,
(35)   and not in the least disease or depravity, so that at last all desire
in me to struggle against this depravity passed. It ended by my
almost believing (perhaps actually believing) that this was perhaps
my normal condition.

EXAMPLE 1: LEVEL 4
What does the author seem to imply in lines 1 and 2 (*I . . . tell you . . .
become an insect*)?

(A)   He wishes to transform into a bug.
(B)   He believes that insects are higher social beings.
(C)   He feels burdened by his human awareness.
(D)   He is using the word insect as a euphemism for a ruler.
(E)   His dreams about insects are becoming repetitive.

This is a perfect example of what might happen if you answer a question
from the sentence itself and not the sentence in context. If you dig back into
the passage only to read: "I tell you solemnly, that I have many times tried to
become an insect," you've got problems and may go with option A. However,
the author is not actually longing to become a beetle; in fact, he immediately
follows the statement with the idea that "it would have been quite enough to
have the ordinary human consciousness." Even if you haven't completely figured out what he's getting at, it should be clear that he's discussing consciousness, not changing bodies. Therefore, you should be able to eliminate the words
into a bug, *for a ruler*, and *dreams . . . repetitive*, as these are overtly incorrect
details. This way you'd already have it narrowed down to B and C.

For me, the word that makes B specifically wrong is *social*. For a bug to
be a higher *social* being, it would need to reflect moral and spiritual behavior
beyond that of humans. Since there is no evidence of that, we strike it. We're left
with C, the correct answer.

EXAMPLE 2: LEVEL 4
The author most likely regards this "most normal condition" in line 34 as

(A)   an easily surmountable urge
(B)   an uncharacteristic problem
(C)   a rudimentary study
(D)   an over-arching falsehood
(E)   a typical experience

When questions refer to pronouns, which they frequently do, you may have
trouble answering the question if you don't dig back to specifically identify the
pronoun. This excerpted quote is actually within the phrase "*it was as though
it were my most normal condition.*" If we don't go back to figure out what it is,
we're stuck. What was his normal condition? We need to dig back farther into
the passage—about four sentences back, in fact—to find out that the author is

referring to struggling between being good or being evil. It is that *struggle* that he considers "most normal...."

Now that we've defined the *most normal condition* as *struggling to do the right thing*, we can use our own little definition to think more carefully about each answer choice. Let's look at A. Is *struggling to do the right thing* "easily surmountable?" Of course not! That's what makes it a struggle. The word *easily* makes this incorrect.

In B, we see the *struggle* defined as something *uncharacteristic*, but the author specifically points out in line 28 that these are actions that *all commit*. When something is uncharacteristic, it is unusual or out-of-character; our author says he struggles like this all the time. Strike B.

I immediately strike C because we're not dealing with a *study* here. Likewise, I lose D because we're not defining something as true or untrue. Plus, an "overarching falsehood" sounds really over the top; it's an enormous lie. That's just too much here.

We reach E and find that it's actually very straightforward—a typical experience. Just as we used the author's statement that this struggle is something that *all* experience up in B, it's exactly the reason that we like E. It's *typical*, something that everyone deals with. So the correct answer is E.

PASSAGE 2

The following passage is adapted from a nineteenth-century novel. A man is flipping through a home medical book that is intended to help people diagnose their own illnesses.

I sat for awhile, frozen with horror; and then, in the listlessness of despair, I again turned over the pages. I came to typhoid fever— read the symptoms—discovered that I had typhoid fever, must have had it for months without knowing it—wondered what else

(5) I had got; turned up St. Vitus's Dance—found, as I expected, that I had that too—began to get interested in my case, and determined to sift it to the bottom, and so started alphabetically—read up ague, and learnt that I was sickening for it, and that the acute stage would commence in about another fortnight. Bright's disease, I was

(10) relieved to find, I had only in a modified form, and, so far as that was concerned, I might live for years. Cholera I had, with severe complications; and diphtheria I seemed to have been born with. I plodded conscientiously through the twenty-six letters, and the only malady I could conclude I had not got was housemaid's knee.

(15) I felt rather hurt about this at first; it seemed somehow to be a sort of slight. Why hadn't I got housemaid's knee? Why this invidious reservation? After a while, however, less grasping feelings prevailed. I reflected that I had every other known malady in the pharmacology, and I grew less selfish, and determined to do with-

(20) out housemaid's knee. Gout, in its most malignant stage, it would appear, had seized me without my being aware of it; and zymosis I had evidently been suffering with from boyhood. There were no

more diseases after zymosis, so I concluded there was nothing else the matter with me.

(25)   I sat and pondered. I thought what an interesting case I must be from a medical point of view, what an acquisition I should be to a class! Students would have no need to "walk the hospitals," if they had me. I was a hospital in myself. All they need do would be to walk round me, and, after that, take their diploma.

EXAMPLE 3: LEVEL 2
In line 26, the word *acquisition* most nearly means

- (A)   achievement
- (B)   asset
- (C)   purchase
- (D)   question
- (E)   calculation

This is an example of the only question type that doesn't focus so much on deductive reasoning as on your ability to find the meaning of the word contextually and then find its synonym on the list of answer choices. When there is no parallel structure to steer you toward the definition, the easiest way to find the correct answer is by simply popping each option back into the sentence. Keep in mind that it is most important to find the right answer *in context.* For example, you'd likely think that an *acquisition* out of context could be a *purchase*, something acquired. However, in our sentence the author claims that he would be such an "interesting case" for the class to look at—that is, he'd *benefit* the class. Of the words in the answer choices, B, *asset* works the best.

EXAMPLE 4: LEVEL 3
In lines 4 and 5, the phrase "it seemed somehow to be a sort of slight" refers to the author's feeling that

- (A)   he rationalizes and decides his situation is mild
- (B)   he thinks this is the work of a magician
- (C)   he considers things lightly
- (D)   he feels entitled to something undesirable
- (E)   he wonders if his circumstance is mild

This is another issue of checking back on those pronouns . . . *it seemed to somehow be a sort of slight* alerts us to an appositive. What seemed to be a slight? Again, we need to look back (into the previous paragraph, no less) to see that the author is disappointed that he does not have one of the afflictions, housemaid's knee, listed in his book. The *it*, then, is his lack of that affliction. According to the satirical tone of the passage, the author ends up feeling offended that he does not have every illness in the book, even though any illness is undesirable. This makes the correct answer D.

EXAMPLE 5: LEVEL 4

The passage could be characterized as

- (A) a satirical look at medical history
- (B) a diatribe about the importance of maintaining health
- (C) an exploration of disease
- (D) a comical essay on hypochondria
- (E) a rant about the failure of health care

Removing an answer choice's concept from its passage's context can often clarify its meaning. Whenever you're struggling to find the overarching theme of a passage, consider the answer choices as though you had not seen the passage—what would a *satirical look at medical history* sound like? It would, at the very least, need to incorporate elements of the development of the study of medicine (like, we used to treat colds this way but now we treat them that way). If the passage doesn't include anything along those lines, A cannot be correct.

By the same token, whether or not you know what a *diatribe* is, you would know that anything about *the importance of maintaining health* would likely list what to do to keep healthy and the benefits one receives from doing so. Because those concepts are nowhere in our passage, we can exclude B, as well. Eliminating answers like this will help you quickly narrow down main ideas from other distracting options.

Let's keep going. If the passage had been "an exploration of disease," it probably would be about different types of disease, where they originate, and how they impact health and culture. An "exploration" of something usually reviews all of the facts and implications of that topic. That's certainly not what's going on here—as we read in the italicized background information, this is a story of a man reading a doctor's guidebook. We eliminate C.

Now we look at D. What if we don't know what *hypochondria* is? The best bet is to look at other elements of the phrase and see if they eliminate the choice. In this case, though, we find "comical essay." We know it's that, so we're going to have to leave D. Let's come back to it (since, again, we don't eliminate answers just because we don't know what a word means).

Moving on to E: if this essay had been a "rant about the failure of health care," what would it have sounded like? It probably would have been about how society is full of sick people and how health care professionals have failed to treat them; that's what a rant is—a long-winded complaint or accusation about something. Again, that doesn't at all match up; we have to go back to D.

Now, D is, in fact, the correct answer. A *hypochondriac* is someone who always thinks he is sick and coming down with every disease in the book. This is a good example of a time when you can confidently say that an answer is correct even though it has elements that are possibly unfamiliar.

Going forward, make a special effort to focus on eliminating specific words in every answer choice you encounter. This process can initially feel a little labor intensive; the only way to make it second nature is to work on it continually while you take practice tests. Ultimately, you'll speed up your overall analytical thinking skills—and raise your score!

WRITING

WRITING OVERVIEW

Your Writing section score is calculated based on two components: a 25-minute essay and two multiple choice sections. The essay is always the very first thing you'll do when you take the SAT; you'll be given a prompt, like a quote or another author's observations about a particular topic, and then you'll be asked to respond to it. Technically, you do not need to study for the essay in that it's not a test about a particular book or poem, but it's important that you do take several steps to prepare for it, which we'll cover later.

Teams of volunteer readers, usually English teachers and other writing professionals, spend about three minutes reading your essay. Two graders read each essay, and each grader gives the essay a score between 0 and 6, meaning your final score will be between 0 and 12. If the two graders disagree significantly about the score, a third grader will read the essay and decide the score. Remember that less than 1 percent of students will receive a perfect score, a 12; however, to earn a 0 you'd have to write on a topic other than that being tested, write nothing, or write your essay in ink.

You'll also need to answer a total of 48 multiple choice writing questions of three types: Improving Sentences (this is the most popular question style), Identifying Sentence Errors, and Improving Paragraphs (there are usually about six of these). An Improving Sentences question asks you to replace an underlined portion of a sentence with a better portion from a group of options below. Answer A will always be a duplicate of what's underlined in the original, while options B through E will be alternatives. Rather than ask you to replace errors, an Identifying Sentence Error question offers you four underlined, possible mistakes within a sentence or—always option E—no error. You simply need to choose which portion of the sentence is incorrect or select E, no error—you don't have to actually fix the sentence. You'll see several examples of each of these question styles throughout the lessons in this chapter.

There are two multiple choice writing sections in which the questions are organized very predictably. In the 25-minute section, you'll first see a chunk of Improving Sentences questions, then Identifying Sentence Errors questions, and finally, Improving Paragraphs. Within the subchunks of Improving Sentences and Improving Paragraphs, the questions *do* become increasingly difficult. This means that the last Improving Sentences question you see will be significantly more challenging than the next question, which will be the first, easy Identifying Sentence Errors question. However, the Paragraph Improvement questions are *not* listed in order of difficulty because they, like the Critical Reading questions, follow the structure of the passage on which they are based.

The last section of the test is always 10 minutes long and includes roughly 14 Improving Sentences questions. You'll want to be particularly careful on this section because you can rest assured that you'll be exhausted by the time you reach it.

Your score on the multiple choice section is combined with your score on the essay; your essay is worth 30 percent of your score, and the multiple choice questions make up the other 70 percent. Therefore, it's very important that you focus on learning and understanding grammar, as a high multiple choice score can profoundly affect your ultimate score.

Shooting for Your Goal Score

It's a little challenging to set raw score goals in the Writing section. Below you'll find some combinations of scores in which I assume your multiple choice skills and your essay-writing skills are about equal. These are the scores that, according to the College Board, you need to earn to score *at least* the following, but likely more. However, if you know that you're far better at the essay or the multiple choice, I suggest you look up the Writing Composite Score Conversion Table that appears at the end of every sample test created by the College Board, so you can calculate your own raw score goal.

To score at least 500:
Answer 38 questions (28 correct/10 errors), for a raw score of 26
and receive a total score of 8 on your essay

To score at least 600:
Answer 48 questions (38 correct/10 errors), for a raw score of 36
and receive a total score of 9 on your essay

To score at least 700:
Answer 49 questions (46 correct/3 errors), for a raw score of 45
and receive a total score of 9 on your essay

Again, you should see that to receive a competitive score on the Writing section, it's not even entirely necessary that you receive a 10 on your essay. However, if you struggle with multiple choice and have a limited grammar background, please pay careful attention to this section. The simple knowledge of the grammatical rules I'll cover here can change your score entirely.

the essay

Why do we have to write an essay, anyway?

Ever thought about why the essay is on the SAT? If your parents took the SAT, they never had to write a single word. When I took it in high school, my SAT was essay-free, too. What changed in 2005 that made the College Board decide that it was worthwhile to read hundreds of thousands of essays? Well, nothing really. Nothing changed specifically right then that instantaneously precipitated the essay's arrival on the SAT. However, one big thing began happening in the late 1990s that had not being going on before: internet usage. Before 1997 or so, students used the library card catalog, books, and printed magazines to research for school. There was no getting on your laptop and finding thirty-seven different pages about the life cycle of the wasp on Google in the comfort of your room.

So? So the basic problem is that these days we're all reading Wikipedia (which is written by anyone who wants to contribute) and blogs, we're using cute shorthand while we beam text messages all over the planet, and suddenly no one knows how to write anymore. It makes sense: if we're seeing incorrect grammar on the Web and hearing horrible syntax on TV, we're less likely to know what's correct and what isn't.

Reality television has probably contributed to our collective grammatical decline, too. I'm not saying that because you like a little late-night *Real World/ Road Rules Challenge* or *Pimp My Ride* you are no longer able to write coherently; it's just probably not quite as good for your writing style as curling up with, say, a copy of *The Economist*.

This is the entire point of the essay: colleges need to be sure that when you arrive as a freshman on their campuses, you're going to be able to do your homework—and very often that means reading assigned texts and writing papers—*good* papers.

How to Prove You Can Write Good Papers

The SAT essay is not a 25-minute opportunity to show how much you know about the Korean War or metaphysics or the finer points of *War and Peace*. In fact, if you check out the grading rubric distributed by the College Board in *The Official SAT Study Guide*, you'll see five key ingredients that the readers look for:

1) Appropriate Examples
2) Organization and Focus
3) Language and Usage (i.e., glitzy vocabulary)
4) Varied Sentence Structure
5) Grammar

Or you could read the list like this:

1) What you think
2) Technical stuff
3) Technical stuff
4) Technical stuff
5) Technical stuff

The essay is your opportunity to show the grader (and colleges) that you know how to organize your thoughts quickly and write a solid rough draft of a paper. Think of your essay as the skeleton of something really great and as an opportunity for you to show that you know where all of the different bones connect.

By the way, someone out there has started a rumor that these essays aren't even read and the grading is relatively random. Don't believe it. I personally know several people who grade SAT essays, and I promise you, they read them . . . carefully.

Getting Ready to Write a Great Essay

Before I show you how to build the perfect essay, we're going to do some serious, organized brainstorming. Since we're given only 25 minutes to write this thing, it makes sense that we have as much as possible figured out long before the clock starts ticking.

If you've spent any time in drama class you may have heard your teacher talk about figuring out the "arc" of the character you're playing. It's pretty much just a method of mapping out what your character feels and acts and how he changes—if he does at all—during the play. As it turns out, this is a perfect way to analyze literature, history, and personal experience for this type of essay. The SAT essay prompt always asks these vaguely ethical, somewhat moralistic, sort of philosophical questions about things like personal motivation, power, change, technology, hard work, and so on. Tracking how people behave and how they respond to circumstance is a perfect way to learn to address these topics.

Creating a Character Arc

Creating a character arc is a pretty systematic process: first, you articulate what your character knows, how he feels, and what he wants at the beginning of the play. Inevitably something happens to your character or your character does something. He tries to accomplish something, he suffers some loss, or he gets lucky. That experience or behavior challenges the character, and then he either stays just the same as he was in the beginning or (more likely) makes a significant change by the end of the play.

Let's look at how to map this out for any simple storyline.

Basic Character Arc

Stage I: Jack is happy and wants to eat lots of cookies.

Stage II: Jack doesn't listen when his mother tells him he can only have one cookie. Instead, Jack eats twenty cookies.

Stage III: Jack is sad and feels sick.

Moral: Jack learns he should listen to authority.

What you're going to do is put together a giant list of possible examples for the essay that will serve as memory jogs on test day. Your list should include books that you've read in high school, historic situations (like wars or famines) that you've learned about, and maybe some influential and/or inspiring people. If you've been through any extraordinary experiences (travel, surviving a hurricane, wilderness camp—that kind of thing), we can map those out to be effective examples as well. What's great here is that you don't have to go back and read the books over again; you can read a certain famous website's online summary, reviewing the plot summaries and character overviews. Or you can research people and events online and get a ton of info.

To get you started, I have included some sample character arcs drawn from a couple of books, and a few people. They are all accurate, and you can use them as a foundation to develop your own character arcs. Don't count on these, though. It really is an abbreviated list and it's important that you do your own work so you sound like you know what you're talking about. The purpose of these arcs is to serve as a memory jog—you'll need to include more details in the essay itself.

Sample Character Arcs

Here are a few more examples of basic character arcs.

Darth Vader in Star Wars

Stage I: Anakin Sykwalker is born with a remarkable amount of "The Force."

Stage II: He gets a taste of power and becomes consumed with garnering more for himself.

Stage III: Anakin becomes Darth Vader and the Republic falls.

Moral: Power motivates people more than anything.

Peter Keating in The Fountainhead

Stage I: Keating has been pushed into a career for which he is not suited; the only true thing in his life is his love for Catherine.

Stage II: Just when Keating is about to marry Catherine, Dominique, who is more beautiful and dynamic (and underhanded), convinces him to marry her.

Stage III: Keating throws away his only opportunity for true happiness and ends the novel miserable and alone.

Moral: Eternal dissatisfaction and constantly looking for an upgrade leads to eternal unhappiness.

Gandhi—The Great Salt March

Stage I: The British imperialist government made it illegal for anyone other than the British to produce salt in India.

Stage II: Gandhi led a march across India to promote civil disobedience and to encourage his followers to make their own salt from the sea.

Stage III: The march ultimately mobilized the Indian people to unify and declare their independence from Britain.

Moral: Sometimes going against the rules and being disobedient can be a good thing, or sometimes the ends justify the means.

Many tutors recommend steering clear of personal examples, but that isn't because they're not valid examples of situations and experiences. The risk with these is that you're more likely to write about the experience as if the reader already knows you, or you'll assume the reader knows certain pieces of information from her own experiences that she'll plug in to relate to yours. When you write about books, movies, or history, you're more inclined to explain (and more in the habit of explaining) the ins and outs of a situation; if you write about your own life, you'll need to approach your personal experiences with this same objectivity, using a character arc to fully explain the example. That means if you're going to discuss something as grave as a family member's experience with cancer, you should not focus on the fact that it was really sad and hard on the whole family. It's very difficult to write about situations that are so profoundly important to you on an analytical level, and unfortunately you don't receive a higher score on the essay because you've been through some extremely trying times. There is no mercy scoring.

That being the case, believe me when I tell you that when it is Saturday morning at 8 AM and you are preparing to write a timed essay, you will be extremely grateful that you assembled your list of possibilities. Your middle two paragraphs will use these character arcs as the meat and potatoes of your examples.

Constructing a Foolproof, Solid Essay

Since we're now all on the same page about the essay being a skeleton—a structural, technical exercise—we should also agree that the bones will always be more or less identical. This is great, because not only can we plan examples, but we can also actually plan the structure of the essay well ahead of time and then just pop in appropriate examples on the day of the test.

Now, because I would never ask you to do something on the test that I don't do myself, I have included, as an example that the format works, my own essay from an actual SAT that received a perfect score of 12. My sample essay pretty much, sentence for sentence, follows the format I'm about to show you. My students have done extremely well with this format, as well.

Note: Any errors that were made in the essay have been left in—I want you to understand that this really is a *rough draft* of an essay and that it's possible to receive a top score even with a few obvious errors.

It's really basic.

You're going to put together a four-paragraph essay with a beginning, a middle, and an end. What's important about this tactic is that all of the components of your essay are extremely identifiable; the structure of the essay counts the most, and we (meaning the English-teacher types and I) want to make sure that you really get it. That means it serves you well to write in such a way that screams: "OK! I GET THIS!" Get it?

Here's a basic sentence-by-sentence outline of how your essay will come together.

Paragraph 1: The Beginning

Once you get into your dream college, you can use this SAT essay format to write five-page, twenty-page, or hundred-page papers.

We're going to write an introductory paragraph that addresses the topic: "What brings success: determination or luck?" To keep it somewhat interesting, why don't we argue that people who are really successful are actually just very lucky?

Here's what we're going to write:

- Sentence 1: The Hook
- Sentence 2: Explanation of or Comment on the Hook
- Sentence 3: Introduction to the Topic
- Sentence 4: Introduction to Your Answer to the Question
- Sentence 5: Old-School Thesis Statement

First: The Hook

A *hook* refers to anything catchy that grabs a reader's attention. There are hooks in advertising and hooks in pop music, too. Your hook can be any kind of quote, fact, or saying that you think somehow relates to the topic you'll be writing about. We're just showing that we know it's a good idea to grab the reader's attention.

> "Today's preparation determines tomorrow's achievement,"
> declares a poster that hangs in many high school classrooms.

This may or may not be true. I actually saw that quote on the wall of the room in which I took an SAT relatively recently, and I used it for my essay right then and there. It sounds good. We'll leave it.

Second: Explanation of or Comment on the Hook

This is probably going to be just a little sentence to help you ease into the topic.

> The ideology that effort expelled results in guaranteed results is pervasive among the American populace.

This sentence just says, "Lots of people think hard work yields success," only it says it using really fancy language. Let me be the first to say that *expelled* is not the best word in this context; however, I didn't edit my essay after the fact, so there it is. What's important about this sentence, though, is that now I've focused your attention on thinking about what causes success as opposed to just leaving a blanket statement. That's key.

Third: Introduction to the Topic

This means that I'm going to get you to think about success overall. I'm not going tell you what I think about it yet; I just want to make sure that we're all clear that the essay is about the concept of success and not about the poster in the classroom that I used to get your attention in the first place.

> But sadly, the achievement of success per the American people
> is not as cut and dry.

Obviously. But perhaps now I have you wondering about what defines success . . . or at least you're onto the fact that I'll be telling you more about it.

Fourth: Introduction to My Answer to the Question

Now I'm going to get you thinking along the same lines as I am without yet introducing my examples. It's the big preparation sentence that keeps your thesis from sounding like it came out of thin air.

> In the United States today, success is defined by celebrity,
> wealth, fame, and power.

See how I did that? I've got you thinking about how we define success—it's my first step in actually answering the question. I defined my terms.

Fifth: Old-School Thesis Statement

This is where I tell you two things: (1) My direct answer to the question, "What brings success?" (2) The two examples I'll be using to support that claim in the order they will appear in my essay.

> Those who pursue the ultimate in the American dream, although
> their dreams may be as disparate as success on Broadway to
> attaining the most powerful position in the world—the United
> States presidency, find that success is largely determined by luck.

My Introductory Paragraph

Here it is, all strung together:

> "Today's preparation determines tomorrow's achievement,"
> declares a poster that hangs in many high school classrooms.
> The ideology that effort expelled results in guaranteed results is
> pervasive among the American populace. But sadly, the achieve-
> ment of success per the American people is not as cut and dry. In
> the United States today, success is defined by celebrity, wealth,
> fame, and power. Those who pursue the ultimate in the American
> dream, although their dreams may be as disparate as success on
> Broadway to attaining the most powerful position in the world—
> the United States presidency, find that success is largely deter-
> mined by luck.

Paragraphs 2 and 3: The Middle

Again, because the point of this essay is to show you know how to structure essays and arguments, here's what we expect to see in a solid body paragraph—no more, no less.

- ○ Point 1: Intro and Brief Background
- ○ Point 2: Character Stage I
- ○ Point 3: Character Stage II
- ○ Point 4: Character Stage III
- ○ Point 5: Summarizing comment that relates directly to your thesis

Unlike the points in paragraph 1, these points are not necessarily a single sentence each. However, since we're writing a whole paper in twenty-five minutes, try to keep it relatively bare bones.

Point 1: Intro and Brief Background

Becoming a "star" in modern culture is deemed a valuable vocation to pursue. There is no better example of the iconic rise to the top than current Broadway leading lady Sutton Foster. Ms. Foster, Tony award-winner and nominee, finds herself at the top her profession, but not through hard work alone.

Point 2: Character Stage I

Her career started at seventeen when she auditioned for the National Tour of "Les Miserables." She was offered the job promptly—even as an unknown. So started her road to success.

Point 3: Character Stage II

Not long after, she found herself in the chorus of a Broadway workshop.

Point 4: Character Stage III

There her luck proved significant again: the lead actress was unable to fulfill her commitments, was fired, and Foster found herself cast as the title role.

Point 5: Summarizing Comment

Your summarizing comment relates directly to your thesis.

Although Ms. Foster is a highly talented and well-trained individual, no amount of training guarantees the luck—and precipitate success—that she currently experiences.

Paragraph 2

Here it is, all strung together:

Becoming a "star" in modern culture is deemed a valuable vocation to pursue. There is no better example of the iconic rise to the top than current Broadway leading lady Sutton Foster.

Ms. Foster, Tony award-winner and nominee, finds herself at the top her profession, but not through hard work alone. Her career started at seventeen when she auditioned for the national tour of "Les Miserables." She was offered the job promptly—even as an unknown. So started her road to success. Not long after, she found herself in the chorus of a Broadway workshop. There her luck proved significant again: the lead actress was unable to fulfill her commitments, was fired, and Foster found herself cast as the title role. Although Ms. Foster is a highly talented and well-trained individual, no amount of training guarantees the luck—and precipitate success—that she currently experiences.

Paragraph 3 will have the same fundamental structure as Paragraph 2.

Point 1: Intro and Brief Background

The same success of attaining the job of United States president requires the same final dose of luck.

Point 2: Character Stage I

Potential presidents are groomed from childhood to be dynamic individuals with exceptional social skills and fundamental political acumen.

Point 3: Character Stage II

They attend the best education institutions and travel in the best influential circle they can in the interest of "earning" the nomination.

Point 4: Character Stage III

Ultimately, though, preparation succumbs to luck, as the decision is not made by the candidate.

Point 5: Summarizing comment

Again, this is a comment that relates directly to your thesis.

Earning a nomination and the election are the product of circumstance, the media, and, again, luck.

Paragraph 3

Here it is, all strung together:

The same success of attaining the job of United States president requires the same final dose of luck. Potential presidents are groomed from childhood to be dynamic individuals with exceptional social skills and fundamental political acumen. They attend the best education institutions and travel in the best influential circle they can in the interest of "earning" the nomination. Ultimately, though, preparation succumbs to luck, as the decision is not made by the candidate. Earning a nomination and the election are the product of circumstance, the media, and, again, luck.

Paragraph 4: The End

Listen to me! The final paragraph is a sentence or two that ties everything together. It is simply a rephrasing (not an exact copy) of the argument in your thesis. You can get a little reflective or clever in your conclusion if you've gone deep and philosophical and that's your style, but it's probably not necessary for a solid score. The concluding paragraph that follows refers back to my original definition of success. I want to make sure you understand, though, that although it brings into question the topic itself, it does not allude to the other side of the argument (that is, it does not in any way say, "well, *maybe* success is earned"). Instead, it is intended to make the reader think more about the question from this perspective.

The End

> It is interesting that modern culture defines success in terms that are circumstantial. Perhaps if success were redefined as personal happiness and peace, the world would be populated by a significantly larger number of "successful" people.

The single biggest error I see students make—and this is classic—is introducing an entirely new example in the last paragraph. It happens all the time: you've been writing for twenty minutes and then all of the sudden it hits you that discussing the events surrounding Winston Churchill's famous "Never, never quit" address (or whatever) would be just perfect for this particular topic. Let me remind you again: 80 percent of the points you earn on the essay are gained by your exhibiting that you know the technical aspects of Good Paper Writing. You would never suddenly bring out your best example at the very end of a ten-page research paper. Now is your opportunity to show the College Board that you know that presenting new ideas at the very end is bad.

So don't do it. Don't bring Winston Churchill or Chernobyl or *American Idol* or any new examples into the last paragraph. Although you may think the examples you have already chosen aren't as strong as the one you have miraculously thought of in the nineteenth minute, the strength of your paper is really found in its organization, and you will ultimately be better off just leaving out the idea.

The Full Essay, All Strung Together

> "Today's preparation determines tomorrow's achievement," declares a poster that hangs in many high school classrooms. The ideology that effort expelled results in guaranteed results is pervasive among the American populace. But sadly, the achievement of success per the American people is not as cut and dry. In the United States today, success is defined by celebrity, wealth, fame, and power. Those who pursue the ultimate in the American dream, although their dreams may be as disparate as success on Broadway to attaining the most powerful position in the world—the United States presidency, find that success is largely determined by luck.

Becoming a "star" in modern culture is deemed a valuable vocation to pursue. There is no better example of the iconic rise to the top than current Broadway leading lady Sutton Foster. Ms. Foster, Tony award-winner and nominee, finds herself at the top her profession, but not through hard work alone. Her career started at seventeen when she auditioned for the national tour of "Les Miserables." She was offered the job promptly—even as an unknown. So started her road to success. Not long after, she found herself in the chorus of a Broadway workshop. There her luck proved significant again: the lead actress was unable to fulfill her commitments, was fired, and Foster found herself cast as the title role. Although Ms. Foster is a highly talented and well-trained individual, no amount of training guarantees the luck—and precipitate success—that she currently experiences.

The same success of attaining the job of United States president requires the same final dose of luck. Potential presidents are groomed from childhood to be dynamic individuals with exceptional social skills and fundamental political acumen. They attend the best education institutions and travel in the best influential circle they can in the interest of "earning" the nomination. Ultimately, though, preparation succumbs to luck, as the decision is not made by the candidate. Earning a nomination and the election are the product of circumstance, the media, and, again, luck.

It is interesting that modern culture defines success in terms that are circumstantial. Perhaps if success is redefined as personal happiness and peace, the world would be populated by a significantly larger number of "successful" people.

Emergency Situations—aka Making Stuff Up or Talking about Yourself

Objectively, making up examples, names, places, facts, or even dates for the SAT essay is totally kosher. Not to belabor this, but the whole point of the essay is to prove your strong rough-draft technique—and to prove that technique using "appropriate examples." The College Board doesn't say "true" examples; the examples must simply be appropriate.

There are two things you need to keep in mind while mulling over the appropriateness of an example, especially if you're going to fabricate it. One, is that example actually related to the essay topic? Two, is it neither stupid (say, the personal experiences of your dog Astro) nor in bad taste? If you pass both those tests, you're golden.

That's not all you need to worry about. The real, honest reason we don't encourage you to make up examples: you're probably not very good at it. You're super at explaining to your folks why you were out three hours past curfew, but what you need on the SAT is a solid, relevant example for which you have developed believable details and a character arc for the person or situation. If you're making up a movie, it needs to sound as if you have actually seen the movie and taken note of all of the important elements. Let's cut to the chase: your example has to be awesome. If you'd like to practice this, write a few example paragraphs and show them to a friend or a teacher and have them critique your ideas. You may be surprised at what you don't see in your own argument.

How the Essay Is Graded and What You Can Do to Up Your Score

Two people will read your essay, each giving your essay a score between 0 and 6. A score of 0 meaning you didn't address the questions, wrote nothing, or wrote in pen and 6 meaning it's one of the strongest that they read. The two reader's combined scores produce the score you see on your score report, which is why you can receive up to a 12. If the two reader's scores differ by more than a point, a third reader reads the essay and decides the score. For our purposes, let's stick to talking about essays in terms of the range of scores you could receive from each reader: between 1 and 6.

If you follow the format I've just described and trace a character arc using an appropriate example, it's more or less a shoo-in that you'll receive a score of at least 4 from each reader for a total score of 8. Keep in mind that during some test administrations *less than 1 percent* of students who take the test receive a perfect 12 on the essay. Moreover, the essay makes up only 30 percent of your total score. The essay should be considered, but there is no need to be frantic about it, particularly if your multiple choice section is really good. I knew a student who received a perfect score on the Writing multiple choice, received only a 9 on her essay, and still received a 780 on the Writing section. The moral: be diligent about the essay but do not make yourself crazy over it.

Here's what you need to do to up your score:

Important: I mentioned this earlier, but please remember that you must write your essay in #2 pencil. If your essay is written in ink, it will be given a score of zero—no ifs, ands, or buts. Count on it.

Vary Sentence Structure

One of the best ways to make any paper more interesting is to vary your sentence structure. Not sure how? Try starting sentences with the changeup words we talked about in the Sentence Completion section. Starting a sentence with *despite, in spite of, although,* or even *though* will force you to subordinate a clause and put the subject in the middle of the sentence rather than at the beginning. To the English buffs who grade these tests, this is scintillating stuff.

Language Usage Tips

It's also important that you show the SAT reader that you know the difference between commonly misused words and that you make wise decisions about word use.

Use the Right Word the Right Way

Know when to use *there, their,* and *they're*:

○ You should use *there* to indicate placement: "*There* are only three donuts left" or "Put the dishes over *there.*"

○ You should use *their* to indicate the possessive: "They took *their* dog to *their* house."

○ Avoid using *they're*, a contraction of *they are*. A sentence like "The boys are sure *they're* going to the movies." is too informal for the SAT.

Know when to use *your* and *you're*:

○ You should use *your* to indicate the possessive: "*Your* jeans are ripped."

○ Avoid using *you're*, a contraction of *you are*, like "*You're* a funny guy."

Know when to use *its* and *it's*:

○ You should use *its* to indicate the possessive form of *it*: "The cat licked *its* fur."

○ Avoid using *it's*, a contraction of "it is" as in "*It's* not my fault."

Replace lame words:

○ Don't use *a lot* (note, that's not "alot"); instead use *many* or *multiple* or *often* or *frequently*.

○ Avoid using *get* and *try*; instead use *attain*, *attempt*, or *works to achieve*.

I always feel a little melodramatic when I berate students for not following these guidelines, but misusing these simple words—or using lame words instead of the smarter option—is like reaching out from your essay and punching your reader in the face. Everyone who reads these essays is an expert writer and has mastered the English language; they freak out about the smallest details.

Don't Use "Don't" or Any Other Contractions

It was important to me to show you the differences between all those words, but you'll notice I told you not to use any contracted forms. Because we're supposed to be exhibiting formal writing on the SAT essay—far more formal than the writing in this book—we want to avoid contractions at all costs.

No Slang

Just as we want to avoid informal contractions, we also want to avoid informal speech, specifically slang. This means that a character won't be *bummed*; he'll be *disheartened*. The general rule of thumb is to use the most formal, uppity, professional-sounding language you can muster, the more prim the better.

Better Vocabulary

One way to preplan your quest for a more formal essay is to have a selection of broad words that can be applied fairly universally. Here's a list of broad words to have on hand:

Ultimately	Fundamentally	Significantly
Quintessentially	Consequently	Demonstrably
Remarkably	Broadly	Generally

Words like *ultimately*, *quintessentially*, and *remarkably* can be thrown into almost any piece of writing and can make your writing feel more powerful and effective.

No Personal Pronouns

Avoid using the words *I think* and *you* like the plague. Once you begin the pattern of referring to yourself, the general language you use will likely not be as strong. Instead of saying, "I think Dickens is implying that. . . ." just say, "Dickens implies. . . . " Moreover, if you stick to the "no you" rule, instead of saying, "When you really want something, you tend to work hard for it," you're more likely to think twice and write something more powerful: "desire produces effort."

Avoid Passive Voice

Passive voice isn't so much a grammatical error as it is a remote, drawn-out way of saying something, usually by putting the subject of the sentence after the verb. For example,

Passive is: The game was played badly by the team.

Better would be: The team played badly.

Changing sentence structure by putting a subordinating clause (a *despite* or *although* clause) at its beginning is a good idea—making the sentence murky by hiding the subject is not. (For more on the passive voice, check out page 61.)

Avoid Extra Words

Steer clear of phrases like "because of the fact that" and "being as she is" that are unnecessarily wordy. Either of these phrases could be replaced with the word *because*. Keep in mind that the most powerful writing often uses the fewest words.

Learn, Study, and Know the Rules from the Grammar Lesson

I don't want to be repetitive, but it's important that you recognize that the sentence-structure rules for the sentence-editing questions on this test apply to the essay, as well. Learn them, own them, and use them. They will help!

Another Real-Life Sample

There is no better way to show you the effectiveness of the essay format than to show you another real SAT essay. The following is one of my students' responses to the same question about success that he wrote on the same test date on which I wrote the previous sample. He also received a score of 12 by modifying the format a bit.

Note: Again, any errors that were made in the essay have been left in—I want you to understand that this really is a *rough draft* of an essay and that it's possible to receive a top score even with a few overt errors.

Austin's Essay

This essay was written by my student Austin Dosch, Wake Forest University class of '10.

Though success is often viewed as sheer luck, the truth behind genuine success lies with one's own perseverance and hard work. Throughout history, success has been achieved by a variety of individuals. However, many of the successes which these figures achieve is a direct result of the hard work they endure. The Wright Brothers and their endeavors are a valid example of pure success through hard work. In literature, Henry David Thoreau considers true success as one's own satisfaction from intense labor. Thus, it is clear that success cannot be measured in luck, it is spurred from the passion of an individual through work.

Before the famous flight, Kitty Hawk, North Carolina was just an empty town filled with average citizens. However, held within its dull confines were the minds of two shrewd bicycle shop owners. Wilbur and Orville Wright had studied the art of flying for years and were determined to put their own genius into flight. The men were ridiculed for the dreams and passion, yet they persevered despite criticism Their one, ten second flight was miraculous and the embodiment of their hard work. However this one success was the product of a great many failures. The Brothers took the "hard way out" and kept trying despite each failure which ensued. Hard work paid off; the Wright Brothers can be thanked for an incredible invention today.

Walden displays a keen view of human achievements. Written by Thoreau, it is an early piece of American literature which advocates the usage of one's own ability to complete any task. "Self-Reliance" was his motto, meaning each man should rely on himself for progress in any activity. Thoreau claimed good work ethic would bring true success, despite wealth or fame. His insight was that a man would not gain satisfaction only by the completed product, but that the journey which pieced the product together would sequester the true treasure. It was a spiritual enlightenment in which Thoreau sought men to persevere through labor an hard work; a man who buys his way into anything has no true sense of self satisfaction, and therefore in reality, no success.

"Opportunity is missed by most people because it comes dressed in overalls and looks like work." Thomas Edison could not have said it better. True opportunity and success lie within one's own hardships. Each person possesses an infinite potential for greatness and success; work, education, and self-insight are just the pathways to discovering it.

How Austin Got a 12

Let's talk briefly about what makes this essay a 12, addressing each of the grading criteria.

- *Appropriate Examples:* Austin used excellent examples that illustrate his point that success is the product of hard work. The Wright brothers are a great example of two people who toiled endlessly until they had perfected their original designs and goals. He challenges the reader by introducing *Walden*, which provides him with an opportunity to argue that work not only leads to success, but also that people do not enjoy their successes if they do not feel that they have worked for them.

- *Organization and Focus:* The organization here is very simple—we see a clearly defined introduction, two body paragraphs, and a concluding paragraph. By introducing his final paragraph with a quote relevant to work and success, he retains the readers' attention throughout the final paragraph and avoids the need to repeat ideas from earlier in the paper.

- *Language (i.e., glitzy vocabulary):* Remember that peppering your essay with interesting vocabulary doesn't mean that it needs to be difficult to understand. Let's look at a few places where Austin opted to use more formal words:

  > *endeavors* rather than *work*
  > *is spurred* rather than *comes out of*
  > *shrewd* rather than *smart*
  > *embodiment* rather than *the thing that finally happened*
  > *advocates* the usage of rather than *says it's a good idea to use*

  See if you can find some other words in the essay that jump out at you as examples of stronger language and keep them in mind while you write your own essay.

- *Varied Sentence Structure:* The first sentence begins with a subordinate clause (it begins with *though*), and there are other examples of varied sentence structure, including the use of a semicolon. More importantly, you'll never find two sentences that start with the same word positioned right after each other. Keep an eye on your own writing—do sentences often start with *The* or *I think*? Learning to break that habit will dress up your writing.

- *Grammar:* While the essay is sprinkled with mistakes that are clearly the fruit of a very short time limit, overall the work is grammatically correct. Semicolons are used properly and the work is free of fragments and run-ons. Austin also steers clear of comma splices, and he placed periods inside the quotation marks.

Overall this essay is strong and generally free of errors. When you write your own essay, focus on staying organized and using language and sentence structure that will keep your reader's attention. Show your practice essays to someone who has seen the grading structure for the test, like your English teacher, and ask her if she'll identify the areas on which you need to work the most.

Remember, the essay is only 30 percent of your score, so you should spend 70 percent of your time working on the multiple choice material that follows. However, practicing the essay in timed conditions can easily influence your achievement on the entire test. How? The essay is always the first task you encounter on test day, and feeling like you weren't as successful as you could have been has been known to cause some students' confidence to flounder. A solid essay can be an excellent springboard for a fantastic SAT.

identifying
sentence errors
and improving
sentences

It's extremely unlikely that you've had a proper grammar course in high school. This is both wonderful (because grammar courses are not known for being thrilling) and awful (because, well, you need grammar badly). What we're going to do here is address the vast majority of the grammar that appears on the SAT as succinctly as possible, learning as much as is necessary but not more. That means that I need you to know how to use all this stuff and recognize it in sentences, but I do not care if you never actually utter the words *coordinating conjunction* or *idiomatic preposition*. I'm doing my best to keep this from being a total drag. I've included questions of both styles throughout the chapter to be efficient and keep things interesting.

The most important, timesaving, streamlining tip I can give you is that you should always read answer choices in order of shortest to longest. Why? The short answer is "efficiency." Streamlined writing is not wordy and garbled; it simply says what it needs to say. You'll find you encounter much less confusion if you zero in on the short answers and work your way up to the longest options.

I'll cover two types of questions in this chapter: Identifying Sentence Errors and Improving Sentences. In the latter, you need to select the answer choice that will correct the grammatical mistake in the sentence. The Identifying Sentence Error questions format is different; parts of the sentence are underlined, and the answer letters appear below. I happen to think that the best part about this question format is that you don't need to develop a "fix" for the incorrect segment; you just need to know what works and what doesn't.

Sentences 101

Each and every sentence has a subject and a verb, which is sometimes called a *predicate*. Every sentence must have those two parts, the subject and the verb; otherwise you've got a fragment.

Granted, you are unlikely to leave an obvious, unmodified subject just sitting out in space without a verb, like this one:

The cat.

"The cat" is not a sentence—it's a fragment. That's pretty obvious. On the other hand, some folks might not notice that the following is not a sentence, either:

> The group of friends whose party was held in a limousine on the way to the prom.

The subject here is "the group"—everything else in that fragment is modifying or describing the group. We never find out what the group did or made or ate or drank (or for what reason they were expelled).

No Verb, No Sentence

You're likely to read commas where there aren't any to make a sentence sound good in your head. It's actually a pretty dirty trick your brain plays on you—the way it reads is actually largely based on what it *expects* to see, not what it *actually* sees, so the test makers sneak in long-winded sentences with no verb and hope you don't notice. This means that when you're thinking subject-verb agreement, you also want to make sure that a sentence contains both a subject and a verb in the first place!

EXAMPLE 1: LEVEL 2
The Peace Treaty of 1868, following two years of war between the Sioux and the United States, <u>violated by General Custer in 1874</u>.

(A)   violated by General Custer in 1874.
(B)   violating General Custer in 1874.
(C)   violated in 1874, it was General Custer.
(D)   was violated in 1874 by General Custer.
(E)   in 1874, General Custer was a violator.

This sentence, as long as it is, is a fragment. Because that huge modifier is thrown in (*following two . . . United States*), you may be distracted from the need for a verb. What you've got, though, is an extended version of a fragment: *The Treaty violated*. Pop in a verb, *was*, and you're golden. So the answer is D.

EXAMPLE 2: LEVEL 2
Scientists claim that giant squid <u>swimming deep below the surface of the ocean</u>, scaring and thrilling researchers and students alike.

(A)   swimming deep below the surface of the ocean
(B)   swimming deeply below the surface of the oceans waves,
(C)   swim deep below the surface of the ocean,
(D)   swims deeply and below the waters of oceans,
(E)   below the deep surface of the ocean, swims,

If we leave this sentence as it is we have the same problem—it's an extra-strength fragment. However, because *scaring and thrilling* is not underlined, it is imperative that we replace the underlined portion with something that includes a verb in the correct form. The other more challenging element of this problem is that the word *squid* is being used in its plural form, which means we need the word *swim*, not *swims*. Correct answer: C.

Subject-Verb Agreement

Not only does every sentence have to have a subject and verb, but the subject and verb also have to agree, or match. You may not normally pay much attention to this when you're speaking and writing, but you pair subjects with different forms of the same verb depending on whether they are singular or plural. If you speak a language other than English, particularly one of the four Romance languages, you'll notice that you conjugate verbs differently for different subjects all the time; there are almost always different verb forms for *he/she* and *they*.

For example, in English the verb "to be" is conjugated differently depending on who is doing the "being": I *am*, you *are*, he/she *is*, we *are*, and they *are*. Each of those italicized words is a form of the same verb, and that's what the subject-verb agreement section tests: your ability to choose the correct form of the verb to match the subject.

The trick to matching a subject and its verb is—usually—to assess whether the subject is plural or singular. In fact, some subjects sound plural but they're actually singular. The words *committee, school, business, duo, group, number, every,* and *each* all demand singular verbs because, for example, a committee is a single entity—it's one committee.

Check out the difference here:

Plural: The <u>members</u> of the committee <u>agree</u> with the president.
             S   V

Singular: The <u>committee</u> <u>agrees</u> with the president.
                S   V

These matching rules apply to both the official subject of the sentence and its corresponding verb as well as all of the other subject-verb pairs that appear in the sentence.

A note about prepositional phrases as filler: Prepositions are the little words that generally introduce those phrases that tell us where things happen or when things happened, like *under the refrigerator* or *after the concert*. What's great about prepositional phrases (*under the refrigerator* is the complete phrase) is how easily they can be compartmentalized and ignored, which is the key to isolating subjects and verbs to make sure you've got proper agreement.

For example, see the prepositional phrases here:

The bird (on the ground) (in the midday sun) eat worms.

I managed to keep that subject and verb seven words away from each other. On the SAT you may find worse. However, if you simply bracket those phrases away, you can easily see that we have a souped-up version of the sentence, "the bird eat worms," which you would immediately notice is wrong.

EXAMPLE 1: LEVEL 3

The principal's <u>insistence on</u> qualified teachers and spacious classrooms
A

<u>were intended</u> to foster a positive <u>outlook</u> and higher grades
B   C

<u>for the students</u>. <u>No error</u>
D   E

This is a perfect opportunity to cross out those prepositions and enclose them in parentheses:

The principal's <u>insistence (~~on qualified teachers and spacious classrooms~~)</u>
A

<u>were intended</u> (~~to foster a positive outlook and higher grades~~)
B   C

(~~for the students~~). <u>No error</u>
D   E

We're left with *The principal's insistence were intended.* See the problem? The trick here is that we would conversationally say, "the insistence was intended"; however, that *were* in the sentence comes after two plural words, *classrooms* and *teachers*, so we tend to expect the plural form of the verb. You must keep an eye out for prepositional phrases and make sure that you're matching subjects and verbs. That makes the answer B.

EXAMPLE 2: LEVEL 3

Neither of the puppies <u>are interested</u> <u>in playing</u> with the toy carrot,
A   B

despite <u>their</u> owner's attempts to capture their attention <u>with it</u>. <u>No error</u>
C   D   E

Example 4 is really just like example 3, except that once you get rid of the prepositional phrases with parentheses you need to know that *neither* is singular—meaning the sentence needs to read *Neither of the puppies is interested.* . . . So A is correct.

EXAMPLE 3: LEVEL 4
A pair of rivers, the Ashley and the Cooper, <u>delineate</u> the peninsula on which the city of Charleston is located.

(A) delineate
(B) delineating
(C) which delineating
(D) rivers that delineate
(E) delineates

The important element here is more esoteric—the word *pair* is singular, just like committee, league, or team. Even though *pair* refers specifically to two of something, it's still a singular word. Therefore, *A pair (of rivers) delineates*. . . . Correct answer: E.

Verbs: Conjugation and the Infinitive

When we've got two related verbs, we conjugate the first and leave the second as an infinitive (the verb in its "to _____" form). You'll find that in simple situations you apply this rule all the time.

> She is trying *to cut* paper.

However, in conversation we are prone to ignore this rule, presumably to make things sound fancier.

> Wrong: The new security tag *uses* human DNA *in the identification of* entering employees.

> Correct: The new security tag *uses* human DNA *to identify* entering employees.

This topic isn't tested very often, but it's a good, simple rule to file away.

EXAMPLE 1: LEVEL 3

Kimberly <u>says</u> some forms of massage <u>employs</u> hot stones <u>in the relieving</u>
      A   B   C
of <u>sore</u> muscles. <u>No error</u>
    D   E

As we discussed earlier, the first verb stays conjugated and the second form must be in the infinitive—so we need "some forms of massage <u>employ</u> hot stones to relieve sore muscles." The answer in this case is B.

Subject and Direct Object Agreement

Sentence subjects are always aspiring to things in the SAT questions. Why? Because it's a perfect opportunity to test whether you know that when someone wants to *be* or *become* something, that goal—the object of the verb—must match the subject, particularly in number.

You'll see this tested with objects that are both plural and singular, for example

> Wrong: John and Mark were hoping to become <u>a professional pilot</u>.

> Correct: John and Mark were hoping to become <u>professional pilots.</u>

A pilot is an individual person, so John and Mark are *each* hoping to become an individual *pilot*. They *both* want to become *pilots*.

Likewise, plural subjects can become a singular unit.

> Wrong: Our cockatiels have always been <u>twosomes</u>.

> Correct: Our cockatiels have always been <u>a twosome</u>.

This refers back to those singular subjects we talked about earlier, as when a number of people form a singular committee or a club or an organization.

EXAMPLE 1: LEVEL 2

Many students <u>would like</u> to <u>believe that</u> high grades <u>guarantee</u> that they
          A   B   C

will be <u>a successful business person</u> later in life. <u>No error</u>
         D   E

Just like we discussed earlier, many *students* (plural) will want to be business *people* (plural), not a single, collective *business person* later in life. To that end, *business person* is incorrect, so the answer is D.

Pronouns—That's What "They" Say

Pronouns are the great stand-in words in language—they're little representative words that keep us from having to use a noun's specific name over and over. Pronouns are words like *I, you, he, she, we, they, them,* and *it.* Because of pronouns, we don't have to write sentences like this:

> Susan packed Susan's belongings into Susan's grandmother's
> bag for the safari. Susan had been dreaming about this trip since
> Susan was six.

Be grateful for pronouns. They make life less annoying.

All pronouns have a relationship with the word for which they stand in. The word the pronoun represents is called its *antecedent.* You don't need to remember the word *antecedent* (although it's a good vocab root word), but you do need to understand that, at least on the SAT, every sentence with a pronoun must include its antecedent. SAT test question sentences are not to be treated as though they have been pulled out of some other piece of writing; these are standalone sentences, created just for the test, for which we need to have all information included right in the sentence.

The point here is that you have to know who *they* are if *they* appears in the sentence. If the antecedent for *they,* meaning the *archers* or the *ice cubes* or the *pack of mice,* doesn't appear in the original version, the correct answer will edit the sentence to include the antecedent. This is one of the rare cases in which your answer choice may be significantly longer than the original underlined portion of the sentence.

Pronouns need to be kept consistent. If a sentence uses the pronoun *one,* then *one* must be used every time throughout the sentence. This makes a sentence sound very prophetic:

> If one chooses not to wash one's hands, one may find one gets
> sick more frequently.

When you write, you may choose to introduce *one* and then switch to *he or she.* This is fine but much more cumbersome:

If one chooses not to wash his or her hands, he or she may find
that he or she gets colds more frequently.

You may also, in your own writing, choose to just use *he* or *she*, whichever
you prefer, which is completely fine; you don't have to be politically correct
here. But in the SAT multiple choice, if you see *one*, stick with *one*. Likewise,
if *you* is the standard, stick with *you*. Consistency is the top priority when it
comes to SAT pronouns.

EXAMPLE 1: LEVEL 4

In many states, <u>they have laws that ban gun sales</u> without a three-day
waiting period, but Arizona is one of the exceptions.

(A) they have laws that ban gun sales
(B) they have laws banning gun sales
(C) laws ban gun sales
(D) laws banning gun sales
(E) there are laws there banning the sales of guns

The first thing to do here is identify to whom *they* refers. Don't get sucked
in—a state is a single, collective place that can never be represented by *they*. In
fact, in this sentence there is no antecedent for *they*—we have no idea who *they*
could be. We need to find an answer choice that either clarifies the pronoun
or avoids it altogether. Because, as you may recall, it saves time to read answer
choices in order from shortest to longest, you should look at choice C first.
Conveniently, this answer works perfectly. It doesn't have a pronoun, and we
retain the verb (which, you may have noticed, some other choices do not do).
Choice C is correct.

EXAMPLE 2: LEVEL 4

<u>For those people</u> living in rural areas, <u>hunting</u> is a relaxing way to spend
      A   B

<u>your</u> time that <u>developed from</u> a necessity for survival. <u>No error</u>
  C   D   E

This question is theoretically more difficult because of two elements: One, it
includes a limiting statement "For those people," which confuses students but is
grammatically correct. Two, the pronoun *your* is not only wrong, it's unnecessary. In this case, answer C identifies the incorrect part of the sentence.

EXAMPLE 3: LEVEL 3

Wayne, Dan, and Paul were riding their motorcycles when, <u>sailing over a speed bump, he was suddenly suspended in midair.</u>

(A) sailing over a speed bump, he was suddenly suspended in midair.

(B) sailing over a speed bump, Wayne was suddenly suspended in midair.

(C) a speed bump having been sailed over, he was suddenly suspended in midair.

(D) he was suddenly suspended in midair after having sailed over a speed bump.

(E) Wayne was suddenly suspended in midair sailing over a speed bump.

Sometimes both a pronoun and an antecedent can appear in a sentence, but it's still not clear to which noun that pronoun refers. In these cases it's better to replace the pronoun with the noun (even if you're saying it twice) for the sake of clarity. As this example stands now, we have no idea if it's Wayne, Dan, or Paul who is suspended. Select those answer choices that include one of those names, then choose the option that offers the most clear modification. In answer E, it is not entirely clear what is *sailing over a speed bump*. That leaves answer B as the correct choice.

EXAMPLE 4: LEVEL 5

<u>With hundreds of cases left to be shipped,</u> the supply company felt that its paper sales were declining.

(A) With hundreds of cases left to be shipped,

(B) Having hundreds of cases left to be shipped,

(C) With hundreds of cases of loose-leaf left to be shipped,

(D) Shipping loose-leaf, leaving hundreds of cases,

(E) With hundreds left to be shipped,

It should bother you to select the longest answer choice in the writing multiple choice section because efficient writing is usually more condensed. That's exactly why a question similar to this one appears at the end of the section. Because we don't have options beyond the passive voice (notably used in each answer choice), instead we have to know that the word *cases* is not a sufficient pronoun. The *cases* in this sentence could be of towels, pencils, or deodorant, for all we know. Unless you are given a choice with a proper pronoun, you must specify. Words like *cases*, *tons*, and *shipments* don't always cut it as a clear stand-in. Here, C is the correct choice.

For more on the passive voice, check out page 61.

Direct Object Pronouns versus Subject Pronouns

It was always about the grammar at my house. This brings us to subject pronouns and direct object pronouns, or the "When to use 'I' and when to use 'me'" lesson. There are two different lists of pronouns to be used depending on the capacity in which the word is functioning. Just hear me out:

The official subject pronouns are *I, you, he/she, we, they,* and *who.* The official direct object pronouns are *me, you, him/her, we, them,* and *whom.*

> "Hey Mom, can me and Leigh Ann have popsicles?"

> "Can Leigh Ann and I have popsicles?"

It seems to me that because the English-speaking world's collective mother has forbidden us to say "Me 'n' Leigh Ann," (and rightly so), we've totally gone off the deep end and stopped using direct object pronouns altogether. This is nuts. There are times when using *me* is not only acceptable, but it's also the only correct option. That's why it's on the SAT.

Cleverly, these subject pronouns and direct object pronouns are named thusly because they stand in for—you guessed it—subjects and direct objects. Not sure what a direct object is? Let's not get technical; just think of it as the person or thing that the verb is being done to.

You'll find you use them fairly reflexively in obvious situations:

> I rode my bike.

> . . . here *I* am the subject of the sentence.

> Albert gave me a rose.

> . . . here the rose is being given *to* me.

In one, I'm doing the action. In the other, I'm receiving the action. Subject, object.

In the same vein, just as you would say, "Come sit next to me," if you add additional people to the sentence, you use the same direct object pronoun:

> Mark sat between Bernie and me.

"Me" is correct in this context; "I" would be wrong. Let's look at how you'll be tested on this.

EXAMPLE 12: LEVEL 4

<u>Excited by</u> the invitation sent by the National Science Fair to my
  A

<u>partner and I,</u> <u>we</u> spent the afternoon <u>working on</u> perfecting our project.
  B   C   D

<u>No error</u>
  E

You'd naturally say "the invitation . . . sent to me"; adding a partner to the mix is no different. The "invitation sent to my partner and *me*" is the only correct grammar. I know. Everyone objects. Believe me, *me* is correct; so the answer is B.

EXAMPLE 2: LEVEL 4

After perusing <u>its</u> contents, the president <u>asked</u> to <u>who</u> the letter <u>had been</u>
           A   B   C   D

addressed. <u>No error</u>
            E

Here's a quick rule of thumb for deciding between *who* and *whom*. If you can say, "the letter was addressed to Norman" (Norman being a direct object), then you would ask the question, "to *whom* was the letter addressed?" (not *who*). Likewise, you would ask the question, "To *whom* are you speaking," if the answer is "I am speaking to Marvin." It's a quick and easy test. So we choose answer C.

Passive Voice and Subject Pronouns

Passive voice is a tricky construction that refers to times when a writer causes the subject of the sentence to receive the action of the verb. That's mucky; it's actually much easier to see than to express, so let's just check out an example:

    Active voice: The team won the game.

    Passive voice: The game was won by the team.

Now, either of these is technically correct, but active voice is always considered stronger and preferable. You'll want to avoid passive as much as possible while writing your essay. However, the passive voice does appear in the multiple choice grammar section, particularly using subject pronouns. I think the idea behind that is, "If you're going to do something annoying, you might as well do it right."

Either way, here's what you need to recognize when using pronouns and passive voice: put simply, we use subject pronouns (*I, she, he*) when the word they're replacing is the subject of the sentence. That's why, when someone calls me on the phone and asks for Elizabeth, I respond, "This is she," *not* "This is her." Let's look at a few examples.

EXAMPLE 1: LEVEL 5

Jason <u>confessed</u> that the surprise party <u>had been</u> planned by <u>him</u> and <u>his</u>
        A   B   C   D

friends. <u>No error</u>
      E

I'll come out and say right off the bat that is an example of a question in which there is no error. In this sentence Jason is the subject of the sentence, right there at the beginning. If the subject is already defined we don't use it elsewhere (if we were to sub in *he* for *him*, we would essentially have two subjects in the sentence). So, the answer is E.

EXAMPLE 2: LEVEL 5

No one is more excited than me that we have decided to stop taking
 A   B   C   D
racquetball lessons. No error
                        E

It's unlikely that you'll see a question for which you'll need to replace *excited than me* with *excited than I* or *excited than I am,* as you'd need to do to fix this sentence. However, you will need to recognize the fundamental differences in the structure of the sentence. We could pare it down to: *I am excited that we have decided to stop taking racquetball lessons.* The *no one* bit is modifying that excitement: *No one is more excited than I am that we have decided to stop taking racquetball lessons,* so B is the correct choice.

Reflexive

Misuse of the reflexive kills me, so I love that it's tested on the SAT. This makes me a huge nerd. Nevertheless, the reflexive is chronically substituted for both subject and direct object pronouns, most likely because folks think it makes them sound fancy or important or something. It doesn't. It makes them sound wrong.

Here are some classic misusages of the reflexive, particularly of the reflexive pronoun *myself*:

> A guilt-ridden student, trying to sound very adult and heroic, explains to the teacher, "Jack and myself were just trying to fix the DVD player that spontaneously fell off its stand."

> A snotty student says to her rival student government candidate, "The principal prefers that my best friend and myself handle the decorations for the homecoming dance. We don't need your help."

Both of these instances call for the subject pronoun *I,* not the reflexive pronoun *myself.*

> Jack and I were just trying to fix the DVD player. . . .

> The principal prefers that my best friend and I handle the decorations. . . .

In fact, there are only two situations in which reflexive pronouns are used:

1) When the verb's action is being done *to* the subject

   Carol pulled *herself* together.
   Sam gave *himself* a birthday card.

2) For emphasis:

   The queen *herself* addressed the pauper.
   The factory workers *themselves* called for longer workdays.

Other than these two usages, subject and direct object pronouns are the only correct options. Seriously.

EXAMPLE 1: LEVEL 4

Jonathan and <u>myself</u> <u>were</u> the proud <u>recipients</u> of the annual award <u>for</u>
    A B   C   D
community service hours. <u>No error</u>
          E

Not to beat a dead horse, but this should read *Jonathan and I,* so your choice is A.

EXAMPLE 2: LEVEL 2

The circus performers <u>theirselves</u> <u>announced</u> that they were
        A   B
<u>convinced that</u> the tiger was safe, <u>despite</u> the rumors. <u>No error</u>
 C   D   E

This is a situation in which the reflexive pronoun should be used for emphasis. You can often tell that a word is being used emphatically when you can pop it out and the sentence is still structurally and grammatically sound. You can't use anything but the reflexive for this kind of emphasis, so the nonexistent "theirselves" could not possibly be correct. We need to correct the sentence by using the real reflexive, *themselves,* so we choose option A.

Past Participles and Past Tense

Not everything is continually happening right this very second. Because of this, we need past tense as well as past participles, which are the forms of verbs that take the word *had.* Yes, there are even rules for when to use *had.*

 Let's look at this nifty time line that shows the order in which we went swimming, ate breakfast, and went for a bike ride:

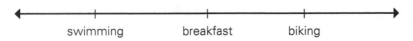

    swimming   breakfast   biking

 So, first we went swimming, then we ate, and then we went out biking. According to the chart, all of this stuff is happening in the past. Check out these thrilling example sentences of how we would express that in writing:

We *had already* swum for three hours by the time *we ate* breakfast that morning.

We *had already swum* and *eaten* breakfast when Dad *was ready* for the family bike ride.

We *had been swimming* since sunrise when Dad *decided* we should eat breakfast.

In that last example, the swimming was ongoing. We were still swimming when Dad showed up on the edge of the lake, wanting to have breakfast.

swimming ~~~~~~~~~~→ breakfast

Admittedly, I chose swimming and eating because they both happen to have past participles far different from their regular past tenses—many students are disinclined to use words like *swum* in conversation. *Swum* may sound weird, uncomfortable, and a little too proper. Nevertheless, this brings us to the list of peculiar past participles that you need to know because, of course, these are what the SAT people are most likely to test.

Present Tense	Past Tense	Past Participle
Eat	Ate	Eaten
Lie	Lay	Lain
Arise	Arose	Arisen
Swim	Swam	Swum
Drink	Drank	Drunk
Bring	Brought	Brought

Learn these and your score—and your writing—will improve. Let's look at some questions.

EXAMPLE 1: LEVEL 2

Because Amy <u>does not</u> vote in yesterday's election, <u>she is</u> concerned <u>that</u>
          A   B   C
her preferred candidate <u>will not</u> win. <u>No error</u>
                            D   E

This is a very basic tense question that uses the context of the sentence to guide your answer choice. Because the election was *yesterday*, the sentence must read that *Amy did not* vote in yesterday's election. The answer is A.

EXAMPLE 2: LEVEL 4

<u>Without doubt</u>, one of the <u>most</u> pervasive changes in the nineteenth
      A   B
century <u>will be</u> the collective departure from <u>idealizing</u> the nuclear family.
           C   D
<u>No error</u>
   E

This is a more difficult version of the same issue—however, it's less likely to register with you that that *the nineteenth century* refers to the eighteen-hundreds. If we're talking about 1837, we need to use *was*, not *will be*. So the correct choice is C.

EXAMPLE 3: LEVEL 3

Wanting to avoid the possibility of a snow storm, the Smiths <u>had chose to schedule their snowboarding trip in the spring</u> so as to enjoy warm, sunbathed slopes.

- (A) had chose to schedule their snowboarding trip in the spring
- (B) have chose to schedule their snowboarding trip in the spring
- (C) have chose to schedule a spring snowboarding trip
- (D) have chosen to schedule their snowboarding trip in the spring
- (E) will have scheduled their snowboarding trip in the spring

This basic example could use either *have chosen, had chosen,* or *chose,* just not a combination of those choices. Remember that even when there are multiple ways to correct a sentence, only one correct option will be available among the SAT choices; in this case, it's D.

EXAMPLE 4: LEVEL 2

For the past twenty years, the wooded area behind Forest Hill School <u>was slowly bulldozed to make room</u> for new housing developments.

- (A) was slowly bulldozed to make room
- (B) were slowly bulldozed to make room
- (C) slowly were bulldozed
- (D) got bulldozed to make room
- (E) to make extra room got bulldozed

An area is a singular region that calls for the verb form *was,* so A (which is the same as the phrase in the question) is correct.

EXAMPLE 5: LEVEL 2

Our vacation <u>was</u> so <u>carefully</u> planned <u>that</u> on the morning of our
           A   B   C

departure, Dad <u>already</u> packed the car and filled the gas tank. <u>No error</u>
           D   E

The planning in this sentence has already happened, and we can tell that when we departed (which also happened in the past), the gas tank *had already* been filled. Here, the answer is D.

EXAMPLE 6: LEVEL 2

<u>The marathoner coming so far</u>, she <u>decided</u> that she <u>would continue</u> to run
           A   B   C

and complete the race, <u>despite</u> her broken collarbone. <u>No error</u>
                        D   E

Another two-step past tense: the marathoner had already been running in the past, and then she made a decision. *The marathoner having come so far,* [at that point in the race] *she decided she would continue to run and complete the race.* So we choose A.

EXAMPLE 7: LEVEL 5

<u>Even</u> some house cats <u>hunt</u> actively, <u>laying</u> <u>in wait</u> for hours for their prey.
  A   B   C   D

<u>No error</u>
  E

I just tossed this in as an example of the nit-picky meanness that can appear on the test. We misuse *laying* and *lying* all the time—what better opportunity to make your life more difficult? Because this is an ongoing, present tense commentary, the verb should be *lying*. So C is the correct choice.

Conjunctions

Conjunctions join clauses. As I said earlier, the most important thing to understand is that a comma without a conjunction is not strong enough to hold two independent clauses (little mini-sentences) together.

One-Word Conjunctions: The Coordinating Conjunctions

Although this is not necessarily an exhaustive list of conjunctions, it's about as much as you need to know for the SAT.

For	Or	Nor
But	Yet	So
While	And	Whereby

Basically, if two independent clauses are being connected in one sentence, you must include a conjunction if you're using a comma, like this:

Eat your cake today, *for* tomorrow your mouth will be filled with low-calorie diet food.

Two-Word Conjunctions: Correlative Conjunctions or Constructions

Correlative conjunctions are these paired words or phrases that tie sentences together; in particular, you can't have one without the other. If one part of a pair is used in a given sentence, you must make sure that your answer choice includes the other part of the conjunction if it does not already.

Not only . . . but also	Between . . . and
Either . . . or	Neither . . . nor
At once . . . and	As much by . . . as by
Whether . . . or	No sooner had he . . . than he
Just as . . . so also	

This means that I *not only* chose to teach you grammar *but also* attempted to make it tolerable. *Whether* I have been successful *or* not, I don't know.

IDENTIFYING SENTENCE ERRORS AND IMPROVING SENTENCES

EXAMPLE 1: LEVEL 4

The new alligator refuge, <u>allocated two hundred acres of unspoiled Everglades, and is protected by the Environmental Protection Agency</u>.

(A)   allocated two hundred acres of unspoiled Everglades, and is protected by the Environmental Protection Agency.

(B)   allocated two hundred acres of unspoiled Everglades, protected by the Environmental Protection Agency.

(C)   allocated two hundred acres of unspoiled Everglades, is protected by the Environmental Protection Agency.

(D)   is allocated two hundred acres of unspoiled Everglades, protection by the Environmental Protection Agency.

(E)   the allocation of two hundred acres of unspoiled Everglades, and is under the protection by the Environmental Protection Agency.

Adding in a conjunction can screw everything up. That measly little *and* after the word *Everglades* causes the sentence to read like it should contain another verb and object, like *The new alligator refuge has been allocated two hundred acres of unspoiled Everglades, and is protected by the Environmental Protection Agency.* But we don't have that option in our answer choices. Instead, this sentence can be fixed by merely removing the *and*: *The new alligator refuge. . . . is protected by the EPA.* So answer C is correct.

EXAMPLE 2: LEVEL 3

Lake Okeechobee provides not only irrigation for surrounding communities but <u>it is also</u> a haven for local wildlife.

(A)   it is also
(B)   it also is
(C)   also
(D)   also it is
(E)   as well

This is just a structural question. As soon as you see the words *not only* in the not-underlined sentence, you must also find *but also*. If it's not there, you'll need to put it in. The *but* is already there; answer C provides the missing *also*. It's as simple as that. For every coordinating conjunction you see, strip the sentence down to make sure you have every piece necessary for construction.

EXAMPLE 3: LEVEL 4

Just as citrus only grows in warmer climates, <u>so most cherries only grow in</u> areas with definitive seasons.

(A)   so most cherries only grow in
(B)   most cherries only grow in
(C)   and so most cherries only grow
(D)   only cherries grow
(E)   like them most cherries only grow

This is one I left correct (answer A) because the test maker likes to include things that are likely unfamiliar to you so that you won't realize they are correct in the original sentence. I guess the test maker figures there's no need to mess around with it if you're not likely to be totally clear on it anyway. Read the sentence looking for the following structure: *Just as citrus grows . . . so cherries grow*. If you can find that, you're in good shape.

EXAMPLE 4: LEVEL 4
Students in the dual enrollment program find their schedules at once intellectually stimulating <u>but exhausting</u>.

(A) but exhausting.
(B) but also exhausting.
(C) and exhausting.
(D) but exhausted.
(E) also exhausted.

It's the same issue as for the previous examples: if you see *at once*, think *at once . . . and . . . .* These students find their schedules *at once stimulating and exhausting*—answer C.

Adverbs

Short and sweet—adverbs are adjectives (describing words) that modify (describe) verbs. The vast majority of adverbs are actually just adjectives onto which we tack an -*ly* ending. *Careful* becomes *carefully*. *Silent* becomes *silently*. You get the idea.

Now, there are a few adverbs that do not end in -*ly*, and you should be somewhat familiar with them. Here's a sampling (there are plenty more):

Thereabout	Nowhere	Verbatim	Later
Afoot	Piecemeal	Soon	

The point here is that you need to be particularly careful about identifying all describing words, both adjectives and adverbs, whenever you come across them, specifically in the Identifying Sentence Errors section. Assess whether your word is describing a noun or a verb (using your common sense, not the form of the word given) and then decide if it needs the added -*ly*.

Some adverbs are less obvious—they can sound and act like conjunctions in addition to being adverbs.

Thereby	Whereby	Consequently	Insofar as	As

Take a look:

The owl managed to chew through its leash, thereby interrupting the school assembly on wildlife.

Here, the adverb *thereby* tells us that *by chewing* (and setting itself free to fly around the auditorium), the owl interrupted the assembly. However, if we use *thereby* as a conjunction, we must include a semicolon and change the structure of the second half of the sentence to include a subject and a verb:

> The owl managed to chew through its leash; thereby, it interrupted the school assembly on wildlife.

The bottom line, in this case, is to recognize the role that *thereby* or *consequently* is playing and construct your sentence accordingly.

EXAMPLE 1: LEVEL 3

The shelves <u>full of</u> books in Dan's office <u>attested to</u> how <u>thorough</u> he
        A   B   C

<u>had researched</u> his doctoral dissertation. <u>No error</u>
    D   E

Obviously, we're in the adverb section, so *thorough* needs to become *thoroughly* to be correct (it was the verb *research* that was done thoroughly). To tackle this across the board, though, whenever you run into an underlined adjective, be sure to pause and identify what exactly that adjective is describing. If it describes a verb, make sure you have the *–ly* ending, which is necessary 99.9 percent of the time. The answer is C.

Commas

First, many of you don't know

1) When commas are needed
2) When commas are *not* needed

So let's discuss.

Connecting Clauses

A comma is a great way to connect two independent clauses (two little sentences, each with its own subject and verb); however, you must connect the two clauses with a comma and a conjunction, like *or, and*, or *but*. Without the conjunction, the comma isn't strong enough to hold the two sentences together.

For more about run-on sentences, check out page 72.

> No good: George carried the split firewood around the side of the house, he was careful to avoid splinters.

> Good: George carried the split firewood around the side of the house, and he was careful to avoid splinters.

We'll cover conjunctions further in the next lesson. Just know that without a conjunction a comma is not strong enough to hold two mini-sentences together.

Avoiding Splices

If your sentence has only one subject and *two* different verbs, you should not use a comma:

> On Tuesday Elena spent the afternoon wondering what she would have for dinner and riding around the neighborhood on her bicycle.

In this sentence Elena spent the afternoon doing *two* things: wondering and riding. If we put a comma in after the word *dinner*, we interrupt Elena's action, so we would have two clauses: "Elena is wondering" and "riding." The interruption of those two verbs that center on one subject (Elena) is called a *splice*, and splices are bad.

Lists

You must always use commas for lists of stuff, dates, and activities. Verbs are just fine in lists as well, but remember to keep everything in the same form when you list them.

Strangely, there is actually a bit of flexibility for comma preference when you create lists. This list can be written with or without a comma before the *and*:

> Michael brought a lacrosse stick, a mouth guard, and a change of clothes.

or

> Michael brought a lacrosse stick, a mouth guard and a change of clothes.

While either option is fine, I recommend that you use a comma between each element of a list every time.

Appositives and Restating

An *appositive*, which we discussed earlier, is used when we rename something, like so:

> Mrs. Wegbreit, our principal, pretended to be very strict.

In this example, *our principal* is the appositive. Any time we rename someone or something like this, we need to offset it between two commas. Notice how the sentence works without the appositive:

> Mrs. Wegbreit pretended to be very strict.

or

> Our principal pretended to be very strict.

In fact, not only appositives need to be offset by commas; all bits of descriptive material that get between the subject and the verb need to be sandwiched by commas.

> Mrs. Wegbreit, although actually very kind, pretended to be very strict.

EXAMPLE 1: LEVEL 4
The nylon supports kept the oldest structure in the state from crumbling, <u>this was a misfortune many preservationists had feared.</u>

(A)   this was a misfortune many preservationists had feared.

(B)   this was unfortunate and a fear of many preservationists.

(C)   a preservationist-feared misfortunate thing.

(D)   a misfortune many preservationists had feared.

(E)   preservationists have feared this misfortune.

In this case we're fixing two standalone sentences that should have been connected by a semicolon (but weren't) by turning one of the clauses into a modifying phrase, kind of like an appositive. Lose the words *this was*, and we revise the sentence so that *crumbling* is *a misfortune many preservationists had feared*—answer D. Often the most challenging sentences require that the entire structure be shifted around.

EXAMPLE 2: LEVEL 3

Florists are not the only establishments in the business of selling flowers; <u>there are also wholesalers and importers and exporters, as well.</u>

(A)   there are also wholesalers and importers and exporters, as well.

(B)   there are also wholesalers and importers, exporters, as well.

(C)   they also have wholesalers, importers, and exporters.

(D)   there are also wholesalers, importers, and exporters.

(E)   wholesalers, importers, and exporters are also.

Keep it simple and stay married to the commas-in-lists rule. Unless you absolutely require more words in a list, paring it down to the ____, ____, and ____ format is the way to go. Answer D fills the bill.

Other Punctuation

Naturally, you'll also need to know how to use colons, semicolons, and dashes—the royalty of punctuation. Colons, semicolons, and dashes are used to help us avoid a run-on sentence situation. In short, a run-on is any sentence in which two independent sentences have been slammed together without enough punctuation. The punctuation must be strong enough to connect the smaller clauses but also to set them off from each other.

The Colon (:)

A colon is great for introducing an extended list of things (although it is not required and might be going a bit overboard if you don't use it correctly). We also use colons to notify the reader that a quote follows.

> Bob's Beach Shack has everything needed for a day at the beach: towels, beach chairs, snacks, and sun block.

See how in this example I could have just ended my sentence after the first word *beach*? Using a colon at the end of a self-sufficient, completed sentence is the most effective way to use it. In the following sentence, you do not need a colon after the word *children*:

Mrs. Adams gave the children apples, raisins, and chocolate milk.

Here, *Mrs. Adams gave the children* is not a complete sentence, so putting a colon after it would be wrong.

The Semicolon (;)

A semicolon could be considered an upgraded period that emphasizes the relationship between the two sentences it joins. Part of that little definition, though, is a requirement: the clauses on either side of the semicolon must each be a legitimate, standalone sentence. If they're not, you'll need to do some adjusting.

You can either join two closely related sentences with a semicolon and no conjunction—literally just stick them together with the semicolon—or use a semicolon and a *conjunctive adverb*—a word like *however, moreover,* or *furthermore.*

By law no animals are permitted in supermarkets; however, guide dogs are the exception.

EXAMPLE 1: LEVEL 3

Standing among the shelves, Ezekial announced that *A Heartbreaking Work of Staggering Genius* <u>was his favorite novel, he bought five copies</u> for his friends.

(A) was his favorite novel, he bought five copies
(B) being his favorite novel, he bought five copies
(C) having been his favorite novel; he should buy five copies
(D) is his favorite novel, therefore, he bought five copies
(E) is his favorite novel; therefore, he bought five copies

As the sentence stands now, with only the comma binding everything together, we're left with a run-on. Commas alone are not strong enough to hold two independent clauses together, so we need to bring in the semicolon. Of our two options that do include a semicolon, C creates an incomplete sentence in the first clause: "Standing among the shelves, Ezekial announced that *A Heartbreaking Work of Staggering Genius* having been his favorite novel." So the clear choice is answer E.

The Dash (—)

Not many students use dashes, most likely because dashes do something so obvious that we don't realize we need special punctuation—they offset thoughts. These additional thoughts or details can be either complete clauses, including a subject and a verb, or fragments. Either way, that thought or detail can just be tacked onto the end of anything.

Sara rode her first roller coaster at age seven—and loved it.

EXAMPLE 2: LEVEL 2

Store sales increase with holiday <u>shoppers—in some establishments as much as forty percent.</u>

(A) shoppers—in some establishments as much as forty percent.
(B) shoppers in some establishments by as much as forty percent.
(C) shoppers and some establishments as much as forty percent more.
(D) shoppers, establishing as much as forty percent more.
(E) shoppers and their establishments get forty percent extra.

This is another example of giving you the option to correct something that doesn't need correction. It's based on the simple fact that many students don't know how to properly use a dash. Now that you know, you won't be fooled—and you'll choose answer A.

Efficient Speech

Good writing is all about presenting your ideas so your readers will understand your points. If they're confused about what you mean, they won't be persuaded.

Dangling and Misplaced Modifiers

Let's talk about the ways modifiers can be problematic.

Dangling Modifiers

Dangling modifiers are the scapegoats for a lot of unintended comedy (or maybe just accidental stupidity) in sentences.

First, whenever a sentence starts with something like this

> *Singing loudly in the shower* or
> *Running as fast as he could* or
> *Able to leap over a building in a single bound* or
> *Lying on the bed*

a comma must come right after the phrase *and* whoever is doing that singing or running or lying must appear directly after the comma. But watch out for this

> Caroling in the winter snow, the neighborhood holiday lights twinkled.

Although this sentence may sound charming, it states that the neighborhood holiday lights are trolling the streets singing songs. For it to be correct, we need whoever is doing that caroling to, again, come directly after the comma.

> Caroling in the winter snow, the children smiled as the neighborhood holiday lights twinkled.

Learn this single rule, and your raw score will go up at least 2 to 3 points.

EXAMPLE 1: LEVEL 3

Famous for its collection of Egyptian art, <u>visitors to New York frequent the Metropolitan Museum.</u>

(A) visitors to New York frequent the Metropolitan Museum.
(B) New York visitors frequent the Metropolitan Museum.
(C) the Metropolitan museum frequents visitors.
(D) the Metropolitan Museum of New York attracts frequent visitors.
(E) the Metropolitan Museum attracting frequent New York visitors.

What's famous? The museum. The museum must come directly after the comma, as in answer D, which also has the necessary verb for what the museum does as a result of its fame, making it the correct choice. On a side note, the word *frequent* can be an adjective or a verb, so it's a likely culprit to appear on the test. Choice C uses *frequent* as a verb for the subject *Museum* and makes *visitors* the object, which makes that answer incorrect.

EXAMPLE 2: LEVEL 3

Looking forward to the weekend getaway she had planned with her friends, <u>Marlene's last day at work seemed to go on forever.</u>

(A) Marlene's last day at work seemed to go on forever.
(B) Marlene's last day seemed to go on.
(C) the last day at work seemed to go on forever for Marlene.
(D) Marlene was frustrated that the day seemed to go on forever.
(E) Marlene was frustrated with the day going on forever.

Who is looking forward? Marlene, not *Marlene's last day*, not *the last day*. The correct choice is D, because the day isn't really going on forever (as in E); it just seemed that way to Marlene.

EXAMPLE 3: LEVEL 4

While learning to make homemade pasta, <u>that was when Dan first discovered his passion for cooking.</u>

(A) that was when Dan first discovered his passion for cooking.
(B) was when Dan first discovered his passion for cooking.
(C) Dan first discovered his passion for cooking.
(D) his passion for cooking was first discovered by Dan.
(E) the passion for Dan's cooking was first discovered by him.

Sometimes you just get lucky like this, and there is only one answer choice that starts with the object of the action—in this case, *Dan*—and that answer is C. However, A is also a tempting choice because it uses something that sounds emphatic—you might read this to yourself dramatically, "*that* was when. . . ." However, it's grammatically wrong.

EXAMPLE 4: LEVEL 5

<u>Contrasting with</u> many other engineers, Charlie <u>maintains</u> professional
    A   B

<u>excellence</u> in an industry <u>characterized by</u> cattiness. <u>No error</u>
    C   D   E

Usually we are asked to correct the subject of the action: the person or thing that comes right after that comma. In this case the level of difficulty is high because you need to pointedly decide whether *Charlie*, the subject of the action, is doing the *contrasting*. The trick here is that he's not—an unnamed person is doing the comparison between the professionals, not Charlie himself. The sentence should really start *Contrasted with*, so A is the answer.

Misplaced Modifiers

Adjectives are words used to describe, or modify, nouns—people, places, or things. They do not have various forms or any other particular details you need to know about, except that you'll need to pay careful attention to *where* they are placed.

Placement of modifiers in sentences is all about efficiency. We always want information to be as accessible and efficient as possible—in writing this means that a descriptive prepositional phrase needs to be placed directly after whatever it describes. Just as a poorly placed adjective can confuse us about a noun, poorly placed prepositional phrases, all of which are mini-modifying phrases, can destroy sentences. This is huge and goes beyond the hard-and-fast rules of grammar; keeping sentences organized, clear, and concise is the A#1 most important aspect of quality writing and communication.

EXAMPLE 5: LEVEL 3

Harvesting Alaskan king crab legs is expensive, but <u>higher is its cost in human life</u>.

(A)   higher is its cost in human life.
(B)   higher is its cost in human lives.
(C)   higher is its human life cost.
(D)   higher is its costing of human life.
(E)   the value of human lives lost is higher.

Many students want to choose C, *human life cost*, because it seems to be more streamlined. However, there is no such thing as "human life cost." E is the correct answer.

EXAMPLE 6: LEVEL 3

Sherrie originally living in the Midwest and then in the South, later settling in the Caribbean.

(A) Sherrie originally living in the Midwest and then in the South, later settling in the Caribbean.

(B) Sherrie first lived originally in the Midwest, in the South, and then settling in the Caribbean.

(C) Sherrie had lived in the Midwest and the South, but she later settled in the Caribbean.

(D) Sherrie first lived in the Midwest, moved to the South, and later settled in the Caribbean.

(E) Sherrie had been living in the Midwest and the South when she was settling in the Caribbean.

The same rule holds true for prepositions. This sentence is best arranged by specifically citing and organizing a list of the sequence of events—it's possible to lose clarity by trying to squish too much information together. We find that clear list in answer D.

Parallelism

By now we should all be aware that efficient writing is all about keeping things concise and organized. More than anything, we don't want sentences that sound sloppy. To that end, parallel structure rules are designed to keep things consistent and orderly, thereby making them more easily understood. *Read:* you should pay attention to this because (1) you'll be tested on it and (2) it will make you a better writer, so your college professors will take you more seriously.

There are three main collections of things we need to keep parallel with each other in a sentence: general structure, lists of verbs, and lists of nouns. To see what I mean by general structure, check out the following sentence:

Mark ate pizza; Elizabeth ate steak.

By stringing those two little sentences together with a semicolon, we create something that sounds a bit less like it belongs in a Dick and Jane book than it would if it were two individual sentences. However, the strong parallelism in that sentence comes from the order *subject verb object*; *subject verb object*. It's a much more efficient and organized option than

Mark ate pizza; steak is what Elizabeth had.

This structural parallelism comes in more refined varieties, too. When a sentence has a single subject and multiple verbs, always make sure that the two verbs are in the same form.

The river meandered through the countryside and emptied into the ocean.

In particular, you'll also see reasons and causes listed all the time—they're the perfect venue for parallel form. It's not unlikely that you've heard in conversation something along these lines:

> The top two reasons students gave for being unhappy at school are too much homework and wanting longer lunch hours.

It shouldn't be shocking news that this is wrong. There are two reasons for student unhappiness in the sentence; (1) the students have too much homework; (2) the students want longer lunch hours. Our sentence structure should reflect these reasons in parallel format:

> The top two reasons students gave for being unhappy at school are that they have too much homework and that they want longer lunch hours.

This parallelism issue can really stretch out, generally into lists of verbs and nouns (with lots of modifiers, naturally). In short, make sure that you have these two situations happening in your sentences:

> Lists of verbs: The children at camp spent time fishing, hiking, and biking.

> Lists of nouns: Mr. Wilson is an author, teacher, and speaker.

EXAMPLE 1: LEVEL 2
Today many young people hope to become fire fighters, teachers, dentists, physical therapists, <u>or other careers.</u>

(A) or other careers.
(B) or pursue other careers.
(C) or work in other professions.
(D) or at work in other professions.
(E) or professionals in other fields.

As it stands in the original sentence, at the very end of the list, the young people hope to become *other careers*, which doesn't make sense. Choice E is correct, because the list identifies each thing they may want to become: become fire fighters, become teachers, . . . or become professionals. Proper lists keep us from having to repeat ourselves and allow us to assign one verb to lots of different objects.

You should notice that I frequently pare down sentences to their core structural elements. The writing test is about structure, not content, so I encourage you to pare down sentences in the same way.

EXAMPLE 2: LEVEL 3

The members of the grass roots organization pledged <u>to return to their respective neighborhoods and they would solicit signatures</u> for the petition by going door to door.

(A)   to return to their respective neighborhoods and they would solicit signatures

(B)   to return to their respective neighborhoods and to solicit signatures

(C)   to return to their respective neighborhoods and soliciting signatures

(D)   to return respectively to their neighborhoods and would be soliciting signatures

(E)   to return respectively and solicitously get signatures in their neighborhoods

The members pledged to do two things: *to return* and *to solicit*. The structure of the sentence must reflect that; if one verb is an infinitive, the other must be. Answer B meets that requirement.

EXAMPLE 3: LEVEL 3

After the boys received their pizza delivery, <u>they began eating immediately, and they continued eating until late in the evening.</u>

(A)   they began eating immediately, and they continued eating until late in the evening.

(B)   they began eating immediately, and the boys continued eating until late in the evening.

(C)   began eating immediately, and continued eating until late in the evening.

(D)   began to eat immediately, and continuing eating until late in the evening.

(E)   they have begun eating immediately, and they continued eating until late in the evening.

The boys *received*, *began*, and *continued*. That parallelism is imperative to the clarity of the sentence. The original sentence repeats "they" twice when it's not necessary. C is correct, as it includes parallelism with no unnecessary words.

EXAMPLE 4: LEVEL 4

The knight could not <u>ask</u> for the princess's hand <u>in marriage</u> until he
　　　　　　　　　　 A　　　　　　　　　　　　　　　　　　　 B

<u>was able to</u> prove his valor <u>and love</u>. <u>No error</u>
　　 C　　　　　　　　　　　　　 D　　　　 E

This is one of the smaller details you'll find helpful to remember. Structurally, you cannot *do this* until you can *do that*. It's one of the finer points of parallelism (and life). The knight *could not* ask . . . until . . . he *could prove* his love. So C is correct.

Rules of Comparison

The old adage "you can't compare apples and oranges" couldn't be truer than it is on the SAT. Comparison scenarios are usually about more people choosing to move to one place rather than another, or comparing one newspaper with another newspaper. Be on the lookout for comparisons in sentences loaded with modifiers and prepositions that are meant to distract you from what you're comparing. We compare people to people, things to things, places to places, and activities to activities. In short, make sure you're comparing the right stuff to the right stuff. Granted, sometimes ensuring that specificity in your sentences can lead to adding extra words for clarity. However, long and clear is better than short and unclear.

When comparing two things, use the word *more* or add *–er*.

Of the two cubs, the older is the *more* aggressive.

Sarah is the *louder* of the two daughters.

You should be able to tell which option you need to use simply based on your familiarity with the language—I dare say it should actually *sound* right. If a word doesn't take *–er* (like, say, *aggressiver*), use *more*. However, no matter what, don't ever say something like "more louder."

When comparing three or more things, use the word *most* or add *–est*.

Baby Bear was the *most* particular member of his family.

Jack expected to make the team because he was the *tallest* of the five boys.

Again, use one or the other but don't use both!

EXAMPLE 1: LEVEL 2

Although she <u>dislikes</u> having too much free time, Ms. Smith complains
         A

that she <u>has never been</u> <u>more busier</u> than she <u>has been</u> this year. <u>No error</u>
      B   C   D   E

Again, one can either be *busier* or *more busy*, but never both. The correct choice is C.

EXAMPLE 2: LEVEL 3

<u>Of the</u> three baseball <u>players</u> <u>featured</u> on the cereal box, Pete Rose is the
 A   B   C

<u>more</u> famous. <u>No error</u>
 D   E

When we compare two things we use *more*; when we compare three things we use *most*. So the answer is D.

EXAMPLE 3: LEVEL 4

Of all the countries attending the informal United Nations reception, the president of the United States was the only one to offer to play the saxophone during cocktail hour.

(A) Of all the countries attending the informal United Nations reception

(B) All of the countries having attended the informal United Nations reception,

(C) The one who attended the informal United Nations reception,

(D) Of all the dignitaries attending the informal United Nations reception,

(E) The reception being full of dignitaries,

Since *the president* is a fixed element of the sentence, we need an introduction to the sentence that says something along the lines of *of all the presidents at the reception, the president of the United States*. . . . Now, while we don't have that exact option, you should see that the beginning of the sentence needs to include all the *people* at the event, not the *countries*. Particularly because the second half reads "the president of the United States was the only one to . . . ," it should be clear that we need that group from which he volunteered. That should lead us straight to D.

EXAMPLE 4: LEVEL 3

While there are so many new ways of creating music, many listeners will maintain that there is no music more beautiful than Mozart.

(A) is no music more beautiful than Mozart.

(B) was never music more beautiful than Mozart.

(C) will never be music more beautiful than Mozart.

(D) is no music more beautiful than Mozart's arias.

(E) are arias no more beautiful that Mozart.

Mozart is not music. His work is music, but Mozart is a human. We could never compare music to a person, so D is the only remotely close possibility.

EXAMPLE 5: LEVEL 4

The children seemed to find their toys equally as fascinating as their meals were delicious.

(A) equally as fascinating as their meals were delicious.

(B) as fascinating as their meals were delicious.

(C) fascinating as their meals were delicious.

(D) fascinating even as their meals were delicious.

(E) equally fascinating even as their meals were delicious.

These comparisons must be *very* concise—you most likely do not use this structure in your day-to-day language, which, again, is why it's on the test. Choice B is correct.

Odds 'n' Ends

Here I've compiled some of the bits and pieces you'll encounter as you work through the sample tests made available by the College Board. Because I like to keep things as simple as possible, I've tossed them all together so you can quickly review them and move forward.

Redundancy

Part of efficient writing is avoiding redundancy. Redundancy can be as obvious as using a word twice (like, Department of Redundancy Department). It can be less noticeable when instructions are repeated: "Don't get dirty; stay clean!" is redundant. When you're not paying attention, it may slip right by you, like "a perpetual motion machine that would never stop." Some SAT questions just check to see if you're paying attention to this important detail.

EXAMPLE 1: LEVEL 3
<u>In the modern world of today exists many</u> instances of the influences of ancient philosophers, artists, and rulers.

(A) In the modern world of today exists many

(B) In the modern world exists many

(C) In the modern world exist many

(D) The modern world of today exist many

(E) Today's modern world has many

In the modern world or *In the world of today* would each be sufficient. *In the modern world of today* is world-class redundancy. To be tricky, the test maker is also seeing whether you'll notice that the verb form must be *exist*, as there are plural *influences*. On both counts, C the winner. It's all in the details.

Which or That versus Who?

This is not commonly tested, but it's not outside the realm of possibility. The fact of the matter is that expert grammarians have been known to argue about the differences between *which* and *that* for hours on end. What you do need to know, though, is that *who* can only be used to refer to a *human*, not a dog, not a teddy bear—nobody but a human can be a *who*. We don't need to get into it beyond that.

EXAMPLE 1: LEVEL 3
FAO Schwartz, <u>who sells toys</u>, has been a major supplier of not only stuffed animals and books but also brand-name items since 1862.

(A) who sells toys

(B) who is selling toys

(C) which is selling toys

(D) which sells toys

(E) those sellers of toys

This topic will never be tested in a more complicated fashion than this on the SAT—FAO Schwartz is a company, so we cannot refer to it as a *who*. C and D both use *which*, but C's *is selling* implies a fleeting event (at odds with the company's long history), so D is correct.

Idiomatic Language Stuff (Including the Archaic) That You May Not Know

This is where things get really challenging—and where students who have been voracious readers get the edge. There are some things in English that are the way they are "just because" that you'd likely only know if you had heard or read them before in at least several different contexts. This includes some out-there permissible grammar, as well as some idiomatic phrases that you need to know.

Random Stuff to Know

It would be impossible for me to list everything in the language that could pop up, but I usually have students jot these down in a notebook under the heading Random Stuff to Know. Here are some strange-sounding, but correct, words and phrases that will show up in both Writing and Critical Reading questions.

○ *Than does* and *as does:* both are legal; they compare one noun (or a verb acting like a noun) to another—for example

> Sometimes speaking quietly catches students' attention more effectively than does screaming.

It sounds odd, but it's correct according to English grammar rules.

○ *One of a kind* versus *one of its kind*: *One of a kind* means that we have one thing and there is no category in which it fits (for example, the duck-billed platypus is a one-of-a-kind creature; it is like no other animal). However, if you're actually referring to, say, a handmade piece of pottery, you'd need to call it *the only one of its kind*, because it has a kind—it's pottery. You can think of the *kind* as a category.

○ *Long since gone:* This is an idiomatic expression that means "that disappeared a long time ago."

○ *Choose to do so:* You could think of this as a reflexive for a verb.

○ *Certain degree of:* This is a measured amount of . . . not fully attained, like a *certain degree of maturity.*

○ *Mutually exclusive:* Freshman year at UC Santa Cruz and freshman year at Yale are *mutually exclusive* in that choosing to attend one automatically excludes the other as an option.

○ *Live vicariously through someone:* This is to experience life and emotions through someone else's experiences rather than to actively live and explore one's own life.

Here's how they ask the question:

EXAMPLE 1: LEVEL 4

The piano teacher argued that consistent yet moderate practice <u>provides more long-term improvement than does extended periods of infrequent practice.</u>

(A) provides more long-term improvement than does extended periods of infrequent practice.

(B) provides long-term improvement more than does extended periods of infrequent practice.

(C) provides more long-term improvement than do extended periods of infrequent practice.

(D) long-termwise, provides more improvement than do longer periods of infrequent practice.

(E) more than do longer periods of infrequent practice, provides more improvement over the long term.

While this may not sound comfortable to you, it's correct to use the singular verb form *does* to compare two verbs. Here, the sentence says that *moderate practice* [provides more improvement] than does *infrequent practice*. It's like a fancy way of saying "this" *does something* better than "that." Nothing that appears in the original sentence is incorrect, so A is the right answer.

Idiomatic Prepositions

Some words only take a specific preposition . . . just because that's what the English language demands. Interestingly enough, even though there's no argument for why these prepositions must be used, if you use a different preposition, you're incorrect. Super, I know. These idioms are what separate the exceptional readers and writers from the pack. There are dozens of examples, but the following pop up most frequently on the SAT.

> Preoccupied *with, by*
> Determine *whether*
> Regarded *as*
> Prefers *to*
> Inconsistent *with*
> Protest (*doesn't require anything else:* "They protested the ruling.")

Let's check out some questions:

EXAMPLE 2: LEVEL 4

Joe has unstable <u>opinions toward</u> different <u>types</u> of paint; nevertheless,
               A   B

he <u>willingly</u> tries new products before <u>making</u> initial decisions. <u>No error</u>
  C   D   E

This should be *opinions of.* That's just the idiom. Choice A is correct.

EXAMPLE 3: LEVEL 5

The docent <u>explained</u> that the historian <u>had been able</u> to identify the
            A   B

painting as surely DaVinci's, as <u>its</u> paint and use of light are <u>consistent to</u>
                                      C   D

his previous work. <u>No error</u>
                            E

This should be *consistent with*, choice D.

The fact is I could never pretend to anticipate every arcane idiom or crazy grammatical trick that may show up on the SAT—the English language is just too vast for that. If you want to bolster your general understanding of English grammar and formal writing, your best bet is to read, read, read. As a high school student your schedule may be tight, but cutting 20 minutes a day out of your social networking website time and devoting it to a national newspaper can do wonders for your writing score.

paragraph
improvement

This is the least important part of the multiple choice test, as far as I'm concerned, primarily because it appears only once and there are only six questions associated with it. However, if you're shooting for a really high writing score, it's important to know what to expect here and how to handle these paragraphs, as the multiple choice questions affect your Writing section score far more than does the essay.

You'll want to briefly skim the passage before you start answering the questions, particularly because you'll find so many questions are based on the main ideas. It's important to remember that, as for the essay, these questions are intended to see if you understand the nuts and bolts of structure and organization. There are very few purely grammatical issues tested in this section, but those that are tested are tested repeatedly. Let's take a look at some of the main question concepts and a few examples.

Understanding the Main Idea:
Passages and Paragraphs

Much of the editing you'll be doing is adding a sentence that reflects the main idea to the existing material, most often as an introduction to or summary of the passage as a whole. Less frequently you'll be inserting sentences as topic sentences for body paragraphs within the passage.

Because this is a multiple choice test and not a creative writing exercise, you'll notice that the potential topic sentences you're offered as answer choices are not exactly scintillating—nor are they anything you'd necessarily write, for that matter. Rather than looking for an answer choice that you find appealing, you'll want to look for the option that is most provable (meaning if you went to court over this question, you'd want the choice that the judge would rule is the "correct" answer). Look for evidence: the correct answer choice will consistently refer to a specific part of the passage—usually the conclusion—even going so far as to borrow words from it.

When the answer choice doesn't borrow exact words, it will include a specific thematic or argumentative element. For example, if a short passage were to begin with the sentence, "Many people have never heard of the long-lost sister of Betsy Ross," it would not be surprising if the concluding sentence was something like: "The importance of Betsy Ross's sister is undeniable." *That* is the straightforward, natural connection you're looking for. The same rules apply to inserting introductory sentences and conclusions: always make sure there is an obvious relationship between the intro and the conclusion and vice versa.

You'll also want to keep in mind that, by offering you choices of topic sentences, the test maker implies that a topic sentence is not yet in the passage. This means it's not a good idea to think you can get a sense of the whole by reading only the first sentence in the paragraph. Take the time to read all three or four sentences as a cohesive whole and choose an introductory sentence that embodies the main point.

Example questions will sound like these:

What is the best choice to add as a concluding sentence to paragraph 2?

It would be most sensible to create a new paragraph before which sentence?

The most appropriate topic sentence for this passage is. . . .

Relevance

Beyond finding and understanding main themes, another basic element of the editing process and improving paragraphs is the ability to articulate why we include some details and choose not to include others. One word sums up the whole concept: *relevance*.

Characterizing Sentences and Paragraphs

These questions explore the purpose of individual sentences and the roles they play in a passage. They will focus on a particular sentence's relevance to the sentence before it or to the paragraph as a whole.

Characterizing a paragraph is very much like characterizing the author's main point in the Passage-Based Reading section. If you're at all confused, you may find it helpful to take answer choices out of context and apply them back to the passage itself. (See page 27 in Passage-Based Reading for a more detailed explanation.)

Creating Relevance

Sometimes two sentences in a paragraph seem unrelated, but including new details will develop relevance. Your replacement answer choice may connect two unrelated sentences, grammatically alter them, or add details to either one of them. Even changing a word like *although* to *therefore* can dramatically change the meaning of a sentence.

Deleting Irrelevance

If a sentence is included that does not improve the clarity or support the main idea of the paragraph or passage, sometimes it's an option to delete it. Don't get spooked—if a sentence seems like it came from left field or if you can pointedly argue why it's not relevant to the point, lose it. However, if the seemingly irrelevant option is grammatically incorrect, search the answer choices for an option that is both grammatically correct and more relevant to the main idea.

Example questions will be along these lines:

What purpose does this sentence serve in the passage?

Why has the author chosen to include this detail?

If the author had not included this paragraph, how would the passage change?

Revision

A common revision is to clarify a pronoun; it's easy for a sentence to become too long, for a pronoun to get so far removed from its antecedent that it's hard to tell what *it* stands for. Often questions challenge you to remove pronouns and replace them with proper nouns for clarity.

Overall, you'll be correcting wordiness (remember we love efficiency and loathe redundancy), tense, fragments, and run-ons. The questions will not directly say: "How do we make sentence 13 not a run-on?" Instead, the questions are vague—laughably vague. Sometimes they only ask how we "deal" with a particular sentence. Just keep in mind that, in this section, if something "sounds bad," it probably is.

If you're asked about what would *not* improve a sentence, often the wordiest, vaguest answer will be the correct choice. You'll find that these questions usually involve ways of cutting down sentences, so be wary if you think it's a good idea to add to what's already there.

Example questions will sound like these:

What is the best way to deal with sentence 8?

Which of the following is the best version of sentence 4?

Let's look at the type of passage you'll see on the test.

Example Passage and Questions

(1) The term "the Netherlands" refers to the European portion of the Kingdom of the Netherlands, which also includes the Netherlands Antilles and the Caribbean island of Aruba. (2) While "the Netherlands" is sometimes used interchangeably with "Holland," the terms are not synonymous. (3) Furthermore, North and South Holland are two of the Netherlands' twelve provinces. (4) Additionally, Holland is well known for its beautiful fields of tulips. (5) Thus, while someone who lives in the Netherlands may not be a resident of Holland, living in Holland is always a considered a resident of the Netherlands.

(6) The popular confusion between the terms "the Netherlands" and "Holland" may be attributable to Holland's considerable

wealth. (7) One of the wealthiest regions in the world, and certainly the wealthiest region in the Netherlands. (8) Another source of the confusion may be the people of the Netherlands themselves, as many have taken to identifying their country as "Holland," perhaps in response to the confusion of outsiders.

(9) Both the people and language of the Netherlands are referred to as "Dutch." (10) A dialect of Dutch, Flemish, spoken in the northwestern part of Belgium. (11) The term "Flemish" is also used to denote all Dutch variants spoken in Belgium. (12) Officially, both Belgium and the Netherlands name "Standard Dutch" as an official language; the difference between Standard Dutch and Flemish is equivalent to the difference between American and British English. (13) While all these details seem difficult to keep organized as an outsider, I imagine people in the Netherlands are not confused at all.

EXAMPLE 1: LEVEL 2

In order to make the passage most effective, which of the following sentences would best be omitted from the passage?

(A) Sentence 2
(B) Sentence 4
(C) Sentence 6
(D) Sentence 11
(E) Sentence 12

Of these five options, sentence 4 includes information not related to the main idea that people find the language and geographical identity of the Netherlands confusing. Because it is irrelevant, we omit it.

EXAMPLE 2: LEVEL 3

What is the best way to deal with sentence 3 (reproduced below)?

Furthermore, North and South Holland are two of the Netherlands' twelve provinces.

(A) Switch sentence 3 with sentence 5.
(B) Replace "Furthermore" with "Rather."
(C) Connect sentence 3 to sentence 2 with a dash, changing "synonymous" to "synonymous—furthermore."
(D) Replace "are" with the phrase "had better be."
(E) Remove the word "Netherlands'."

This is an example of one of those really vague questions I talked about earlier; your objective here is find an answer choice that makes sense and that overtly improves the sentence or the way it fits into the paragraph. Nearly all of our options would make the sentence more confusing, vague, or grammatically incorrect. But check it out: the word *furthermore* is a continuing word, yet sentence 3 is clearly meant to be in contrast with sentence 2. Therefore, we should change *furthermore* to *rather*, which makes choice B correct.

EXAMPLE 3: LEVEL 3

If the author wanted to include the following sentence, where would it best fit in the passage?

Sometimes understanding the organization of kingdoms and languages can be confusing, particularly in the case of the Netherlands.

(A)   Before sentence 1
(B)   Before sentence 5
(C)   After sentence 5
(D)   Before sentence 9
(E)   After sentence 11

While it may not be the best introductory sentence that you could imagine writing, this is still a sentence that introduces the main idea of the passage: how the relationship between the Netherlands, Holland, and their languages can be confusing. It makes the most sense to put this sentence before sentence 1. You'll notice as you work through the answer choices that this broad introductory idea would be more and more out of place as the argument becomes more specific. Also, this sentence uses the word *confusing*, just like the concluding sentence. That bit of evidence should clinch it; this sentence makes the most sense as an introduction, so A is correct.

EXAMPLE 4: LEVEL 4

In context, which of the following is the best version of the underlined portion of sentence 5 (reproduced below)?

Thus, while someone who lives in the Netherlands may not be a resident of Holland, living in Holland is always a considered a resident of the Netherlands.

(A)   living in Holland certainly makes you a resident of the Netherlands.
(B)   living in Holland is a different story entirely.
(C)   but you could also be living in Holland, which is always considered part of the Netherlands.
(D)   you're better off living in Holland.
(E)   someone who lives in the Netherlands is also part of the same country.

You'll want to use the parallel structure of the sentence here to ensure that you choose the right information to follow it. Because the argument pertains to confusion between the Netherlands and Holland—and because the sentence includes the word *while*—we know that we should find an answer that gives us the alternative scenario. Basically, while living in Netherlands doesn't mean you have to live in Holland, living Holland means you live in the Netherlands. That's answer A.

EXAMPLE 5: LEVEL 3

Which revision of the underlined portion of sentences 6 and 7 (reproduced below) best fits the context of the passage?

> *The popular confusion surrounding the terms "the Netherlands" and "Holland" may be attributable <u>to Holland's considerable wealth. One of the wealthiest regions in the world, and certainly the wealthiest region in the Netherlands.</u>*

(A)   to the wealthiness that is Holland and its famousness.

(B)   to all that wealth that Holland has that makes it so famous.

(C)   to Holland's considerable wealth; therefore it enjoys a particularly high profile in world affairs.

(D)   to Holland's wealthy status that makes it famous.

(E)   to the fact that Holland is wealthy and famous for being so wealthy.

Since simply alluding to Holland's wealth may not make it clear why it would be more well known, a good revision to these sentences would be to include what that wealth means: Holland is a major financial player in the world. This *creates* relevance where little is originally apparent. We'll add that fact and then choose the grammatically correct and answer choice, C.

EXAMPLE 6: LEVEL 3

Which is the best version of the underlined portion of sentence 10 (reproduced below)?

> *A dialect of <u>Dutch, Flemish, spoken in the northwestern</u> part of Belgium.*

(A)   of Dutch, Flemish, being spoken in the northwestern

(B)   of Dutch, Flemish, in the northwest is spoken as

(C)   of Dutch, Flemish, is spoken in the northwestern

(D)   Flemish, this is part of Dutch, is spoken in the northwestern

(E)   of Flemish, this Dutch is spoken in the northwestern

This verges more on grammatical editing than general paragraph improvement. Clearly the author has left a fragment in the original, so we need to fix it while retaining the author's intent and ensuring contextual clarity. Answer C simply pops in the word *is*, retaining the meaning of the sentence and fixing its grammatical error.

Remember, even though we think of editing as a flexible, subjective endeavor, the SAT is still a standardized test. You may not always like the "best choice" answer, especially if your English course at school has a writing-heavy curriculum. Approach this section for what it really is: another opportunity for you to prove that you can arrive at the same answer choice as the test maker. Be quantitative in your assessment of the answer choices and you'll be fine.

MATHEMATICS

MATHEMATICS OVERVIEW

The Mathematics section of the SAT contains 44 multiple choice questions that include 5 answer choices and 10 Student-Produced Response questions, often referred to as *grid-ins* because that's what you do—you grid in your own answer. Math topics tested can be grouped into 4 broad categories: Numbers and Operations; Algebra and Functions; Geometry; and Data Analysis, Statistics, and Probability.

The SAT does not test everything you have ever learned in your math classes from the time you were in kindergarten until today. In fact, the list of math topics on the SAT is relatively limited, and I've organized them in simple, progressive chunks. You'll find that each question type is based on a primary math idea or topic, and then each type of question is made more difficult by adding particular details or specific steps. Know what to look for, and your score will go up. There are 2 parts to my explanation of each math topic: What You Need to Know and How They Ask the Questions. The first will give you the math skills you need to know; the second shows you how you'll use them on the test. It's that simple.

Just as building your vocabulary will benefit you long after you take the SAT, building your math skills will take you a long way in college, even if you plan only to take the single math course your school requires. Many test-prep books claim to give you clever ways to narrow down answer choices and select an answer without doing much math at all. Maybe I sound stuffy, but if you really want to excel on the SAT, you're not going to do it by guessing and strategizing your way to the top. You're going to outsmart the test by being prepared, thinking carefully, and knowing your stuff. Besides, if I told you that this test is so difficult that you're going to have to guess your way to success, I would feel like I might as well smack you across the face and tell you I have no faith in you. Forget that. You can do this.

Shooting for Your Goal Score

I'm going to assume that you're all college-bound students shooting for at least 500 points.

To score at least 500:

Answer 41 questions (31 correct/10 errors), for a raw score of 29.

To score at least 600:

Answer 53 questions (43 correct/10 errors), for a raw score of 41.

To score at least 700:

Answer 54 questions (51 correct/3 errors), for a raw score of 50.

Math Fast Facts

○ **Fact:** While you still lose a quarter point for answering a math multiple choice question incorrectly, there is no penalty for incorrect answers to the Student-Produced Response questions (aka the grid-ins). If you feel like you're on the right track but you're running out of time in the grid-in section, go ahead and grid in what you have. You can't lose.

○ **Fact:** Math questions on the SAT do not necessarily get harder by testing more advanced math skills (there won't necessarily be arithmetic at the beginning of a section and Algebra II at the end of the section). Instead, math questions on the SAT get more difficult by involving more steps and a wider variety of skills. Question 1 in a section may ask you something about geometry that involves 1 step; question 25 may also use geometry but will require 4 or 5 steps, or more complex reasoning. Keep in mind that those 4 or 5 steps aren't necessarily harder steps—there are just more of them. Your job is to arm yourself with the skills to tackle the steps.

○ **Fact:** It is best to practice taking the SAT without a calculator. I do not permit my students to use them when we work together. If you force yourself to relearn your multiplication tables (and I *know* many of you don't remember them), focus on using fractions, and pay attention to the work you do, you'll discover math reflexes you may never have known you have.

○ **Fact:** You *must* show some work in your test booklet for every problem you attempt, *especially* if you think you already know the answer. This is not an issue of scoring; it's an issue of accuracy. You *may not* work in your head; this problem is particularly rampant with students who are less skilled at math. This is not a matter of appearing to be "smart" and not needing to write things down—it's about discipline and precision. If you show your work, you can go back and check your answers because you've left yourself a paper trail.

○ **Fact:** To get points for a correct answer on the Student-Produced Response section, you need to both write your answer *and* bubble it in. If your answer is a repeating a decimal, like 0.555555, you can't just write 0.5; you must either shorten it to 0.555 or round up to 0.556. You must also grid-in fractions in fully reduced and improper form: because $4\frac{1}{2}$ would look like $^{41}/_2$ when gridded, you need to enter $^9/_2$ to get credit for the correct answer.

numbers and operations

Baby steps, baby steps. Rather than tackle the most complex topics on the test, let's first go back to the basics. This stuff is a good review, especially for those of you in advanced math classes, because the SAT uses a ton of material that we all did for homework in the fourth grade. Although you may not expect it, even challenging (level 5) problems are created using only basic arithmetic, so please don't just blow past the basics simply because you can already count and add.

Integers

WHAT YOU NEED TO KNOW

An integer is any basic whole number: negative, positive, or zero—no decimals, no fractions, just whole numbers.

Don't get confused: the term *digit* refers to 0, 1, 2, 3, 4, 5, 6, 7, 8, or 9, just like the numbers that appear on your telephone. This means if we're talking about a 4-digit integer, we mean an integer that has 4 slots for any of those 10 numbers. It's important that you know that there are 10 digits available when you're building numbers (from 0 to 9). Don't forget that 0! Conveniently, *digit* is another word for finger; we usually have 10 of those, too.

Integers on the Number Line

The most common place we use integers is on the standard number line which includes positive numbers, negative numbers, and zero. This bit is huge: 0 is neither positive nor negative. That means if you encounter the following question—"How many negative integers satisfy this equation?"—0 is not a viable answer choice.

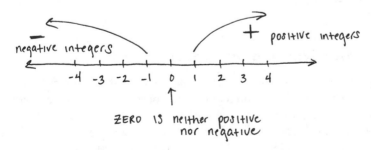

You also need to know what happens to negative and positive numbers when you multiply them together.

$$- \times - = +$$ ⟵ like signs? positive product
$$+ \times + = +$$ ⟵
$$- \times + = -$$ ⟵ opposite signs? negative product

Although there are many ways to hack away at problems involving ordered integers, I want to make sure you have the most elegant (and foolproof) method of solving them. That being said, here's how to represent ordered integers on the number line.

Consecutive Integers

Consecutive integers are integers that start somewhere on the number line and count up in single steps. Say we're going to represent 5 consecutive integers using variables. Rather than calling these consecutive integers *v*, *w*, *x*, *y*, and *z*, which turns into a math nightmare, let's keep our definitions all in relation to a single variable.

totally unrelated variables : BAD for consecutives

←—+—+—+—+—+—+—+—+—→
    v w x y z

Let's call the first integer x.

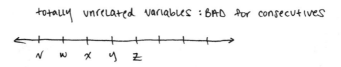

consecutive? keep everything in terms of 1 variable

←—+—+—+—+—+—+—+—→
  x x+1 x+2 x+3 x+4 ....

When we start counting up from x (or moving to the right along the number line), we can call the next integer we hit $x + 1$. Count up again, and we get $x + 2$. We always keep the term we're defining in relation to the first term (meaning we always want to use x if that's what we picked in the beginning). Continuing with that pattern, we can represent 5 consecutive numbers using a single variable: x, $x + 1$, $x + 2$, $x + 3$, and $x + 4$, which can make for some super-easy math.

Consecutive Even and Odd Integers

Consecutive even integers and *consecutive odd integers* should be represented using a single variable. If we represent the first consecutive even integer with x, this time we're going to count up 2 places on the number line to find the next even integer, so we'll call that $x + 2$. Count up 2 again and we reach $x + 4$. This time, 5 consecutive even integers will be represented by x, $x + 2$, $x + 4$, $x + 6$, and $x + 8$. Let's look at our number line again.

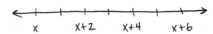

consecutive odd integers ALSO count by 2s

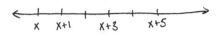

Listen up! Consecutive odd integers are represented by *exactly the same pattern* as consecutive even integers.

Do NOT ADD ODDS, ever.

Because both odd numbers and even numbers count by 2's, each new consecutive odd integer will always be 2 away from the odd integer before it. Add only 1, and your answer will be wrong.

HOW THEY ASK THE QUESTIONS

Positive/Negative/Odd/Even

Integer questions like these focus not only on the definition of an integer but also on its qualities: positive or negative, odd or even. Because different operations can change values from positive to negative or create odd or even numbers, you need to know what to home in on.

EXAMPLE 1: LEVEL 2

If *r* is any negative number, which of the following must be positive?

(A) $4 - r$
(B) $r - 4$
(C) $r + 4$
(D) $4r$
(E) $\dfrac{r}{4}$

These problems come in *must, could be,* and *cannot* varieties. Always be aware of which type you're working with.

As soon as a negative number is manipulated in a problem so that the entire expression *must* be positive, you need to make a beeline for those answer choices in which your negative number is either (1) multiplied by another negative number or (2) subtracted from a positive number. Feel free to choose an easy number to plug into your answer choices.

Let's say $r = -4$, and check out answer choice A, $4 - r$:

$$4 - r \rightarrow 4 - (-4)$$
$$4 + 4 = 8$$

In this case, no matter what negative number you choose as a value for *r*, that value will always be multiplied by another negative (because we distribute the negative sign to what's in the parenthesis), so you'll always be adding something to 4. That means you'll always find a positive value for answer A. Likewise, answers B, D, and E will always stay negative, so they must be wrong.

I do want to talk about answer C, though, because options like C are the options that make this test difficult. This is a *must* question, which means the answer is some expression for which there is never a case that the outcome is negative. If we plug in −1 for r we get −1 + 4, which equals 3. That's positive, so if you started with C and only tried −1, you might think C is correct. However, if we try out −5 we get −5 + 4 = −1, which is wrong.

Whenever you see "which of the following" in an SAT question, you will have to sort through the answer choices rather than doing the math and circling the correct answer. This is about as close to plugging in answer choices as I'd like you to come on this test. When you do see a "which of the following" question, though, always try answer A or E first.

EXAMPLE 2: LEVEL 1

If x represents an odd integer, which of the following expressions must represent an even integer?

(A) $x + 2$
(B) $2x - 1$
(C) $3x - 2$
(D) $3x + 2$
(E) $5x + 1$

Again, this is another "plugging in" question. There is no other way to sort through the answer choices. However, when you work through problems like this, always use an odd number other than 1 to try out, because 1 does interesting things when it's involved in multiplication. Although in this problem it wouldn't make a difference in your answer, in more difficult problems it may. If you choose 3 and plug it in for x, you'll find that only answer E gives you an even integer.

EXAMPLE 3: LEVEL 3

If $\frac{x + 1}{2}$ is an integer, then x must be

(A)   an odd integer.
(B)   an even integer.
(C)   a multiple of 2.
(D)   a positive integer.
(E)   a negative integer.

The only thing that makes this problem a level 3 rather than a level 2 is that you can't just pop in a number (say, choose 3 and see if it works), because the number that you choose may or may not give you enough information to answer the question. We could choose 3 and try it out and get $\frac{(3 + 1)}{2} = 2$, which is an integer, but that doesn't tell us that it's a necessity to choose a positive number; we just happened to do so and it worked out. Instead, this problem involves going a step further. Fortunately, the only thing we need to realize is that we're turning a fraction into an integer—that means that our fraction needs to perfectly reduce to a whole number. If it's not a whole number, it's not an integer. In this problem we need to ensure that the numerator (whatever number we pick plus 1) is divisible by 2 (the denominator), so the correct answer is A, an odd integer.

To make this problem more difficult, the fraction could be written with a denominator of 3 or 5 or 7. If that were the case, we'd need to choose an answer that would consistently make the numerator a multiple of that denominator.

Number Lines

Number-line problems are exactly what they sound like: they are those problems that make sure you understand the relationships between numbers on the line, most often between those to the left of the 0 and those to the right.

EXAMPLE 1: LEVEL 1
How much greater than $t - 3$ is $t + 8$?

There are 3 ways to solve this problem. For starters, we can just assign t a value—any value—and then find the difference between the 2 other values.
Let's say $t = 6$.

$$t-3 \text{ becomes } 6-3 . \quad 6-3 = \underline{3}$$
$$t+8 \text{ becomes } 6+8 . \quad 6+8 = \underline{14}$$

The difference between those values is $14 - 3$, which is $\boxed{11}$.
Or, because these points are relatively near each other, we could simply plot them on a number line and count the distance between them.

Count up and you've got the difference: $\boxed{11}$.
Our third option is simply to subtract $t - 3$ from $t + 8$.

$$t + 8 - (t - 3)$$
$$t + 8 - t + 3$$

The t's cancel, and we're left with $8 + 3 = \boxed{11}$.

EXAMPLE 2: LEVEL 3
What is the coordinate of the point on a number line that is exactly halfway between the points with coordinates 73 and 86?

There are a few ways to answer this question. Most students quickly draw a number line first, so let's do the same.

73   86

"Which of the following" is a popular format for integer-related questions; this "plugging in" style of problem solving is far less common in other question types. Don't expect this in every section.

"Finding the difference between 2 values" means "subtracting."

Be sure to distribute when you subtract parenthetic expressions! Check out the lesson on distribution on page 154 for more information.

Now, we can either find the halfway point by finding the distance from 73 to 86, splitting that in half, and adding it back to 73 . . .

Counting the distance

on a number line between

2 points is the same as

finding their difference.

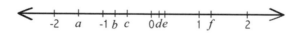

find the difference : 86 – 73 = 13
split the difference : 13 ÷ 2 = 6.5
add the difference : 73 + 6.5 = 79.5

. . . or we can find the average (the mean) of 73 and 86, which will also give us the halfway point.

$$\frac{73 + 86}{2} = \frac{159}{2} = \boxed{79.5}$$

Here are some key things to think about on number-line estimation problems: always remember that as you move left from 0, numbers become increasingly negative. If you're moving along from 0 toward –1, just before you hit –1 you're at a value like $-\frac{7}{8}$ — not $-\frac{1}{8}$. This seems to throw everyone off.

Worse comes to worst, you could feasibly count up the number line to find the midpoint. However, this problem is intentionally designed to have a midpoint between 2 whole numbers, which often forces you to double-check your counting, cancel notches, and waste time. I say focus on solving problems using those options that include calculation so you can be confident that you didn't miscount.

More difficult number-line questions require assigning values to notches on the line rather than working with numbers that are already labeled. As usual, even this comes in varying degrees of difficulty.

EXAMPLE 3: LEVEL 3
Which of the letters on the following number line could represent the product when point B is multiplied by point E?

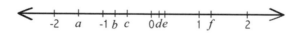

This type of question is always drawn to scale. It has to be; it's all about estimation. These problems are inherently simple, but somehow they often go awry for students.

Because we're finding the value of the product of point b and point e, it's only important that we estimate their values. On our number line it seems like point b could be roughly $-\frac{3}{4}$ and e is $\frac{1}{2}$. Be very careful when multiplying these values together, being most vigilant about the sign of your final answer— in this case,

Did you notice that I used fractions? By putting your values into fractions you'll increase the accuracy of your estimation.

$$-\frac{3}{4} \cdot \frac{1}{2} = -\frac{3}{8}$$

Remember, on the number line $-\frac{3}{8}$ is just to the right of $-\frac{1}{2}$. Therefore, the product of point e and e is closest to the value of point c.

EXAMPLE 4: LEVEL 4

The intervals on the following number line are equally spaced. What is the value of p?

You may notice in this illustration that there are not 10 notches on the line. This matters, particularly because the line has been drawn to scale. Most number lines (that is, metric rulers) are divided into tenths—there are 10 notches between each set of big notches. On these questions we cannot assume we have 10 notches; we have to count them.

Many students have trouble actually counting the notches—they're not sure what to include and what not to include in the count. Here's how to do it:

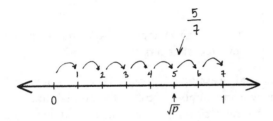

So it turns out that on my line here I have 7 notches total. Next we find which of these is our marked notch. If we count over (again, from the same point) we see that our notch is number 5. This value, $\frac{5}{7}$, is equivalent to the value of the variable after it has been square-rooted. Now, because our variable is $\sqrt{p}$, we say that $\sqrt{p} = \frac{5}{7}$.

Then, just solve for p by squaring both sides: $(\sqrt{p})^2 = \frac{5}{7} \times \frac{5}{7}$. We end up with $p = \boxed{\frac{25}{49}}$. That's it.

Adding along the Number Line

There is a particular way of working with a string of numbers on the number line, usually starting from a given point and adding. Although this will come up in other types of "consecutive integer" problems, understanding how numbers cancel on the line is the most important element of these problems.

EXAMPLE 1: LEVEL 5

If the sum of the consecutive integers from −18 to n, inclusive, is 60, what is the value of n?

If we were to rephrase this problem, here's what we'd find it's really saying: Start at −18. Moving to the right along the number line, add −17 to −18. Then add −16 to that sum. Continue adding all the way along the number line until your final sum equals 60. The value of n is the last number you add to the ongoing sum that gives you the value 60.

What would happen if we simply added up all of these values? Let's see. We begin at −18 and start adding. As we progress and approach 0, our sum is very big and negative: −171 to be exact. We add 0 to −171 and we still have −171. This is where things start changing, though. Next we add 1 to –171, yielding –170. Add 2 and we have –168. Continue adding and we finally approach positive values. When we add 18, our sum finally equals 0. Add 19 and the sum is 19; add 20 and the sum is 39; add 21 and the sum is 60.

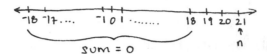

If a problem calls for 2 consecutive odd integers, you'll need to be careful. Choosing 1 can be a problem—when you square it, its value stays the same! As you know, multiplying other numbers by 1 has no effect on them either. Your best bet is to choose 3 and 5. Bigger numbers are fine too, but they'll be just that: bigger.

Fortunately, we don't have to do all that adding—all the numbers between –18 and 18 cancel each other out, so we know the sum starting at 18 must be 0. You never need to add through the entire list! Instead, start with 19, add 20, and add 21. Bingo. The answer we're looking for is 21—the last value we added to find 60.

EXAMPLE 2: LEVEL 5

The least integer of a set of consecutive integers is –30, and the sum of that set of integers is 31. How many integers are in the set?

This problem operates just like example 1, except that we are interested not in the sum itself but in how many numbers were on the number line that got us to a sum of 31. Again, the emphasis is on recognizing that adding from –30 up to 30 gives a total sum of 0; they all cancel out. Add 1 more number, the 31, and there's your sum of 31. Although that's pretty intuitive, there is a twist here. Let's look at the line:

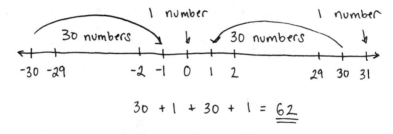

$$30 + 1 + 30 + 1 = \underline{\underline{62}}$$

This really is just a counting problem. There are, in fact, 30 numbers from –30 to –1. Zero counts as an additional number: even though it didn't change the sum as we added up the line, it still counts as a number. There are another 30 numbers from 1 to 30. So far we're up to 61 numbers. Add that 31 to the pile, and we have 62 numbers on that line, all told. Tricky.

Consecutive Integers without the Number Line

These consecutive integer problems require using the definition (or relationships) between consecutive integers to define the elements of your problem. These problems employ the "$n, n + 1, n + 2, n + 3 \ldots$" and "$n, n + 2, n + 4, n + 6 \ldots$" patterns we talked about earlier.

EXAMPLE 1: LEVEL 1

If a and b are positive consecutive even integers where $a > b$, which of the following is equal to $a^2 - b^2$?

$$\textcircled{A} \quad a$$

$$\textcircled{B} \quad b$$

$$\textcircled{C} \quad 2b + 2$$

$$\textcircled{D} \quad 2b + 4$$

$$\textcircled{E} \quad 4b + 4$$

This is an example of the easier problems of this type because we do not need to list a string of 5 or 6 consecutive even integers to solve the problem; instead, we're just going to choose 2 integers and work with them.

In this case the problem calls for consecutive even integers, so we'll choose 2 and 4. Be aware that we are told that $a > b$, so this time around $a = 4$ and $b = 2$. We are looking for an answer choice whose value is equal to $4^2 - 2^2$, which can be simplified to $16 - 4 = 12$. Just like with any other "which of the following" problem, we're going to have to plug in and check answers based on our chosen numbers. In this case, when we use our chosen value of b, 2, we'll find that $4b + 4 = 12$, which makes the answer E.

In short, this is another situation in which we plug in values for the original problem and find an answer choice that matches our result using the values we chose. We chose 4 and 2, so our answer must match using that 4 and 2.

EXAMPLE 2: LEVEL 3

What is the greatest integer on the list of six consecutive integers whose sum is equal to 147?

Everyone, and I mean everyone, picks up a calculator at this point. I always ask the same question: "What on earth are you planning to put into your calculator right now?" and I always get the same response: "I dunno. I was going to plug in some numbers until I found something that worked."

Forget that. This is so simple, and we don't have time to waste plugging in numbers until something works. This problem calls for "six consecutive integers," so the first thing we do is write down the pattern that represents those 6: $x, x + 1, x + 2, x + 3, x + 4, x + 5$. Now, the problem tells us that their sum equals 147, which means that we add them up and set them equal to 147:

$$x + x + 1 + x + 2 + x + 3 + x + 4 + x + 5 = 147$$

We just use algebra to solve this:

$$6x + 15 = 147$$
$$6x = 132$$
$$x = 22$$

Now, *answering the question* is the most important part of the problem (and the part that the test maker most often manipulates to make these problems more tedious). The problem specifically asks for *the greatest number on the list*, not x. Whenever we use the consecutive integer pattern, the x value we find is always the smallest value on the list. In this case the greatest number on the list is represented by $x + 5$, so we must add 5 to our answer: $22 + 5 = \boxed{27}$.

It is important that you notice that this problem says "positive consecutive . . ." When any SAT problem does not stipulate that a number must be "positive" or must be an "integer," or any other limiting feature for that matter, you must be very careful to try values that include negatives— and even 0, if the problem doesn't rule it out.

Always make sure you are

answering the question

with consecutive integer

problems—sometimes

they ask for the least

value, sometimes the

greatest, and sometimes

the value in the middle.

Pay attention!

EXAMPLE 3: LEVEL 4

The sum of three consecutive even integers is 198. Using p to represent the least of the three integers, which of the following equations represents the relationship among the three integers?

Rather than reproducing answer choices, I'd like to focus instead on the fact that the College Board rewards you for knowing how to write out the equation I keep mentioning—it's simple, just like the other "consecutives" problems. Opportunities to win another raw point, like the example just shown, are a perfect excuse to learn how to do the math rather than pick up the calculator and take ballpark stabs at finding an answer.

This time we're working with 3 consecutive even numbers, and they've told us p represents the least, so our 3 will be p, $p + 2$, and $p + 4$. Their sum is 198. Just like in easier problems, we simply set it up according to the pattern: $p + p + 2 + p + 4 = 198$. Simplify that to $\boxed{3p + 6 = 198}$ and voilà, we have our answer.

Because problems like this appear at the end of the test, I'd encourage you to commit to really knowing your stuff—you'll be amazed at how many concepts are repeated in the problems on the last pages of the math section.

Number Behavior

WHAT YOU NEED TO KNOW

We're going to use the term *number behavior* to cover a couple of skills and concepts that are often tested but aren't so easily classifiable on the test. I've tried to include this stuff alongside the other topics to which they're most applicable, so you'll see number behavior questions in many forms throughout this book. For example, when a fraction between 0 and 1 is squared, it gets smaller—that's counter-intuitive, so it appears more often on the test. When a negative number is squared, cubed, raised to the fourth power, and so on, it switches back and forth from positive to negative. That's another key ingredient in SAT questions. In this section we'll talk about a few more.

First, you need to be aware of the transitive property—what it does and what it means. As usual, you don't need to know what it's called. The transitive property (which I hope will sound familiar to you) is the rule that says if $a = b$ and $b = c$, then $a = c$. The focus of these questions will be about the relationship between the a and c components.

You'll also want to be aware of the very big roles that 0 and 1 play in very small problems. The problems often focus on established relationships between numbers (usually represented by variables) and how plugging in 0 or 1 for those variables changes those relationships, particularly when you multiply by them or involve exponents.

Transitive Property

These are simple questions; to solve them, you'll mainly rely on knowing the transitive property rule.

EXAMPLE 1: LEVEL 2
If $2x = 7y$ and $7y = 8z$, then what is z in terms of x?

First, let's make sure we're clear on what "z in terms of x" means. Finding z in terms of x means to find the value of z but use x to express it. Because both $2x$ and $8z$ are equal to $7y$, then $2x = 8z$. We then divide both sides by 8:

$$2x = 8z \quad \text{so:} \quad \frac{2x}{8} = \frac{8z}{8} \quad \rightarrow \quad \frac{x}{4} = z$$

So our answer for z in terms of x is just $\boxed{\frac{x}{4}}$.

EXAMPLE 2: LEVEL 3
If a is $\frac{1}{7}$ of b and b is $\frac{3}{11}$ of c, a is what fraction of c?

The first step here is to translate all this English into math so we can see the relationships more clearly:

$$a = \frac{1}{7} \cdot b \quad \text{and} \quad b = \frac{3}{11} \cdot c$$

Or, because I'm obsessed with keeping everything organized and in its place:

$$a = \frac{b}{7} \quad \text{and} \quad b = \frac{3c}{11}$$

Let's jump back to that $a = b$, $b = c$, then $a = c$ thing. See how in this problem the first b is being divided by 7? We've got to fix that before we can compare a and c. They both need to equal b to be comparable. So I'll fix it with some multiplication:

$$7a = b \quad \text{and} \quad b = \frac{3c}{11}$$

Now we can set them as equal to each other and compare. Keep in mind, however, that this problem asks "a is what fraction of c?" That means we need to reorganize our information to find $\frac{a}{c}$.

Set them equal to each other and solve for $\frac{a}{c}$:

$$7a = b \quad \text{and} \quad b = \frac{3c}{11}$$
$$7a = \frac{3c}{11}$$

First, get that 7 away from the *a*:

$$\frac{1}{\cancel{7}} \cdot \cancel{7}a = \frac{3c}{11} \cdot \frac{1}{\cancel{77}}$$

$$a = \frac{3c}{77}$$

Then move the *c* over to get to that $\frac{a}{c}$:

$$\frac{1}{c} \cdot a = \frac{3\cancel{c}}{77} \cdot \frac{1}{\cancel{c}}$$

$$\frac{a}{c} = \frac{3}{77}$$

Zero and One

EXAMPLE 1: LEVEL 2
If *abcd* = 3 and *abde* = 0, which of the following must be true?

Ⓐ $a = 3$
Ⓑ $b = \frac{1}{3}$
Ⓒ $c = 1$
Ⓓ d is negative
Ⓔ $e = 0$

As soon as different combinations of variables are being multiplied together and sometimes they equal 0 and sometimes they equal something else, the first thing you should think is that a variable in there has got to equal 0. You can multiply thousands of different numbers together, but if you throw in 0, the whole thing equals 0. Because *a*, *b*, *c*, and *d* are all part of the first equation—the equation that multiplies to 3—none of those can equal 0 (because if they did, that whole first equation would equal 0, not 3).

It's also important to keep in mind that this is a *must* problem, not a *could* problem. It's entirely possible that choices A, B, C, and D are true. However, we know that *e* must be 0 (since we decided that *a*, *b*, and *c* can't be), so answer E is correct.

EXAMPLE 2: LEVEL 2
If $x = 5y$, for what value of *y* is $x = y$?

Many students jump the gun and immediately choose $\frac{1}{5}$ as a value of *y*, mistakenly thinking that they want *x* and *y* to multiply together to equal 1. This question asks us to find a single number than can be plugged into both sides of the equation that will make it true. As we've said, only 1 number multiplied by anything always stays itself: 0. So *x* and *y* must equal 0.

A similar question will ask about a variable multiplied by a constant that always remains that variable (that is, that looks like $xa = x$); this time they're checking to see if we'll know that the constant, *a*, needs to be equal to 1.

Order of Operations

WHAT YOU NEED TO KNOW

Now that you know all the operations involving integers that you'll see on the SAT, you need to know the order in which you should work. I've been working like this throughout the section, but I just want to double-check that we're clear before we move on. When you have a string of operations (like adding or multiplying), you can't just work from left to right; you need to use the official Order of Operations. This is simple, and the questions are simple; you just have to get the order right.

So, when presented with any equation or expression, if you're going to simplify it you're going to

P: Simplify the expressions in the **P**arentheses.

E: Work out the **E**xponents.

M: Complete the **M**ultiplication.

D: Complete the **D**ivision.

A: Wrap up the **A**ddition.

S: Wrap up the **S**ubtraction.

There are a few mnemonic devices for remembering the order of operations, but the word "PEMDAS" usually works for me—spell it, and there's the acronym for the order.

HOW THEY ASK THE QUESTIONS

EXAMPLE 1: LEVEL 1
$[(3 + 2^3)(6 \times 2)] + 8 \div 2 = ?$

Visually, you should quickly see that all of that stuff inside the brackets will be added to $8 \div 2$. Brackets are like the granddaddy of parentheses—they block off large chunks of math. I'm going to simplify everything systematically, not skipping steps or doing anything in my head. That's the most important element of ensuring we get to the correct answer:

$$[(3+2^3)(6 \times 2)] + 8 \div 2 =$$

$$[(3+8)(12)] + 4 =$$

$$[(11)(12)] + 4 =$$

$$132 + 4 = \boxed{136}$$

I won't spend time on more examples here, because order of operations is the foundation you'll use to solve so many other problems.

Greater-Than and Less-Than Expressions

In this section we're going to talk about the uses of $<$, $>$, $\leq$, and $\geq$ signs in expressions—apart from inequalities, which we'll talk about more in the algebra section. Here I just want to focus on their smaller uses; they show up pretty frequently and can be fairly challenging.

So let's quickly talk about what these things mean. First, the signs *without* the lines underneath them, $<$ and $>$, are used for comparing 2 values. You can imagine those are little open mouths; whichever way the mouth faces points to the bigger value. All the information is found in the direction in which the mouth faces.

The signs *with* the lines underneath them, $\leq$ and $\geq$, work the same way except that the lines underneath them means the values could also be equal, like this:

$$\text{BIGGER} > \text{smaller} \qquad \text{smaller} < \text{BIGGER}$$

$$\underset{\text{or equal}}{\text{BIGGER}} \geq \underset{\text{or equal}}{\text{smaller}} \qquad \underset{\text{or equal}}{\text{smaller}} \leq \underset{\text{or equal}}{\text{BIGGER}}$$

They're not necessarily equal, but they can be.

That means that the following statements are true: $7 > 5$ and $7 \geq 5$, because 7 is definitely bigger than 5, and although they're not equal to each other, the second statement is true because it says bigger *or* equal. That *or* is key—sometimes a question will focus only on the direction in which the mouth faces, and sometimes the question will want you to use the possibility that they might be equal.

Using Number Theory

These questions focus on the departure from normal number behavior.

EXAMPLE 1: LEVEL 4

What value for x makes $4x^2 < (4x)^2$ a false statement?

I just used the order of operations, commonly referred to as PEMDAS, to simplify that equation—if you're not sure why I'm doing what I'm doing, check out the order of operations lesson on page 109.

This is really a number behavior question; as you'll see later in the lesson about exponents, that 2 exponent in the $(4x)^2$ chunk distributes to everything inside the parentheses. You could rewrite what we've been given as $4x^2 < 4^2x^2$ or $4x^2 < 16x^2$. That would mean that in most circumstances this expression is always true—16 times something squared will always be bigger than 4 times that same something squared. But not if you put in 0. If you throw a 0 in for x, both sides multiply to 0, and $0 \not< 0$—they're equal—so 0 is the answer we're looking for here.

Organizing Lists of Increasing or Decreasing Values

EXAMPLE 1: LEVEL 1

Sara (*s*) is taller than Karen (*k*). Jeff (*j*) is taller than Sara but shorter than Greg (*g*). Which of the following expressions represent the heights of these four people?

OK, I'm not showing the expressions here because I don't want to distract you. I just want us to figure it out and move on. What I would do in a situation like this is read through the problem carefully and take some notes.

Sara is taller than Karen

$$S > K$$

Jeff is taller than Sara . . .

$$J > S > K$$

. . . but he's shorter than Greg

$$G > J > S > K$$

So now I'd refer back to the multiple choice list (which, again, I did not provide here) and we'd look for either $g > j > s > k$ or $k < s < j < g$. *Triple check* the direction in which those arrows face, and you're in great shape.

EXAMPLE 2: LEVEL 4

If $5a = 8b = 7c = 9d > 0$, which of the following expresses the relationships of the values of a, b, c, and d?

Again, we don't want to let the answer choices guide us, so we're going to pretend that we don't have answer choices. We're just going to do the problem, arranging these variables using the > sign.

We've been given these values that are all equal to each other: 5 a's are the same as 8 b's. Let's stop there. If I told you: "5 of these cookies are equivalent to 8 of those," which cookie is bigger? Right, cookie a, which we have 5 of. That's how we know that $a > b$.

Now we'll use that thinking to define the relationship between b and c: 8 b-sized cookies are the same as 7 c-sized cookies. This tells me that those c cookies are larger than the b's, but still not as big as the a's: $a > c > b$.

Finally, we have to look at the 9 d cookies. It takes 9 d's to have the same amount as 5 a's, 7 c's, and 8 b's. These d's are the smallest, so we indicate them as less than everything else: $\boxed{a > c > b > d}$.

Let's take a quick look at the following expression: $3n < m < 0$. In this expression, $3n$ is less than m, and both of those values are less than 0. However, it's important to recognize that n and m could both be the same value and that multiplying n by 3 is what makes $3n$ less than m. For example, if both m and n were -1, $3n$ would be -3 so the statement $3n < m < 0$ would remain true. Again, in this case n and m could be equal, which can be the key to unlocking the most challenging questions.

Using Extremes to Define Ranges

EXAMPLE 1: LEVEL 1

There are 11 rows of parking spots outside the grocery store. Each row has room for at least 75 cars and at most 123 cars. Which of the following could be the number of parking spaces in the lot?

Often students will find the average of 75 and 123 and multiply that by 11. This is a good idea if you're looking for the dead-middle possible number of spots in the lot. The problem is that the amount you calculate might not be listed in the answer choices. So instead, we need to limit the range—the name of the game on problems like this is always to find the lowest possible number of spots and the highest possible number of spots. There will only be 1 answer choice between that range.

We find the range by multiplying 75 by 11 and 123 by 11: $75 \times 11 = 825$ and $123 \times 11 = 1{,}353$. We calculate that our number of parking spaces must be between those 2 values: $825 < \text{number of spaces} < 1{,}353$.

EXAMPLE 2: LEVEL 4

If $0 \le a \le 7$ and $-1 \le b \le 5$, what inequality expression represents the range of possible values of ab?

This is challenging because everyone homes in on the 0 rather than the -1. However, the negative is the key to this problem—we could choose 0 for a and any value for b to get $ab = 0$. But we want to find the greatest range, so we'll choose the greatest and smallest numbers possible—7 for a and -1 for b—so we get that ab value down to -7. We actually use that 7 value to create both the greatest and the least values in the range, because we'll multiply 7 and 5 to find our greatest value of ab: 35. So an expression representing this range would be: $\boxed{-7 \le ab \le 35}$.

Divisibility Rules and Old-Fashioned Long Division Refresher

WHAT YOU NEED TO KNOW

Rather than reaching for your calculator or writing out a long division problem, there are a few quick ways to check for divisibility.

A number is divisible by

- O 2 if it ends in 0 or an even number; that is, if it ends in 2, 4, 6, 8, or 0
- O 3 if the sum of its digits is divisible by 3 (that is, we know 324 is divisible by 3 because $3 + 2 + 4 = 9$ and 9 is divisible by 3)
- O 4 if its last 2 digits are divisible by 4 (that is, 4,827,516 is divisible by 4 because 16 is divisible by 4)
- O 5 if it ends in 0 or 5
- O 6 if it is even and divisible by 3 (that is, use the rules for both 2 and 3)
- O 7 . . . forget it—just use your calculator for 7

○ 8 if the last 3 digits are divisible by 8 (it's probably not a bad idea to use your calculator for this, too)

○ 9 if the sum of its digits is divisible by 9 (that is, we know 327,168 is divisible by 9 because $3 + 2 + 7 + 1 + 6 + 8 = 36$ and $3 + 6 = 9$)

A word about long division: using it on this test will be extremely helpful for several different problem types, so let's quickly review how to do it (since you most likely haven't used it in 10 years).

$3\overline{)841}$

how many times does 3 go into 8?

$\begin{array}{r} 2 \\ 3\overline{)841} \end{array}$

multiply 2 by 3

$\begin{array}{r} 2 \\ 3\overline{)841} \\ 6 \end{array}$

subtract and bring down the 4

$\begin{array}{r} 2 \\ 3\overline{)841} \\ -6\downarrow \\ 24 \end{array}$

how many times does 3 go into 24?

$\begin{array}{r} 28 \\ 3\overline{)841} \\ -6 \\ \overline{24} \end{array}$

multiply 8 by 3

$\begin{array}{r} 28 \\ 3\overline{)841} \\ -6 \\ \overline{24} \\ 24 \end{array}$

subtract and bring down the 1

$\begin{array}{r} 28 \\ 3\overline{)841} \\ -6 \\ \overline{24} \\ -24\downarrow \\ \overline{01} \end{array}$

how many times does 3 go into 1?

$\begin{array}{r} 280 \\ 3\overline{)841} \\ -6 \\ \overline{24} \\ -24 \\ \overline{01} \end{array}$

multiply 0 by 3

$\begin{array}{r} 280 \\ 3\overline{)841} \\ -6 \\ \overline{24} \\ -24 \\ \overline{01} \\ 0 \end{array}$

Subtract

$\begin{array}{r} 280 \\ 3\overline{)841} \\ -6 \\ \overline{24} \\ -24 \\ \overline{01} \\ -0 \\ \overline{1} \end{array}$ ← Remainder.

note: * the remainder **must** be smaller than the divisor
* you may put the remainder over the divisor to create a fraction if necessary, like $280\frac{1}{3}$

If you have a remainder that's bigger than your original divisor, you've made a mistake

Relying on Remainder

These problems use remainder rules to get you to the right answer.

EXAMPLE 1: LEVEL 2

Which of the following could be the remainders when 5 consecutive integers are each divided by 4?

(A) 1, 2, 3, 4, 5
(B) 0, 1, 2, 3, 4
(C) 2, 3, 4, 4, 1
(D) 1, 2, 3, 0, 1
(E) 2, 2, 3, 3, 4

As we just learned in the long division refresher, a division problem's remainder can never be bigger than the divisor itself (what you're dividing by). Of these answer choices, only answer D is made up of remainders that are less than 4. Also, because we're dividing by consecutive integers, the group of remainders needs to reflect that and change consecutively as well.

EXAMPLE 2: LEVEL 3

If r is an integer and 5 is the remainder when $2r + 9$ is divided by 6, which of the following could be a value of r?

(A) 3
(B) 4
(C) 5
(D) 6
(E) 7

These problems are honestly just tedious—you have to use the answer choices to plug in for a value of r. Once you get that value, divide it by 6 and see if you get a remainder of 5. If you do, that's the right choice. In this case, the answer is E.

$$2r + 9 \rightarrow (2 \cdot 7) + 9 \rightarrow 14 + 9 = 23$$

$$\begin{array}{r} 3 \\ 6\overline{)23} \\ -18 \\ \hline 5 \end{array} \leftarrow \text{remainder } 5 \checkmark$$

EXAMPLE 3: LEVEL 4

When 16 is divided by the positive integer t, the remainder is 2. For how many different values of t is this true?

This question seems pretty straightforward: do some division, find some values that give us a remainder of 2, and move on. Here's how students usu-

Many students ask me about those questions that include something like " . . . and $x \neq 0$ " or " . . . $rs \neq 0$" or whatever variable from the equation. This phrase is included not to overload you with information but to preemptively respond to those students who say, "Well, if x were 0, that denominator would be undefined . . ." or "Well, if rs were equal to zero, there would be no solution to the problem." You can consider it a math compliance phrase and nothing to stress about.

ally attempt this problem: "OK, 16 ÷ 2 = 8, no remainder. That's not it. OK, 16 ÷ 3 = 5 R1. That's not it. OK, 16 ÷ 4 = 4, no remainder. Wrong again. 16 ÷ 5 = 3 R1. Nope. 16 ÷ 6 = 2 R4. No. 16 ÷ 7 = 2 R2. That works! OK . . . 16 ÷ 8 goes in evenly, and 16 ÷ 9 will have a huge remainder. Great. I'm done. Only 1 value gives us remainder 2." *That* is why this is a hard problem: everyone reads "integer" in the question as "single integer" and stops checking values after they have used all the single-digit numbers. And true, it is a little tedious to keep checking answers, but in this case 16 ÷ 14 = 1 R2.

So there are 2 values of *t* that leave us with the remainder 2. The moral of the story: don't stop checking at 9.

Divisibility Rules

Forget your calculator for these problems. Just use divisibility rules to find the right answer quickly.

EXAMPLE 1: LEVEL 2

If *n* is a positive integer that is divisible by 6 and $n < 80$, what is the greatest possible value of *n*?

(A) 75
(B) 76
(C) 77
(D) 78
(E) 79

Naturally, since we're looking for the greatest possible value of *n*, we should begin with the largest option available. Don't pick up your calculator yet! The quickest way to solve this problem is to use divisibility rules. As we learned, numbers that are divisible by 6 are divisible by both 2 and 3. First we can eliminate all odd answers (75, 77, and 79) because our answer must be divisible by 2. To check for divisibility by 3 we add the digits in our possible answer choice. Adding the digits in the largest answer choice, 78, first gives us 15 (that's just 7 + 8). And 15 is divisible by 3, so we've found our answer.

Primes, Factoring, and Multiples

WHAT YOU NEED TO KNOW

Primes

If we've applied all our divisibility rules to a number and we still haven't found a divisor, we need to consider that the number may be prime. Prime numbers have a really specific definition: each prime number is divisible only by 1 and itself.

Here are some things to note:

1 is not prime

2 is the only even prime number

recognize this pattern: 2, 3, 5, 7, 11, 13, 17, 19, 23

Prime Factors

Understanding primes is really helpful, as every other whole nonprime number can be created by multiplying lots of little primes together. For example, 63 can be created by multiplying 3 × 3 × 7. Coming up with a list of the primes that create a number is important in several types of questions; you can always find the list of prime factors by using a *factor tree*. A factor tree is created by simply dividing up a number until you can't divide it any longer—until you produce a list of indivisible *prime factors*.

For example, let's build a factor tree for 63. I happen to know off the top of my head that 9 × 7 = 63, so I'll make those my first branches.

factor tree refresher

63
∧
9 × 7

In that step alone I've already found 1 of my prime factors, 7. However, 9 breaks down too, so I create a new row and bring down the 7 so everything stays organized.

63
∧
9 × 7
∧
3 × 3 × 7

you're done when the bottom row is made of prime numbers

Some students learn to create factor trees and leave each prime factor as a "leaf" on the tree; I prefer to bring each number down to the bottom row every time I create a new row so that I know I won't overlook any factors at the end.

Anyway, my bottom row now reads 3 × 3 × 7—my complete list of the prime factors that make up 63. Now, if I hadn't been so up on my times tables, I might have used divisibility rules to realize that 63 is divisible by 3 and subsequently started my branches with 3 and 21. Even if I had, I still would have worked down to 3, 3, and 7. It always works.

A cool thing you can do with these factor trees is analyze or create square numbers and perfect cubes on the fly.

Here are some things to note:

- ○ Every perfect square has an even number of each of its distinct prime factors.
- ○ Every perfect cube's distinct prime factors come in groups of 3's.

That means if I want to find out if a number is a perfect square, I can just create a factor tree and make sure I've got an even number of each distinct prime. If I factor and I have 3 of each distinct prime, I've got a cube.

how to be sure a number is a perfect cube

```
        27000
         /\
       27  1000
      /\    /\
    3  9  10  100
   /  /\  /\   \
  3  3  3  2  5  10  10
  |  |  |  |  \  /\   |
  3  3  3  2  5 2 5  2 5
```

fully factored we get

3: 3's   3:5's   and   3:2's.   cube ✓

Factors

Now, if you're not specifically asked about prime factors, you're being asked about plain old vanilla factors. Factors are all of the numbers that divide evenly into a particular number. For example, the factors of 63 are 1, 3, 7, 9, 21, and 63.

A great way to be pretty foolproof in your attempts to find all the factors of a number (rather than doing it in your head) is to use the prime factors to build pairs of factors.

finding all the factors of 63

```
┌─────────────────────────────────────────────┐
│  1. create factor tree    2. group prime factors
│                              to create all pairs
│          63
│         /\                 1 × 63 →   1, 63
│        9 × 7
│       /\                   3; 3 × 7 →  3, 21
│      3 × 3 × 7
│                            3 × 3; 7 → 9, 7
│
│                          final list:
│                    ➡    1, 3, 7, 9, 21, 63
└─────────────────────────────────────────────┘
```

Basically, you can work your way across the row of prime factors to create each factor: keep the 3 and use the 3 × 7 to create the pair 3 and 21; use the 3 × 3 to create 9 and keep the 7 to create the pair 9 × 7; and, most important, don't forget to include the pair 1 and 63. Keep it organized and you'll be sure you've got them all.

Defining Primes and Finding Factors

These factor and prime problems focus on defining primes and finding factors. More challenging problems that use these skills will be in the exponents lesson.

EXAMPLE 1: LEVEL 3

What is the smallest three-digit integer that has a factor of 5?

This problem directly relates to those divisibility problems we were looking at earlier. *Having a factor of 5 is the same as being divisible by 5.* We know, then, that our 3-digit integer is going to end in either 0 or 5. A 3-digit integer means we're building a 3-slot number: _ _ _. We must make this whole number as low as possible, so we'll need to pay careful attention to each digit.

In the first slot we enter a 1, since 0 is not an option for the first digit in a whole number: 1 _ _. The next digit needs to be as low as possible as well, but this time we can use 0: 1 0 _. Now, the last part is tricky because the question asks for a multiple of 5. Don't jump to the conclusion that this number ends with a 5 just because it's a multiple of 5 . . . we have both 0 and 5 at our disposal. Because 100 is less than 105, we choose 0 as the last digit. So we end up with 1 0 0.

EXAMPLE 2: LEVEL 3

If *a* is the greatest prime factor of 46 and *b* is the greatest prime factor of 72, what is the value of *ab*?

Remember, the greatest prime factor of a number is the biggest number you have in the final row of your factor tree. To create a factor tree for 46, it's probably easiest to start by dividing 46 by 2, as 46 is obviously even.

$$46$$
$$\wedge$$
$$\textcircled{23} \times 2$$

We've already found the value of *a*, because 23 is prime. Now let's do the tree for 72:

$$72$$
$$/\backslash$$
$$9 \times 8$$
$$/\backslash \quad /\backslash$$
$$3 \times 3 \times 2 \times 4$$
$$| \quad | \quad | \times /\backslash$$
$$\textcircled{3} \times 3 \times 2 \times 2 \times 2$$

Interestingly enough, even though 72 is a bigger number than 42, 72's greatest prime factor is only 3. So 3 is our value for *b*.

Let's remember to answer the question!

$ab = 23 \times 3$

$ab = \boxed{69}$

Multiples and Least Common Multiples

Multiples

Multiples are just the opposite of factors; they're all the numbers you get when you multiply a given number by anything else.

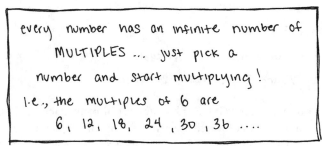

every number has an infinite number of MULTIPLES ... just pick a number and start multiplying! i.e., the multiples of 6 are 6, 12, 18, 24, 30, 36 ....

→ btw, all negatives have multiples, too!

Least Common Multiple

The least common multiple (LCM) of 2 numbers is found by listing the multiples of 2 different numbers and finding the very first multiple they have in common. For example, if we're looking for the LCM of 6 and 9, we start by creating a list of the multiples of 6 and a list of the multiples of 9. Compare the list and, lo and behold, they have the number 18 in common.

However, sometimes finding the LCM isn't that easy. Say we're looking for the LCM of 30 and 108. We could start multiplying each of them by 2, by 3, by 4, and comparing our products. The lists would get pretty long before we found the LCM, and creating the lists would burn a ton of time on the calculator, which we really want to avoid on a timed test. Those factor trees from earlier are about to become pretty helpful.

Let's create factor trees for 30 and for 108. So 30 is the product of 2 × 3 × 5, and 108 is the product of 2 × 3 × 3 × 3 × 2. Let's compare these lists:

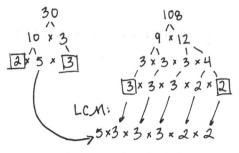

finding the LCM of 30 and 108

30
/\
10 × 3
/\   \
[2]× 5 × [3]

108
/\
9 × 12
/\   /|
3 × 3 × 3 × 4
/   /   / / \
[3]× 3 × 3 × 2 × [2]

LCM: / / / / /
→ 5 × 3 × 3 × 3 × 2 × 2

include enough of each prime factor
to create 30 and 108 from your
list, but don't include duplicates.
I boxed 2 and 3 to mark the repeats.

Here's what to do to find the LCM: See how the list of prime factors of 108 already contains a 2 and 3, both of which are prime factors of 30? Get this: since 108 already has a 2 and a 3, if I simply tack the 5 onto 108's prime factor list, I'll have created the lowest common multiple for both numbers.

5 × 3 × 3 × 3 × 2 × 2 = <u>540</u>

540 is the LCM of 30 and 108.

Let me reiterate. The least common multiple of any 2 numbers will contain all of the factors needed to create each of our original 2 numbers. The list 5 × 3 × 3 × 3 × 2 × 2 includes all the prime factors I need to create 30 and all the prime factors I need to create 108.

Greatest Common Factor

The greatest common factor (GCF) of 2 numbers is simply the greatest factor, or number, that divides into each of them. For example, the GCF of 15 and 60 is 15, because 15 goes into each without a remainder. It's that simple. We'll see more about this in later sections.

HOW THEY ASK THE QUESTIONS

There are 2 ways you'll use multiples and, in particular, LCMs on the SAT. For starters, we can use LCMs to find a common denominator for a fraction, which we'll get into in the very next lesson. If you are asked specifically about the LCM of 2 numbers, more often than not, that question will be a more challenging version of what we have seen here that will use variables and exponents. So to be efficient, I included the example with the exponent questions, on page 149.

This is me sticking to my promise that I wouldn't give you unnecessary work.

Fractions and Decimals

You're going to hate me for this, but . . . you should use fractions instead of decimals whenever possible on the SAT. It actually makes things easier.

Fractions are great because

○ They reduce.

○ They cancel.

○ They give us tons of information.

○ They don't require the use of a calculator.

First, let's start with some decimals you should be able to convert to fractions right off the top of your head.

fraction and decimal exchange

$.2$	$.25$	$.\overline{33}$	$.5$	$.\overline{66}$	$.75$	$.8$
↓	↓	↓	↓	↓	↓	↓
$\dfrac{1}{5}$	$\dfrac{1}{4}$	$\dfrac{1}{3}$	$\dfrac{1}{2}$	$\dfrac{2}{3}$	$\dfrac{3}{4}$	$\dfrac{4}{5}$

Know them. Love them. Memorize them.

If you've got a decimal other than these, you can always use place value to quickly convert it to a fraction. For example, rather than reading 0.72 as "point seventy-two," read it as "seventy-two hundredths." Simple: $\frac{72}{100}$, seventy-two hundredths.

convert any decimal to a fraction

$$.72 \quad = \quad \frac{72}{100}$$

"seventy two   "seventy two

hundredths"   hundredths"

Likewise, 0.328 isn't "point three two eight"; it's "three hundred twenty-eight thousandths." Read it properly and you'll read the fraction: $\frac{328}{1000}$.

There are 3 main circumstances in which you'll find your basic fraction problems: you'll be adding them, you'll be multiplying them, or they'll be set equal to each other. Let's cover the basics here; the rest of the rules and fraction exceptions will pop up in other topics.

Parts of Fractions

The top part of the fraction is the *numerator*; the bottom part is the *denominator*. We refer to $2\frac{1}{2}$ as a *mixed fraction* and $\frac{9}{4}$ as an *improper fraction*.

$\frac{3}{4}$ ← numerator
← denominator

$2\frac{1}{2}$ ← mixed fraction

$\frac{9}{4}$ ← improper fraction

Whenever you're writing out fractions, keep your numerators over your denominators, like this: $\frac{\text{numerator}}{\text{denominator}}$. Don't use a slash between them, like this: $^{\text{numerator}}/_{\text{denominator}}$. I know, the slash looks fancier, but you'll have a much easier time quickly canceling, reducing, and working algebraically if everything is visually exactly where it belongs.

Finding a Common Denominator to Add Fractions

Fractions cannot be added together if they don't have the same denominator. Finding a common denominator is as simple as finding a common multiple—or even the LCM—of the denominators you're adding (whether there are 2 different denominators or 10), adjusting the numerators accordingly, and then adding the numerators. By "adjusting the numerators," I mean that we can't just leave the numerators as they are; they have to be related to their new denominators. To adjust the numerator, simply multiply the numerator by the same number by which you multiplied the denominator to create the common denominator.

$$\frac{2}{3} \rightarrow \frac{2}{3} \times \frac{5}{5} = \frac{10}{15}$$

Multiplying Fractions

To multiply fractions, multiply straight across the top and across the bottom of your problem.

$$\frac{3}{7} \times \frac{2}{5} = \frac{3 \times 2}{7 \times 5} = \frac{6}{35}$$

Dividing Fractions

It's important to know that $\frac{x}{x}$ (any value over the same value) is always equal to 1, except when $x = 0$.

To divide anything by a fraction, multiply instead by the fraction's reciprocal.

$$\frac{3}{7} \div \frac{2}{5} \rightarrow \frac{3}{7} \cdot \frac{5}{2} = \frac{15}{14}$$

Cross-Multiplying Fractions

When fractions are equal to each other, always cross-multiply.

$$\frac{3}{7} = \frac{x}{35}$$
$$3 \cdot 35 = 7x$$
$$105 = 7x$$
$$15 = x$$

Another important feature of a fraction is that its denominator can never be equal to 0. We refer to any fraction whose denominator is 0 as "undefined."

Canceling and Reducing Fractions

On the SAT, if you don't answer a question with a fraction in its most reduced form, it's wrong, so let's be clear about what you need to do. A fraction is a relationship: $\frac{1}{3}$ of a pie is the same as $\frac{3}{9}$ of a pie. Likewise, $\frac{1}{4}$ of the senior class could be $\frac{4}{16}$, $\frac{5}{20}$, $\frac{200}{800}$, and so on. In fact, the relationships can get infinitely large, so the rule in math is to keep them as small as possible.

In light of this, we *always* have to fully reduce fractions. What we're doing when we reduce is technically canceling the common factors of the numerator and denominator.

Let's look at canceling $\frac{15}{20}$. When we reduce the fraction, we're treating it as though it says this:

$$\frac{15}{20} = \frac{3}{4} \cdot \frac{5}{5}$$

Because $\frac{5}{5} = 1$, what's happening here is that $\frac{3}{4}$ is being multiplied by a form of 1. It's totally legal to ignore multiplication by 1 (since multiplying by 1 doesn't change anything), so it's safe to say that $\frac{15}{20} = \frac{3}{4}$. The value of the fraction—the relationship between the numerator and denominator—doesn't change; just the numbers change. That's canceling and reducing.

In general, you should use your divisibility rules to see if the numerator and denominator of any given fraction are divisible by the same number. If they are, divide them both, and you've reduced. A fraction is reduced when the numerator and denominator no longer have any factors in common. I don't want to go nuts about this, but always double-check that you've fully reduced an answer choice before you grid it in.

Real convenience happens when you cancel fractions that are being multiplied rather than multiplying enormous numbers together.

Case in point: $\frac{3}{46} \times \frac{46}{2}$. For heaven's sake, please, please do not multiply 3 and 46 in the numerator and 46 and 2 in the denominator—you'll get $\frac{138}{92}$ and have to reduce, which is (1) not intuitive and (2) just plain awful. Instead, we can merely cancel the 46's (because they're about to become factors of our giant numerator and denominator) and simply multiply 3 × 1 and 1 × 2.

$$\frac{3}{46} \times \frac{46}{2} \quad \text{is the same as} \quad \frac{3}{2} \times \frac{46}{46}$$

$$\frac{3}{2} \times \frac{\cancel{46}}{\cancel{46}} \rightarrow \frac{3}{2} \times 1 \rightarrow \boxed{\frac{3}{2}}$$

This makes for a much easier life.

This is great for canceling 0's when you have multiples of 10 in the numerator and denominator . . .

$$\frac{32000000}{8000} \rightarrow \frac{32000\cancel{000}}{8\cancel{000}} \rightarrow \frac{32000}{8} \rightarrow 4000$$

and when you have like variables in the numerator and denominator . . .

$$\frac{6abcd}{2ac} \rightarrow \frac{6\cancel{a}b\cancel{c}d}{2\cancel{a}\cancel{c}} \rightarrow \frac{6bd}{2} \rightarrow 3bd$$

HOW THEY ASK THE QUESTIONS

Intro Level Don't-Overdo-It Questions

These problems are basic, basic, basic—the trick is to not think too much and to just be careful.

EXAMPLE 1: LEVEL 1

If $a + \frac{3}{a} = 4 + \frac{3}{4}$, what is the value of a?

Before you do anything here, just look at the problem. You'll actually get into a long bit of algebra if you try to solve it. Instead, just read it: If a plus 3 over a is equal to 4 plus 3 over 4 . . . then, yes, a is just equal to 4.

Any time you have a fraction problem like this at the very beginning of the test, just look at the arrangement of the problem and go from there.

EXAMPLE 2: LEVEL 1

Which of the following decimals is between $\frac{1}{3}$ and $\frac{1}{4}$?

I have specifically left out the answer choices here to make sure we're focused on understanding the problem. Many students will jump right down to the answer choices (which are in decimal form) and start trying to translate those decimals back to fractional form. Instead, we're going to employ perhaps the most important general tip I can give you for this test: *any time you're looking for a "between," find the extremes.*

In this problem, finding the extremes is really simple because you've already memorized that list of exchanges I gave you on page 121 (or at least you will have memorized them before test day). We know that $\frac{1}{3}$ is equal to $.\overline{33}$ and $\frac{1}{4}$ is equal to 0.25.

There will only be 1 decimal answer choice between $0.\overline{33}$ and 0.25.

EXAMPLE 3: LEVEL 1

If the product of b and 0.7 is equal to 1, what is the value of b?

Because I think calculators are great tools for making mistakes, I don't go to my calculator on this problem. Instead, I convert 0.7 into a fraction and go from there. Because 0.7 is "seven tenths," I use $\frac{7}{10}$ in my problem: $\frac{7}{10} \times b = 1$.

Then I just solve for b.

$$\frac{7}{10} \cdot b = 1 \quad \leftarrow \text{keep those numerators on top!}$$

$$\frac{7b}{10} = 1$$

$$7b = 10$$

I always like to use fractions to ensure that I have a simple answer to put in the grid-in section. Not that gridding in decimals is difficult, but I feel like fractions leave less room for error. Moreover, I haven't put anything into my calculator, which means I can easily go back and check my work after I have finished the rest of the section.

Using the Reciprocal

This is a more general skill that I want to make sure we look at. Many problems incorporate the element of "multiplying by the reciprocal when dividing by a fraction," but the skill is not often tested individually. When it is, it will look something like the following.

EXAMPLE 1: LEVEL 3

If $a = \frac{1}{3}$, what is the value of $\dfrac{1}{a-1} + \dfrac{1}{a}$?

This problem is all about keeping things organized. Don't get intimidated by it; just keep your work clear. First, do not try to simplify while you plug in. The first step is just to plug in $\frac{1}{3}$ for a, like this:

$$\frac{1}{\frac{1}{3} - 1} + \frac{1}{\frac{1}{3}}$$

Don't get intimidated. Next, focus on getting rid of the -1 in the denominator of the first fraction:

$$\frac{1}{\left(\frac{1}{3} - 1\right)} + \frac{1}{\frac{1}{3}}$$

$$\frac{1}{3} - 1 = \frac{1}{3} - \frac{3}{3} = \left(-\frac{2}{3}\right)$$

$$\frac{1}{-\frac{2}{3}} + \frac{1}{\frac{1}{3}}$$

> Easier versions of this problem will use fractions that cancel each other out, but they may make you feel less confident because students tend to stress out when an answer is 0 or 1.

This is where we use the reciprocal rule; we're going to multiply those 1's in the numerators by the reciprocals of the fractions in the denominators:

$$1 \cdot \left(-\frac{3}{2}\right) + 1 \cdot \left(\frac{3}{1}\right) \;\rightarrow\; -\frac{3}{2} + \frac{3}{1}$$

Last, we find a common denominator for our fractions and add 'em up:

$$-\frac{3}{2} + \frac{3}{1}\left(\frac{2}{2}\right)$$

$$-\frac{3}{2} + \frac{6}{2} = \boxed{\frac{3}{2}}$$

Canceling

Not canceling everything you possibly can as early on in a problem can cost you, big time. This goes for the simplest fraction multiplication problems and the most difficult.

EXAMPLE 1: LEVEL 1
If $xy = 12$, what is the value of $3 \times x^2 \times \frac{y}{x}$?

Cancel those x's, now!

$$3 \cdot x\!\!\!/^{\,\prime} \cdot \frac{y}{\cancel{x}}$$

$$3 \times y$$

Just like that, you've got 3×12 (because $xy = 12$).

$$3 \cdot 12 = \boxed{36}$$

Dividing Wholes and Fractions

These problems focus on your ability to understand how whole pieces are repeatedly split evenly; they usually measure things like lengths, amounts of liquid, or areas of surfaces.

EXAMPLE 1: LEVEL 3
Four campers are out in the wilderness. Camper A drinks half of the water in the canteen and passes it to Camper B. Camper B drinks half of the water in the canteen and passes it to Camper C. Camper C does the same and passes the canteen to Camper D. What fraction of the original water from the canteen does Camper D get?

This is a pretty standard fraction "concept problem": some whole amount (the water in the canteen) is being divided in half over and over again, and we are interested in a particular measurement of the water (this time, the amount of water that Camper D will have to drink).

So here's what's happening: we're starting with 1 (a whole) and we're going to split that whole up evenly.

$1 \div 2 = \frac{1}{2}$ ← that's camper B's amount. camper B's water is divided in half and given to camper C:

$\frac{1}{2} \div 2 = \frac{1}{4}$ ← camper C gets $\frac{1}{4}$ of the water. we split that in half and give it to camper D:

$\frac{1}{4} \div 2 = \boxed{\frac{1}{8}}$ ← that's camper D.

Again, you will see this concept over and over in the SAT; the main goal is to figure out what the whole is and then find the pieces in relation to that whole. Your answer may be as big as $\frac{1}{4}$ or as small as $\frac{1}{64}$.

EXAMPLE 2: LEVEL 5

A classroom of students is planning to divide a bucket that contains n ounces of candy corn into smaller jars. They have two options that will each hold exactly n ounces: a set of 24 jars or a set of 12 jars. What fraction represents the amount of candy corn the smaller container will hold?

This time we're dividing up a whole, n, but we're not splitting it in half over and over. Instead, we have options about how much we'll divide it up—into 24 jars or into 12 jars. The question asks for the amount that 1 of the smaller containers will hold. Because the same amount of corn will fit into 24 jars or 12 jars, we need to recognize that the 24 jars are smaller.

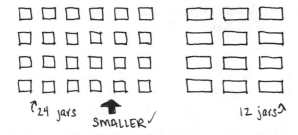

So we need to find *one 24th of the candy corn* and express it as a fraction: $\frac{1}{24}$ of n.

$$\frac{1}{24} \cdot n = \boxed{\frac{n}{24}}$$

Manipulating Fractions

These are the problems that really test your understanding of fractional relationships—they aim to see if you understand everything that's tough about the fraction:

- Understanding part-to-whole relationships
- Finding fractional parts of wholes
- Finding measured amounts of wholes
- Finding wholes based on given pieces

EXAMPLE 1: LEVEL 3

In a survey, 14 people reported that pink is their favorite color, 20 people reported that blue is their favorite color, and 16 people reported that red is their favorite color. What fraction of those surveyed reported that pink is their favorite color?

This type of problem provides all the numbers we need to find the total; all we need to do is total the people surveyed, create a fraction from that value, and reduce.

$$14 + 20 + 16 = 50 \text{ people total}$$

$$\frac{14 \text{ like pink}}{50 \text{ total people}} \longrightarrow \frac{14}{50}$$

$$\text{reduce} \quad \boxed{\frac{7}{25}}$$

This type of problem is made more challenging by translating the parts into fractions, rather than giving us the actual number in each part.

EXAMPLE 2: LEVEL 3

Of the sophomore class at Wellington High School, $\frac{1}{3}$ of the students have math first period, $\frac{1}{4}$ of the students have math second period, $\frac{1}{6}$ of the students have math third period, and the rest of the students have math fourth period. If there are 360 students in the sophomore class, how many students have math during fourth period?

Did you notice this whole problem is given in fractions but we're asked for a number? There are several ways to do this problem, but most students find it easiest to set up a little chart and keep track of info that way:

1st period	2nd period	3rd period	4th period
$\frac{1}{3}$ of 360	$\frac{1}{4}$ of 360	$\frac{1}{6}$ of 360	
$\frac{1}{3} \cdot 360$	$\frac{1}{4} \cdot 360$	$\frac{1}{6} \cdot 360$	
120 students	90 students	60 students	x

Now that we've determined how many students are in each period, we can add them up and subtract them from the total to find x, the number of students in fourth period:

$$120 + 90 + 60 + x = 360$$

$$270 + x = 360$$

$$x = 90$$

EXAMPLE 3: LEVEL 4

Paper clips are available in mixed containers of small, medium, and large sizes. If Javier buys a box of paper clips in which $\frac{1}{3}$ of the paper clips are size small, half as many as are size small are size medium, and 36 are size large, how many paper clips are in the box?

This problem combines skills we used in both examples 1 and 2—we've been given fractions in the first part, a description of another part relative to the fraction, and an integer value for yet another part. We're asked to find the whole amount from all this information.

A chart is probably not a bad idea here, either:

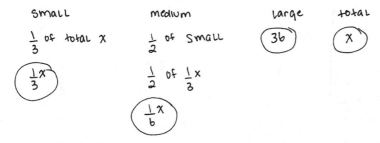

OK, so my whole box of paperclips can be expressed by what we just found:

$$\frac{1}{3}x + \frac{1}{6}x + 36 = x \longrightarrow \frac{x}{3} + \frac{x}{6} + 36 = x$$

I also put everything else into a fractional format so we could really see what we're doing and we're sure everything is where it's supposed to be. Now I'll put everything over the common denominator 6:

$$\frac{2x}{6} + \frac{x}{6} + \frac{216}{6} = \frac{6x}{6}$$

It's extremely important, when you're adding fractions like this, that you put everything over the same denominator—we couldn't just leave that as $\frac{x}{1}$ over on the end there. However, now that we've got everything over the same denominator we can actually drop the denominator and focus on the numerators. (This is legal because it's like we multiplied everything by $\frac{6}{1}$, which cancels the denominators.)

$$2x + x + 216 = 6x$$
$$3x + 216 = 6x$$
$$216 = 3x$$
$$\frac{216}{3} = x$$
$$72 = x$$

So there are 72 paper clips in the box. Don't get intimidated by these problems. The trick is to stay organized and pay attention to each step you're doing without jumping ahead. With practice, you'll start to recognize and predict what's happening in each problem. But be careful: predicting can be the death knell for your accuracy. Don't predict. Solve.

EXAMPLE 4: LEVEL 4

Lola fills a bottle one third of the way with sand. She then fills the rest of the bottle with a mixture that is equal parts sand, glitter, and glue. After she has completed filling the bottle, what fraction of the bottle contains sand?

This time we're given fractions and the problem asks for a new fraction. What's so challenging? Keeping the concept straight. Let's draw this bottle:

She fills the bottle $\frac{1}{3}$ with sand, leaving $\frac{2}{3}$ of the bottle empty. Then she fills the remaining $\frac{2}{3}$ with a mixture that includes $\frac{1}{3}$ sand. So, an additional $\frac{1}{3}$ of $\frac{2}{3}$ is sand.

Sand, then, is repesented by

$$\frac{1}{3} + \left(\frac{1}{3} \cdot \frac{2}{3} \right)$$

$$\frac{1}{3} + \frac{2}{9}$$

Find a common denominator, add, and you've found the amount of sand in the bottle:

$$\frac{3}{9} + \frac{2}{9} = \boxed{\frac{5}{9}} \leftarrow \text{total sand}$$

Proportions and Ratios

Proportions

The most common application of a fraction on the SAT, other than just measuring things, is the proportion. Keeping something "in proportion" means keeping the relationship between the original thing or amount and another thing or amount constant. If I'm mixing muffin ingredients, I always want to make sure that I keep the amount of sugar proportional to the other ingredients, no matter if I double, triple, or quadruple my original recipe. If Marc Jacobs is making a sample-size dress, that dress in all the other sizes must be proportional to the first dress so that they look exactly the same, just bigger. If I commit to running 1 mile for every 2 slices of pizza I eat for dinner, I'll be running 2 miles for every 4 slices of pizza or (cringe) 3 miles for every 6 slices. It's just fancy multiplication.

A proportion is an expression that uses fractions to keep the relationships between 2 values straight. You'll use them to measure increments on maps, lengths of sides of triangles, and parts of mixtures to whole mixtures.

In fact, you can always use the following formula to figure out any proportional relationship:

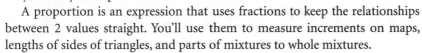

$$\frac{PART}{WHOLE} = \frac{NEW\ PART}{NEW\ WHOLE}$$

Simply fill in the information you have, pop in a variable for the bit you want to find, and cross-multiply. The fractional relationship that you set up between any part and its whole and a new part and its whole will always be true—it is the relationship that's constant, not necessarily the values themselves.

Ratios

Ratios are really just another expression of fractions, but they're used in a specific way on the SAT.

Ratios are often easier to understand if we think about them as ways of talking about a complete group of things rather than relationships between different things. For instance, suppose we go to the grocery store to shop for a prepackaged bag of apples. If we looked carefully at the bags, maybe we'd discover that the orchard bagged the apples such that for every 3 red apples they put in the bag, they also included 4 green apples.

This red-apple-to-green-apple ratio could be expressed as the fraction $\frac{3}{4}$ or with a colon, 3:4. Be careful: because we've stipulated *red* to *green*, our ratio is *3* to *4*, not 4 to 3. Anyway, the most important piece of info to pick up on here is that these apples are packaged in groups of 7. For every 3 red apples we have 4 green apples, which means we can only have packages that contain groups of 7 apples.

We will never have a piece of a whole apple in these situations (either it's an apple or it's not), which also means that each bag will need to contain a multiple of 7 apples: these bags come with only 7, 14, 21, or 28 apples at a time.

More advanced ratios will divide a complete group up into more than 2 parts. A ratio that reads 3:4:5 means we have 12 pieces of something, which are being allocated in groups of 3 pieces, 4 pieces, and 5 pieces.

HOW THEY ASK THE QUESTIONS

Using the Proportion Format

These problems make sure you understand the "2 fractions equal to each other" format and how to use and interpret it.

EXAMPLE 1: LEVEL 2
If $\frac{a}{6} = \frac{3a}{x}$ and $x \neq 0$, what is the value of x?

This is the mantra: whenever fractions are equal to each other, cross-multiply. Here, $\frac{a}{6} = \frac{3a}{x}$ cross-multiplies to $ax = 18a$. Don't think too much about this: if $ax = 18a$, then x must equal 18. Mathematically the a's just cancel and leave you with $x = 18$.

> Are fractions equal to each other? Cross-multiply!

Maps, Measurements, Recipes, and Miniatures

These problems involve using a basic proportion to solve for a value in a given relationship.

EXAMPLE 1: LEVEL 1
A recipe for chicken soup that serves 4 people calls for 3 quarts of broth. At this ratio, how much broth is required to make soup for 132 people?

All we're going to do is set up an equation that expresses the little relationship in the problem:

$$\frac{4 \text{ people}}{3 \text{ quarts}} = \frac{132 \text{ people}}{x \text{ quarts}}$$

See how I used the relationship I was given to create the new relationship? If 4 people need 3 quarts, then 132 people need x quarts. Now we simply cross-multiply to solve for x.

$$4x = 132 \cdot 3$$
$$4x = 396$$
$$x = 99$$

We need 99 quarts of broth to serve 132 people this particular chicken soup. The fact of the matter is that plain old proportions just aren't that challenging, so you won't see many problems as simple as the first example. Instead, the given values will be fractions or decimals, which will involve a little tricky math.

EXAMPLE 2: LEVEL 3

It takes $\frac{1}{3}$ of a yard of velvet to make 2 pairs of gloves for the school play. How many yards of velvet will it take to make 47 pairs of gloves for the cast?

This problem is more challenging than the first example simply because the first measurement is in fractional form. However, I'd still like you to set up 2 equivalent fractions and work from there, just to make sure you keep everything organized.

$$\frac{\frac{1}{3} \text{ yard}}{2 \text{ pairs}} = \frac{x \text{ yards}}{47 \text{ pairs}}$$

$$\frac{1}{3} \cdot 47 = 2x$$

$$\frac{47}{3} = 2x$$

$$\frac{\frac{47}{3}}{2} = x$$

Remember here that dividing with fractions is like multiplying by the reciprocal. We just flip that 2 around and write:

$$\frac{47}{3} \cdot \frac{1}{2} = x$$

$$\frac{47}{6} = x$$

Also remember that on the SAT, particularly in the grid-ins, you'll want to leave your fraction in fully reduced, yet improper, form. Therefore, we'd say that it will take $\frac{47}{6}$ yards of fabric to make gloves for the whole cast.

Ratio Problems

Ratio problems usually focus on the individual components of the relationship and then require you to gather and apply information about the whole to solve the problem.

EXAMPLE 1: LEVEL 3
The ratio 1.4 to 1 is equivalent to what fraction?

The ratio we've been given (if this were legal in math land) is $\frac{1.4}{1}$. The first thing I'd want to do is get rid of that decimal. Multiplying the numerator and denominator by 10 will give us $\frac{1.4}{1} \times \frac{10}{10} = \frac{14}{10}$, just like that. However, we can't enter $\frac{14}{10}$ in our grid because it's not reduced (I know, I'm saying the same thing over and over). If we reduce down to $\frac{7}{5}$, though, we're good. It's just that simple.

EXAMPLE 2: LEVEL 3
In a certain flower arrangement, the ratio of yellow roses to red roses is 5 to 3. Which of the following could not be the number of roses in the arrangement?

(A) 24
(B) 32
(C) 35
(D) 40
(E) 56

Again, the key to ratio problems is in the sum of the components. In this case, we can't have part of a rose—either a flower is a rose or it's not. So if the ratio of yellow to red is 5 to 3, then these roses are arranged in groups of 8. Therefore, the total number of roses must be a multiple of 8. Of our answer choices, only C, 35, is not a multiple of 8.

EXAMPLE 3: LEVEL 4
Big buttons and small buttons are sold to factories by the pound in a ratio of 7 to 2. How many pounds of small buttons would be in a 5-pound box?

This question is a bit more challenging only because it feels weird—it's meant to freak you out. If we add together 7 pounds and 2 pounds, we get a 9-pound total mixture. But this problem wants to know how many pounds of small buttons would be in a 5-pound box! No big deal. Although we usually think of proportions increasing a value, in this problem we will simply reduce a value.

$$\frac{2 \text{ small buttons}}{9 \text{ pound mix}} = \frac{x \text{ buttons}}{5 \text{ pound mix}}$$

Again, just cross-multiply and solve for x.

Please be very careful to review the language of SAT questions. Often questions use words like *except*, *least*, and *greatest* to guide you to the correct answer choice. If you overlook words like these your answer choice may be a possible value of a variable but *not* what they're looking for. Circle these words when you see them.

$$2 \cdot 5 = 9x$$
$$10 = 9x$$
$$\frac{10}{9} = x$$

So in a 5-pound mixture of buttons, we'd have $\frac{10}{9}$ pounds of small buttons. Again, you'll actually grid-in $\frac{10}{9}$. If the question were multiple choice it would likely be converted to a proper fraction: $1\frac{1}{9}$ pounds.

EXAMPLE 4: LEVEL 4
Miniature golf businesses often order different-colored golf balls in gross cases (144 balls). These cases come such that the ratio of red balls to green balls to yellow balls is 2:3:4. How many more yellow balls than red balls are in a case?

OK, there are a few things going on here. For starters, the sum of the total mixture has been given: 144 balls. The ratio has been given too, but there are more than 2 components here—they are divided into a relationship of 2 to 3 to 4. Using that info, we need to figure out how many yellow balls and red balls we have; then we need to find the difference between those 2 values (which is really just another tedious step to increase the "difficulty" of the problem).

As these balls come in a ratio of 2:3:4, we add the 2, 3, and 4 together to start understanding what's happening: 2 + 3 + 4 = 9. That tells us that the balls are split up into 9 groups and each of those includes: 2 groups of red, 3 groups of green, and 4 groups of yellow. To find out how many balls are in each group, we divide the number of balls we actually have into 9 groups there are: 144 ÷ 9 = 16. In each of our 9 groups are 16 balls. This means that we have 32 red balls (16 × 2 groups), 48 green balls (16 × 3 groups), and 64 yellow balls (16 × 4 groups). The difference between the number of yellow balls and the number of red balls in a case is 64 − 32, which equals 32 .

When you work on a problem like this, keep in mind that it's not more difficult because it involves more *complex* work, but only because it involves *more* work. If you can budget the time to solve the problem, you definitely should.

Percents and Percent Increase

WHAT YOU NEED TO KNOW

Percents

Arguably, the most popular proportion on the SAT is a percentage, because a percentage is a standardized proportion. For example, 24% really means: "if you had 100 of those [points, cookies, cars, shirts, rabbits], 24 of them would be [correct, burned, hatchbacks, collared, brown]." In other words, whatever part you're measuring is going to be expressed as though it were related to 100, or a fraction out of 100.

In terms of solving for a percentage (or a part), I know some of you have learned the phrase "is over of" that I keep hearing about, but I've never had a student be able to effectively explain it in every percent context, so I'm going to ignore it and give you 1 rule by which you can solve every percent problem:

$$\frac{PART}{WHOLE} = \frac{\%}{100}$$

Quick trick: If you're calculating a percent-off sale, rather than calculating how much you're taking off the original price, calculate how much you're keeping. If something is on sale for 25% off, rather than finding 25% and then subtracting that amount from the original, find 75% of the original price. It saves you the subtraction and time.

You can place your variable and given info into the 3 slots (the 100 always stays the same because percentages are always in relation to 100) and solve. This technique is safe and prevents you from rethinking your tactic every time you're approached with a percent. Just plug in the info you have for the part, whole, or percent and solve.

Not all questions that include percents are straightforward "find the part" or "find the whole" problems. Instead, the question may include a percentage that you'll need to incorporate into an algebra equation. This can be really challenging if you don't know how to handle it. It sometimes surprises people to learn that percents are among the biggest stumpers on the SAT, but this is what you need to know: Whenever an equation calls for a percentage, *do not use a decimal*. Use a fraction and stay off your calculator. This means that if your question says that something is 35% of something, use $\frac{35}{100}$ in the equation. If the question calls for "*p* percent" of something, use $\frac{p}{100}$.

Percent Increase

Say you and I decide to pool our resources and invest $100 in the stock market. Turns out things are going well, and we end up with $150. This means that we earned 50% on our original investment: a cool $50. We call this $50 difference the *percent increase*, and it has a special definition. To find the percent increase on the SAT, always use this formula:

$$\frac{CHANGE}{ORIGINAL} = \frac{\%}{100}$$

HOW THEY ASK THE QUESTIONS

Percent Questions That Use % in the Answer

The mere presence of a % sign in an answer choice should direct your thinking.

EXAMPLE 1: LEVEL 4

There are 45 more yellow ears of corn than white ears of corn in a bucket. If there are *w* white ears of corn in the bucket, what percent of the corn are yellow ears?

First, we need to come up with a fraction that uses *w* to represent $\frac{part}{whole}$ for yellow ears of corn. We're looking for $\frac{yellow\ ears}{total\ ears}$. According to the problem, there are *w* white ears of corn and 45 more yellow ears than white; we can use $(w + 45)$ to represent the yellow corn. I still need to find the total number of ears, yellow plus white: $w + w + 45$, which we can simplify to $2w + 45$.

Using my new terms, I can safely say that the proportion of $\frac{yellow\ ears}{total\ ears}$ is $\frac{w + 45}{2w + 45}$. We're nearly done, but most students would stop here. That's what makes this a level 4 problem. However, this is a case for which you should use the $\frac{\text{part}}{\text{whole}} = \frac{\%}{100}$ rule. In this situation we've set our equation equal to $\frac{\%}{100}$, so we need to multiply by 100 to find the actual percentage (which is what the problem asks for).

$$\frac{w+45}{2w+45} \quad \leftarrow \text{multiply this by } 100: \quad \frac{100(w+45)}{2w+45} \%$$

Think of it this way: any fraction is just a numerator divided by a denominator. If we had left our original $\frac{\text{part}}{\text{whole}}$ alone, that $\frac{w+45}{2w+45}$ piece would equal a decimal (just like $\frac{1}{4}$ is equal to 0.25). The question specifically asks for the percent, though, which means that decimal needs to be multiplied by 100 to turn the decimal into a whole number (like how 0.25 is actually 25%—we need to move that decimal point over 2 places by multiplying it by 100).

The lesson here is that whenever a question asks for the percentage and you see "%" in the answer choices, you must always multiply your fraction answer by 100.

Using Percents in Equations

These problems go beyond the proportion and incorporate a percent expression into an algebra equation.

EXAMPLE 1: LEVEL 2
If 40% of n is 60, what is 20% of n?

There are 2 methods here, the long way and the short way. The long way involves using math (which I always support). First, write an equation that represents "40% of n is 60," like so:

$$\frac{40}{100} \cdot n = 60$$

You should ultimately write equations like this with everything in the numerator and denominator already combined and where it should be: $\frac{40n}{100} = 60$. I always think that writing everything like that makes isolating the variable so much more clear.

$$\frac{40n}{100} = 60$$

$$40n = 6000$$

$$n = 150$$

Now that we know the value of n, 150, we can find 20% of it:

$$\frac{x}{150} = \frac{20}{100}$$

$$3000 = 100x$$

$$30 = x$$

Now for the short way. If 40% of something is 60, then 20% of something should be half that: 30.

EXAMPLE 2: LEVEL 3

If 15% of 50% of a number is equal to 20% of m% of the same number, what is the value of m?

Warning: Don't start trying to do this problem in your head. It's really important that we write out an equation and go from there. Again, we're going to use fractions whenever we have to include percent expressions:

$$\frac{15}{100} \times \frac{50}{100} \times \frac{x}{1} = \frac{20}{100} \times \frac{m}{100} \times \frac{x}{1}$$

A couple of thoughts about what I've done there: for starters, as usual I made sure it was clear that my variable (which I called x, but you can call anything you like) is clearly up in the numerator. Also, see how the fraction rule for percents really paid off when I had to represent "m%"? I couldn't write $0.0m$ or something—this was my only option. If you didn't know how to do it, you'd be stuck.

So, moving along, we cancel:

$$\frac{15}{100} \times \frac{\overset{1}{\cancel{50}}}{\underset{2}{\cancel{100}}} \times \frac{\cancel{x}}{\cancel{1}} = \frac{\overset{1}{\cancel{20}}}{\underset{5}{\cancel{100}}} \times \frac{m}{100} \times \frac{\cancel{x}}{\cancel{1}}$$

$$\frac{15}{100} \times \frac{1}{2} = \frac{1}{5} \times \frac{m}{100}$$

$$\frac{15}{200} = \frac{m}{500}$$

$$7500 = 200m$$

$$\frac{75}{2} = m$$

Very often you'll find that you need to write out what may feel like an ever-lasting gob-stopping problem, but if you write it out carefully you'll discover that it was designed to cancel quickly and easily. Put in that little bit of effort at the outset, and it will likely pay off.

EXAMPLE 3: LEVEL 4

If $2a + 2b$ is equal to 140% of $4b$, what is the value of $\frac{b}{a}$?

A few things right off the bat here: this is "harder" because the percent we're asked about is greater than 1 (meaning it's not 20% or 70%—it's 140%). Also, when a question asks for an answer like the value of $\frac{b}{a}$, you can view it as a set of instructions that says "take what we've given you and reorganize it so you've got $\frac{b}{a}$ on its own side of an equation; then give us the info on the other side." So that's what we'll do.

Again, sticking with the fraction to represent the percentage:

$$2a + 2b = \frac{140}{100} \cdot \frac{4b}{1}$$

$$2a + 2b = \frac{7}{5} \cdot \frac{4b}{1}$$

$$2a + 2b = \frac{28b}{5}$$

$$5(2a + 2b) = 28b$$

$$10a + 10b = 28b \searrow \text{ combine terms.}$$

$$10a = 18b \searrow \text{ divide by } a.$$

$$10 = \frac{18b}{a} \searrow \text{ divide by 18.}$$

$$\frac{10}{18} = \frac{b}{a} \searrow \text{ reduce}$$

$$\boxed{\frac{5}{9}} = \frac{b}{a}$$

EXAMPLE 4: LEVEL 3

A pool store's monthly income consists of $2,200 in service contracts plus 30% of the dollar amount of its in-store product sales. In July the pool store's total monthly income was $6,700. What was the total dollar amount of in-store product sales in July?

We're going to do the same thing we always do: write an equation to represent what's in the problem, using a fraction for the percent, and then solve.

$$2200 + \left(\frac{30}{100} \cdot s\right) = 6700$$

$$2200 + \frac{30s}{100} = 6700$$

$$2200 + \frac{3s}{10} = 6700$$

$$\frac{3s}{10} = 4500$$

$$3s = 45000$$

$$\boxed{s = 15000}$$

So in-store sales were $15,000.

EXAMPLE 5: LEVEL 5

An electronics store sells SuperLite handheld devices for $360, which is 20% above the store's cost on SuperLites. During a Black Friday sale, the store sells SuperLites at 15% below their cost. What is the price of a SuperLite on Black Friday?

This isn't hard; it's just tricky! Do not add together the 20% and the 15% and find 35% off of $360. Percents all need to be handled individually—you'll find at the mall that a 30% off and then an additional 20% off is not the same sale as 50% off. That's what we need to be really careful of in this problem.

Additionally, this $360 we've been given is actually more than 100% of the cost; because it's 20% *above* cost, we have to say that $360 is 120% of the cost (which we'll call c to keep things easy). So let's find the store's cost for a SuperLite:

$$\frac{360}{c} = \frac{120}{100}$$

This proportion says that 360 is related to the store's cost and 120 is related to 100. So we know our c value will be less than 360. Solve for c:

$$\frac{360}{c} = \frac{120}{100}$$

$$36000 = 120c$$

$$300 = c$$

We've just established that the store's cost is $300. Now, on Black Friday the store takes 15% off of their cost, presumably to get shoppers into the store. So now we need to take 15% off of $300. I still want you to use the percent proportion, but I'd like to show you how to skip a step here. Normally you'd find out what 15% of $300 is and then subtract that amount from $300. However, a 15% off sale could really be called a "pay only 85% sale." To save yourself some time, find 85% of $300 and you've found yourself the price of the phone on Black Friday.

$$\frac{p}{300} = \frac{85}{100}$$

$$100p = 25500$$

$$\boxed{p = 255}$$

And the sale price is $\boxed{\$255}$.

EXAMPLE 6: LEVEL 4

The price of a desk was first increased by 20% and then decreased by 30%. The final price was what percent of the original price?

This is just like the previous example except we're not given any prices to work with; we're only given percent changes. Here's what you do this in situation: always, always, always choose $100 as your original price. It doesn't matter if you're pricing cars, teddy bears, or oranges, if you're got a percent change problem, you always want to start at 100. Why? Because you can do all this work to the 100 (that is, take it up a percent, take it down a percent, and so on) and then you can simply compare what you end up with to the 100 you started out with.

For example, our desk here is $100. If we increase the price by 20%, we know that the new price will be $120. Easy. You should be able to do that in your head. Now we need to find 30% off of $120. Because I keep harping on this, I'm going to stick with the idea that a 30% off sale is really a "pay only 70%" sale and solve for 70% of $120:

$$\frac{p}{120} = \frac{70}{100}$$

$$100p = 8400$$

$$p = 84$$

Now we've found that $84 is our final price as compared to the $100 original price. So the final price is $\boxed{84\%}$ of the original price.

Calculating the Original Amount

Percent increase questions specifically home in on whether or not you know that the increase is always calculated in relation to the original amount, like we discussed earlier.

EXAMPLE 1: LEVEL 3
Karl finds a young owl that is 12 inches tall living in his barn. In three weeks he returns to the barn to find that the owl is now 16 inches tall. The owl's new height is what percent greater than its height when Karl originally found it?

We're going to use the $\frac{\text{part}}{\text{original}} = \frac{\%}{100}$ method here. You need to focus on how much this owl grew—that's the "part" we're looking for. If the owl was originally 12 inches tall and then grew to 16, his total growth was 4 inches.

$$\frac{4}{12} = \frac{x}{100}$$

$$400 = 12x$$

$$\frac{400}{12} = x$$

We reduce that fraction to $\frac{100}{3}$, which equals .33 or $\boxed{33\%}$.

EXAMPLE 2: LEVEL 4

A grandmother knits 18 socks in a week. The following week she increases her productivity by 50%. How many socks does she knit in the second week?

This problem is just the reverse of example 1; instead of finding the percent increase, we find the new amount produced. Set up your proportion to quickly find 150% of the original.

$$\frac{n}{18} = \frac{150}{100}$$

$$100n = 2700$$

$$n = 27$$

She makes $\boxed{27 \text{ socks}}$ the second week.

Exponents

Exponent Basics

Using an exponent is a way of denoting that a number is being multiplied by itself rather than by any other number.

The exponent is just a small set of directions: multiply whatever that exponent is attached to (the base) by itself however many times the exponent tells you to do so.

$$3^3 = 3 \cdot 3 \cdot 3$$

$$a^3 = a \cdot a \cdot a$$

Basic Exponent Rules You Need to Know

$$x^y \cdot x^z = x^{y+z} \qquad \left(x^y\right)^z = x^{yz} \qquad \frac{x^y}{x^z} = x^{y-z}$$

You can't do anything with exponents that are being added or subtracted, like $3^x + 3^x + 3^x$, even if they have like bases! $3^x + 3^x + 3^x \neq 3^{3x}$ But what you can do is turn that into a multiplication problem and work with it from there. $3^x + 3^x + 3^x$ is the same as $3(3^x)$. If that's hard to see, you could consider that I "factored out" 3^x from $3^x + 3^x + 3^x$, like this: $3^x(3^1)$. Now you can treat it like the multiplication that it is: $3^x \times 3^1 = 3^{x+1}$.

You'll also want to know some quick exponent exchanges off the top of your head.

really important exponent exchanges

$2^1 = 2$ $\qquad$ $3^1 = 3$

$2^2 = 4$ $\qquad$ $3^2 = 9$

$2^3 = 8$ $\qquad$ $3^3 = 27$

$2^4 = 16$

Memorize these.

More often than not, if you're given an equation that involves exponents and different bases you'll be able to sub in those equivalents and solve.

Moving on. It would seem that as the exponent gets larger, the larger the whole expression would be larger, too. This is always true for positive whole numbers—which is why the SAT never asks about them. Instead, it addresses the exceptions.

Now let's compare x^2 and x when $0 < x < 1$. Normally, we square x and it gets bigger. However, when we multiply fractions that are between 0 and 1, just the opposite happens.

$0 < x < 1$ $\leftarrow$ read this as

"x is between zero and 1."

It tells us that x is a

fraction, like $\frac{1}{2}$ or $\frac{3}{4}$.

For example, let's say that $x = \frac{1}{2}$. If we square that, we'd write $x^2 = \frac{1}{2} \times \frac{1}{2}$. Remember, we always multiply straight across when we work with fractions: $\frac{1}{2} \times \frac{1}{2} = \frac{1}{4}$. When we square fractions between 0 and 1, they get smaller: x^2 is less than x itself. If we look for x^3, we find that it's even less than x^2.

Now let's compare x^2 and x when $x < 0$. We'll start with $x = -2$. Square it and we get $x^2 = -2 \times -2 = 4$. So in this case x^2 is, in fact, greater than x. However, solve for x^3: $-2 \times -2 \times -2$ and we get -8. For values less than 0, the even exponents will yield positive numbers, but the odd exponents yield negative numbers. Beware! The signs constantly switch!

Raising a number to a negative power also has an unexpected result. Negative exponents indicate that you need the reciprocal of the exponential expression. That's really fancy math speak for "just put whatever you've got under a 1."

$$x^{-3} = \frac{1}{x^3}$$

Everything stays exactly the same except it's under a 1 and that negative sign goes away.

Square Roots and Other Radicals

Fractional exponents are their own ball of wax. Rather than doing something to the base (multiplying it by itself some number of times), you're undoing something that was done to the base. This is where square roots and the radical sign come into play.

$$x^{\frac{1}{2}} = \sqrt{x} \qquad and \qquad x^{\frac{1}{3}} = \sqrt[3]{x}$$

First, $x^{\frac{1}{2}}$ is exactly the same as $\sqrt{x}$. So $16^{\frac{1}{2}}$ is equivalent to $\sqrt{16}$. The square root of 16 is 4, because $4^2 = 16$. It's important to know that x raised to the $\frac{1}{2}$ is completely interchangeable with the square root of x.

Second, $x^{\frac{1}{3}}$ is the same as $\sqrt[3]{x}$. That little "3" hanging out there in front of the root sign tells you "cube root." This means that $125^{\frac{1}{3}}$ refers to the cube root of 125, which is 5, because $5^3 = 125$.

Simplifying a Radical

While we're at it, let's talk about how to simplify radicals (a *radical* is just the sign that means *root*). Just as every fraction must be reduced to its lowest possible denominator to be correct, so also radicals must have the smallest number possible underneath the root sign. We call this *simplifying the radical*.

Let's look at $\sqrt{18}$. The best way to accomplish simplifying a radical is to look for factors of the number under the root sign that are perfect squares, most likely 4, 9, 16, and 25.

For example, $\sqrt{18}$ is equal to $\sqrt{9} \times \sqrt{2}$. Well, $\sqrt{9} = 3$, so we can reduce $\sqrt{18}$ to $3\sqrt{2}$.

To reduce a bigger radical, we just repeat that process. Let's work on simplifying $\sqrt{2268}$. Because we can use divisibility rules to check for squares, I like to start there. It turns out that, because $2 + 2 + 6 + 8 = 18$, 2268 is divisible by 9. So, $\sqrt{2268} = \sqrt{9} \times \sqrt{252}$ or $3\sqrt{252}$. We're not done there, though: 252 is divisible by 9 as well. $3\sqrt{252} = 3 \times \sqrt{9} \times \sqrt{28}$ or $3 \times 3 \times \sqrt{28}$ or $9\sqrt{28}$.

We're down to $9\sqrt{28}$, but we can still do more. There's a 4 hiding in that 28: $9\sqrt{28} = 9 \times \sqrt{4} \times \sqrt{7}$ or $9 \times 2 \times \sqrt{7}$, which equals $18\sqrt{7}$.

There. $\sqrt{2268}$ fully reduces to $18\sqrt{7}$.

There's a big difference between $\sqrt[3]{18}$ and $3\sqrt{18}$. The first is the cube root of 18 and the second is "3 times the square root of 18."

HOW THEY ASK THE QUESTIONS

Understanding Fraction Behavior

These problems look specifically at the squaring and cubing of fractions or negative numbers. The problems rarely involve more steps or details than the specific skill they test; they are designed only to see if you understand fraction and exponent behavior.

EXAMPLE 1: LEVEL 3

If $0 < x < 1$, which of the following cannot be true?

(A) $\frac{x}{2} > x$

(B) $x > x^3$

(C) $x^2 > x^3$

(D) $x^2 > 0$

(E) $x = \frac{7}{8}$

So your best bet here is to start with the option that's definitive: is it possible that $x = \frac{7}{8}$? Absolutely: x can be anything in between 0 and 1. Because this is a *cannot* be true problem, we can eliminate answer E and move on. That being said, let's choose an easier fraction to plug into the rest of the answer choices. I always like to go with $\frac{1}{2}$ for this type of problem.

Let's look at the options:

A)
$$\frac{\frac{1}{2}}{\frac{1}{2}} > \frac{1}{2} ?$$

$$\frac{1}{2} \cdot \frac{1}{2} > \frac{1}{2} ?$$

$$\frac{1}{4} > \frac{1}{2} ? \quad no. \quad \frac{1}{4} \not> \frac{1}{2}$$

Now, if you were taking the test and you found answer A was the correct choice, in that it *cannot* be true, I'd recommend that you move on and come back and confirm your answer after doing all the rest of the questions that you could in the section.

EXAMPLE 2: LEVEL 3

If $a = -1$ and $b > 0$, which of the following has the greatest value?

(A) $3ab$
(B) $5a^2b$
(C) $7a^3b$
(D) $9a^4b$
(E) $11a^5b$

The reason that $b > 0$ matters is so that you know that the only negative value we've got in any of these expressions is a. That's also why all the answer choices use exponents with the a and not the b. So what you really need to do here is consider the impact the exponents are having on the problem. If you're not paying attention, it might seem like an obvious answer to say, "Well, 11 times anything has to be the biggest." However, that a is being raised to an odd exponent—raising a negative number to an odd exponent will result in a negative final answer. The largest exponent that makes a positive is actually 4, so D has the greatest value of these answer options.

Remember that when x is between 0 and 1:

$x^3 < x^2 < x < \sqrt{x}.$

The hardest version of this problem usually includes $\sqrt{x}$, which actually increases the value of x when it's between 0 and 1: it's easiest to see on a calculator. Plug in 0.5 (or $\frac{1}{2}$ is fine if you're on a graphic calculator) and press the $\sqrt{}$ button. You'll get 0.7071. You don't need to remember these values; just know that rooting these fractions makes them bigger.

Interchangeability

These problems involve using the $2^1, 2^2, 2^3, 2^4 = 2, 4, 8, 16$, and $3^1, 3^2, 3^3 = 3, 9, 27$ rules.

EXAMPLE 1: LEVEL 2
If $3^{3x} = 27$ then $x = ?$

A pretty typical trick in a problem that uses the interchangeability rules is using 16 in the problem—16 is equal to both 2^4 and 4^2. Although it will be obvious when you're looking for everything to be in base 2, in other problems you may reflexively use 4^2 for 16. Be careful that they have not defined in the problem that the exponent is larger than the base; that would mean you would have to use 2^4.

The first thing you always do on problems like this—even the easiest problem—is change the bases so that they match. We're going to turn that 27 into 3^3:

$$3^{3x} = 3^3$$

Now that the bases are the same, we can ignore them and compare the exponents:

$$3x = 3 \quad so \quad \boxed{x = 1}$$

EXAMPLE 2: LEVEL 3
If $2^{3x} = 8^{4-x}$, then $x = ?$

This problem is just like the earlier version except we need to track more details and exponent rules to make sure we get it right. First thing, as always, is to make the problem have like bases:

$$2^{3x} = \left(2^3\right)^{4-x}$$

Because when we raise an exponent to another (like we're doing on the right side of the equation) we multiply, let's multiply $3(4 - x)$ to find the new exponent. Our problem will look like this: $2^{3x} = 2^{12-3x}$. Notice that I went ahead and distributed the 3. Now that the bases are the same, we can drop them and focus on the exponents and solve for x.

$$2^{3x} = 2^{12-3x}$$
$$3x = 12 - 3x$$
$$6x = 12$$
$$x = 2$$

By the way, if you're wondering why we can suddenly drop those bases, it's because a problem that says $2^{3x} = 2^{12-3x}$ means "raising 2 to the $3x$ is exactly the same as raising 2 to the $12 - 3x$," so we know that $3x$ and $12 - 3x$ must be equal.

Solving for Values or Manipulating for Expressions

Simple exponent comprehension problems are made more difficult by including 2 variables in the expressions and then asking for "x in terms of y," "a in terms of b," or "xy." As usual, for "in terms of" questions, you won't be solving for a particular numerical answer. Instead, you'll be solving and rearranging the problem to solve for 1 variable and using the other side of the equation as your answer.

EXAMPLE 1: LEVEL 3
If $a^p \times a^6 = a^{36}$ and $(a^q)^4 = a^{24}$, then what is the value of pq?

Naturally, we need to find values for p and q before we multiply them together.

$$a^p + a^6 = a^{36} \qquad \left(a^8\right)^4 = a^{24}$$
$$p + 6 = 36 \qquad\qquad 4q = 24$$
$$p = 30 \qquad\qquad\quad q = 6$$

Now we multiply those values to find pq:

$$30 \times 6 = \boxed{180}$$

EXAMPLE 2: LEVEL 3
If $r^4 = s^8$, then what is r in terms of s?

Whenever we're looking for a single variable in terms of something else, we need to solve for that variable—in this case, r. Our main objective here is to get rid of the 4 exponent above the r, which means we have to more or less undo that 4. The way we're going to do that is by taking the 4th root of both sides. Hang on, stay with me . . . we're not going to write $\sqrt[4]{r^4} = \sqrt[4]{s^8}$, because the 4th root of 8 probably doesn't mean anything to us. Instead, we're going to do the same thing as "taking the 4th root," but we're going to use exponents to do it; we're going to "raise both sides to the $\frac{1}{4}$," like this:

$$\left(r^4\right)^{\frac{1}{4}} = \left(s^8\right)^{\frac{1}{4}}$$

This way we can just multiply those exponents. The exponential stuff on the left side cancels, and we're left with something pretty recognizable on the right: $r = s^{\frac{8}{4}}$ or just plain $r = s^2$. To answer the question, r in terms of s is s^2.

EXAMPLE 3: LEVEL 4
If a and b are positive integers and $100a^3b^{-1} = 10a^2$, what is a^{-1} in terms of b?

You may want to start here by doing a little quick canceling.

$100a^3b^{-1} = 10a^2$ ← cancel zeros

$10a^3b^{-1} = a^2$ ← cancel a's exponents

$10ab^{-1} = 1$ ← rewrite

$\dfrac{10a}{b} = 1$

note: this canceling
is like division
(and legal because
of division rules)

Starting to look easier? Before we go further, let's make sure we're clear on what we're going for. We're looking for a^{-1} in terms of b, which means we're going to manipulate what we have to get $\frac{1}{a}$ (which is a^{-1}, remember?) on its own side of the equation and b-stuff on the other. I'm going start by just trying to get the a by itself.

$$\frac{10a}{b} = 1$$

$$10a = b$$

$$a = \frac{b}{10}$$

Now, in order to find $\frac{1}{a}$, we're just going to put both sides under 1 (because you can't do anything to 1 side without doing it to the other), like this:

$$\frac{1}{a} = \frac{1}{\frac{b}{10}} \quad \text{...multiply by the reciprocal} \quad \frac{1}{a} = \frac{10}{b}$$
$$\text{on the right side} \longrightarrow$$

So a^{-1} in terms of b is $\boxed{\frac{10}{b}}$.

EXAMPLE 4: LEVEL 5

If a, b, c, and d are all positive integers and $a^{-\frac{2}{3}} = c^{-4}$ and $b^{\frac{2}{3}} = d^4$, what is $(ab)^{-\frac{2}{3}}$ in terms of c and d?

I know: whoa! Everyone hates this type of problem; it's designed to make you balk and make mistakes. However, if you can work up to a pace at which you're completing a math section, you need to know how to capably and quickly do a problem like this. Here's the short summation of what's going on here: we're just solving for 1 thing in terms of the other, just like we've been doing. However, this problem doesn't stop there. Instead of defining 1 term, we define 2 terms and then do something else to those definitions.

Bear with me and read this. Don't check out. You'll get it.

Let's start simply. At the very end of the problem we see the magic words "in terms of c and d." We can use that as a starting place: we've got to solve for the a and b to find them in terms of c and d. So let's start with a. We need that a exponent to equal positive 1, so we're going to raise both sides to an exponent that will multiply with $-\frac{2}{3}$ to do so, like this:

$$\left(a^{-\frac{2}{3}}\right)^{-\frac{3}{2}} = \left(c^{-4}\right)^{-\frac{3}{2}}$$

Multiply the exponents, and we get this:

$$a^{\frac{6}{6}} = c^{\frac{12}{2}}$$

$$a = c^6$$

You'll find that if you know how to attack a problem on this test, it will usually work out to be pretty neat and clean. So let's solve for b using the same process:

$$b^{\frac{2}{3}} = d^4$$

$$\left(b^{\frac{2}{3}}\right)^{\frac{3}{2}} = \left(d^4\right)^{\frac{3}{2}}$$

This time we're using positive $\frac{3}{2}$ to manipulate b's exponent to be equal to 1. It works out nicely, too.

$$b^{\frac{6}{6}} = d^{\frac{12}{2}}$$

$$b = d^6$$

The last part uses what we just did: to find $(ab)^{-\frac{2}{3}}$ in terms of c and d, we just pop in those new values and do the same multiplication.

$$\left(c^6 d^6\right)^{-\frac{2}{3}}$$

$$c^{-\frac{12}{3}} d^{-\frac{12}{3}}$$

$$c^{-4} d^{-4}$$

Let's not leave those exponents in negative form; your answer choice will more likely look like this: $\boxed{\frac{1}{c^4 d^4}}$.

EXAMPLE 5: LEVEL 5

If $\left(x^{\frac{1}{4}} y^{\frac{1}{4}} z^{\frac{1}{6}}\right)^{12} = 54000$ for positive values x, y, and z, what is the value of $x + y + z$?

Before we go any further, let's multiply those fractional exponents by 12 to clean this problem up a bit.

$$x^3 y^3 z^2 = 54000$$

That's so much simpler. Now the question is, how on earth are we supposed to know what x, y, and z are just from that? Let's think creatively. We know that $x^3 y^3 z^2$ is a math shorthand version of $x \times x \times x \times y \times y \times y \times z \times z$. There's a circumstance in which we see a long list of numbers multiplied together that we've already talked about in the book: factors. Whenever we put together a factor tree, we get these long lists of the factors that multiply together to create a number. This time we're going to create a factor tree for 54,000 and use what we find to get us to the answer. Fortunately for us, 54,000 is just 9×6 with a bunch of zeros tacked on the end.

$$54000$$
$$\wedge$$
$$90 \quad \times \quad 600$$
$$\wedge \qquad \wedge$$
$$9 \times 10 \quad \times \quad 60 \times 10$$
$$3 \times 3 \times 2 \times 5 \times 6 \times 10 \times 2 \times 5$$
$$3 \times 3 \times 2 \times 5 \times 2 \times 3 \times 2 \times 5 \times 2 \times 5$$

Now I'm going to reorganize those numbers so we can see how many of each we have:

$$3 \times 3 \times 3 \times 5 \times 5 \times 5 \times 2 \times 2 \times 2 \times 2$$

OK, I've got three 3s, three 5s, and four 2s. I'm looking for 3 x's, 3 y's, and 2 z's. I'm going to go ahead and assign x to those 3's and y to those 5's. However, I need 2 z's, but I've got four 2's. This is another manipulation moment—just multiply them back together, so that instead of four 2's, we'll have two 4's. I've got my 2 z's!

Now that we've decided that $x = 3$, $y = 5$, and $z = 4$, we just do what the problem asked and add them together: $3 + 5 + 4 = \boxed{12}$.

The most important aspect of this problem is that you can always use math facts and rules to make things into what you need them to be. That's the main way this test is different from a test you have in school—on the SAT you just use what you know to get you where you need to go.

Squares: Recognizing and Using Them

EXAMPLE 1: LEVEL 1

Which of the following cannot be the last digit of a square number?

(A) 0
(B) 4
(C) 5
(D) 8
(E) 9

This is just a "know your squares" question. Now, there are a few other options for a correct answer: 2, 3, and 7 could have been on the list. However, even numbers seem like they're more likely to be squares, so the trick here is that despite that instinct, the correct answer is 8. Jot down your rationale for eliminating all the other answers; I certainly would if I were taking the test. Avoiding working in your head makes you much less likely to make a mistake or be confused.

Let's quickly double-check this by finding an example of a square for each of the others on the fly:

$2 \times 2 = 4$

$3 \times 3 = 9$

$5 \times 5 = 25$

$6 \times 6 = 36$

$10 \times 10 = 100$

EXAMPLE 2: LEVEL 3

How many nonsquare integers are there between 1 and 200, inclusive?

Any time you are faced with a list problem in which you need to count up what could be a very large number of items or numbers, always check to see if it would be more efficient to count what's *not* on the list rather than what is. That certainly holds true in this case.

Let's throw together a list of square numbers: 1, 4, 9, 16, 25, 36, 49, 64, 81, 100, 121, 144, 169, and 196. I did the vast majority of that off the top of my head; you should know your squares up to 13. I admit that I did check 196, which is 14 × 14, on the calculator. Otherwise, it was fast and simple—I just wrote them down as I worked up the list.

To answer the problem, I know that I have 200 numbers on the list of 1 to 200. I have just written down 14 square numbers. (Notice how that's the 14 that created the highest number on my list of squares?) so $200 - 14 = \boxed{186}$. That's it. Rather than counting them all up, I just took out what wouldn't make the list. There are 186 nonsquare integers from 1 to 200, inclusive.

Square Roots: Manipulating Them

These problems will simply take what you know about square roots and ask you something you never would have seen in algebra class. For these problems it is always in your best interest to not use your calculator but instead use what you know.

EXAMPLE 1: LEVEL 3

Provided that x is positive, what value of x makes $\sqrt{\frac{9x}{2}}$ an integer?

You'll need to work backward to finish this problem quickly: if the square root of a number is going to be an integer—a whole number—we know that no matter how complex the fraction under the radical may look now, it's going to have to reduce to a whole, square number.

Now, the fact of the matter is, I made this problem really easy. We can just pop in a 2 for x, the 2's cancel, and we're left with $\sqrt{\frac{9 \times 2}{2}} = \sqrt{9} = 3$. On the real SAT this type of problem can be a bit more challenging, but the premise is still the same: use values that make your fraction reduce to a square.

The trick with a problem like this, just like in those integer division problems we talked about early on, is knowing that the correct answer isn't the whole number you end up with (in this case 3), but rather the x value, 2, that

It is important that you pay attention to this word *inclusive*, which means that you *do* include 200 in your count; it's not *up to* 200, it *includes* 200. Pretty tricky, no? This doesn't matter much here, as 200 is not a square, but if the problem went up to 100, it certainly would matter.

you use to get it. The College Board uses the same tricks in all sorts of ways to try to trip you up.

EXAMPLE 2: LEVEL 4

If $27\sqrt{27} = a\sqrt{b}$ and $a > b$, what is the value of $a - b$?

For starters, the way you want to read this phrase is "27 root 27 has the same value as a root b." If you immediately jump to the conclusion that they're equal, you may start thinking that both a and b are equal to 27. But we're told that $a > b$, so you need to understand that you can manipulate that $\sqrt{27}$ into something else by simplifying it.

So we look for squares underneath the root sign:

$$27\sqrt{27} = 27 \times \sqrt{9} \times \sqrt{3}$$
$$27 \times 3 \times \sqrt{3} = 81\sqrt{3}$$

This works perfectly for our $a > b$ rule:

$$a = 81 \quad \text{and} \quad b = 3$$

It's that simple: $a - b = 81 - 3$ so $a - b = \boxed{78}$.

As you've probably noticed, success on Numbers and Operations problems is largely dependent on keeping track of the details. Silly mistakes are usually the roadblocks on these problems—they can seem so familiar and straightforward that students tend to take them for granted and let their guards down. Remember to take problems that are conceptually simple just as seriously as those requiring the most complex mathematical analysis.

algebra and functions

I often ask students, "Which is worse: algebra or geometry?" It turns out that opinion is sharply divided because students often grasp one branch of math far better than the other. To that end, both the Algebra and Geometry chapters begin with the absolute fundamentals—the skills you would learn in the first week of these classes—and proceed from there, as though you'd never taken either class. In the Algebra chapter we'll explore variables in expressions and equations, factoring polynomials, and inequalities. You'll also learn everything you need to know about function problems on the SAT as well as the particular ways all of these topics are tackled. Let's get started.

Solving a Basic Equation

Algebra equations were designed to use letters in place of numbers to find the numerical value of those equations. More simply, finding the value of the letter (the variable) in the equation is the whole point of algebra. All of the algebra you'll do on the SAT is based on being able to solve for the value of these variables—sometimes you're looking for an actual number (like $n = 6$), sometimes you want a range of values (like $3 < x < 5$), and sometimes your answer will use variables instead of numbers. Whatever the case, strong algebra skills are a must.

Solving for a variable in algebra is like undoing what someone else has already done to a variable. For example, in English, $3x = 12$ means: "I had some number x, I multiplied it by 3, and now I have 12." Now, if I asked you to tell me what x is, you'd say "Oh, well, I need to divide it back out: 12 divided by 3 is 4. You must have started with 4 . . . $x = 4$." Bingo. That's algebra.

Now, the formal "math" way of approaching $3x = 12$ is to divide both sides of the equation by 3. It makes sense: x times 3 divided by 3 is just x; 12 divided by 3 is 4; we end up with an x on its own side of the equals sign and a 4 on the other. So $x = 4$.

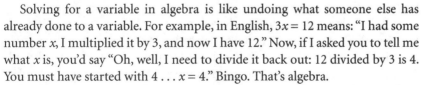

$$3x = 12$$
$$\frac{3x}{3} = \frac{12}{3}$$
$$x = 4$$

A somewhat more complicated equation would read something like $3x - 6 = 12$. In English, that says something like this: "I had some number x and I multiplied it by 3. I took that number and subtracted 6 from it and I ended up with 12." If we were going to think about how to get back to x, we would have to undo what's been done to it. That means the first thing we need to do is put back the 6 that we took away from the answer; because we subtracted it, we'll add it back to the 12. That gives us 18. Fine. Now, whatever number we had in the first place was something that when multiplied by 3 gave us 18. To undo that multiplication, we'll divide 18 by 3 and get 6, so $x = 6$.

This is where I say: Don't Do Algebra in Your Head. It's a train wreck waiting to happen. Let's look at the formal way to solve $3x - 6 = 12$.

$$3x - 6 = 12$$
$$ + 6 + 6$$
$$3x = 18$$
$$\frac{3x}{3} = \frac{18}{3}$$
$$x = 6$$

The basic gist is this: find the value of any variable by "walking backward" to the original equation.

Distributing to a Parenthetic Expression

Algebra equations that are a bit more complex will include numbers and terms in parentheses, like $(2x + 3)$. We might throw something like that into an equation, like $2(2x + 3) = 24$. In English, we read that as "2 times the quantity $2x + 3$ equals 24" ("the quantity" is math-speak that tells you $2x + 3$ are a single unit, so they must be considered a single expression). In other words, 2 multiplies $2x + 3$ in its entirety. In fact, if you needed to, you could treat that $2x + 3$ as a single variable while you're solving, until you can manage to get rid of the parentheses around it.

For a refresher on the order of operations, check out the PEMDAS explanation on page 109.

To solve this equation and find the value of x, we have to "undo" this equation just like the problems we looked at earlier. There are a couple possible directions we can go with this. We can divide both sides by 2 (acting like it reads $2x = 24$) or we can *distribute* the 2 by multiplying each term in the parentheses by 2. Either way we arrive at the same answer. That may sound confusing, so let's look at the math. The equation $2(2x + 3) = 24$ can be worked out like this:

$$2(2x + 3) = 24$$
$$\frac{2(2x + 3)}{2} = \frac{24}{2}$$
$$2x + 3 = 12$$
$$ - 3 - 3$$
$$2x = 9$$
$$x = \boxed{\frac{9}{2} \text{ or } 4.5}$$

... or like this ...

$$2(2x + 3) = 24$$
$$4x + 6 = 24$$
$$4x = 18$$
$$x = \frac{18}{4}$$
$$x = \boxed{\frac{9}{2} \text{ or } 4.5}$$

No matter which way you slice it, you'll get $x = \frac{9}{2}$ or 4.5.

If that equation read $-2(2x + 3) = 24$, it would be hugely important to recognize the negative 2; you would either divide both sides by -2 or distribute -2 to each of the terms inside the parentheses.

HOW THEY ASK THE QUESTIONS

Basic Algebra Examples

These questions give you an opportunity to score points just for knowing some basic algebra.

EXAMPLE 1: LEVEL 2
If $4(x + 2) = 24$, what is the value of $\frac{x-2}{x+2}$?

Here we're going to solve for x and then pop our value of x into that fraction.

$$\frac{\cancel{4}(x+2)}{\cancel{4}} = \frac{24}{4}$$
$$x + 2 = 6$$
$$x = 4 \leftarrow \text{plug in}$$

$$\frac{x-2}{x+2} \rightarrow \frac{4-2}{4+2} = \frac{2}{6} = \boxed{\frac{1}{3}}$$

EXAMPLE 3: LEVEL 1
If $2727 = 27(n + 1)$, what is the value of n?

Don't distribute! The problem is made to look tricky and play with your expectations—they expect you'll try to predict the answer. Don't. Just solve the equation.

$$\frac{2727}{27} = \frac{\cancel{27}(n+1)}{\cancel{27}}$$
$$101 = n + 1$$
$$\boxed{100 = n}$$

In algebra, every term—number or variable—takes its sign with it. They're not independent of each other.

Subbing-In Given Values for Variables

Algebra problems that appear to be more difficult will include a bunch of variables but then give you values for all but 1 and ask you to solve. It's simple algebra in disguise.

Did you notice that I

indicated multiplication

with • instead of × ?

That helps avoid confusion

when a problem has an

x variable.

EXAMPLE 1: LEVEL 2
If $xy + y = x + 3z$, what is the value of z when $x = 3$ and $y = 4$?

I'd quickly plug in and make sure everything remains organized here.

$$xy + y = x + 3z$$
$$3 \cdot 4 + 4 = 3 + 3z$$
$$12 + 4 = 3 + 3z$$
$$16 = 3 + 3z$$
$$13 = 3z$$
$$\boxed{\frac{13}{3} = z}$$

EXAMPLE 2: LEVEL 2
If $3(a + b)(a - b) = 30$ and $a + b = 5$, what is the value of $a - b$?

Before this gets sticky, notice that you've been given the value of $a + b$, so just plug it in!

$$3(a+b)(a-b) = 30$$
$$3(5)(a-b) = 30$$
$$15(a-b) = 30$$
$$\frac{15(a-b)}{15} = \frac{30}{15}$$
$$(a-b) = 2$$

It's important that you notice that we never had to figure out the exact values of a and b; we just needed to pop in a value for a little expression that was already in the equation.

Manipulating Algebra

These questions aren't about finding a value for a variable. Instead, they ask you to find variables in terms of other variables or to use algebra rules to change a given expression and comment on it.

EXAMPLE 1: LEVEL 2
If $4b + c = b + 7$, what is b in terms of c?

This is simply a reorganization problem—because you have only 1 equation, but 2 variables, you could never find a value for either variable. However, you can solve for either variable in terms of the other; in this case we solve for b, and our answer is everything on the other side of the equation.

$$4b + c = b + 7$$
$$-b -b$$
$$3b + c = 7$$
$$-c -c$$
$$3b = 7 - c \quad \leftarrow \text{divide by } 3$$
$$\boxed{b = \frac{7-c}{3}}$$

EXAMPLE 2: LEVEL 3

If $b + 3(c + 2) = f$, then what is $c + 2$ in terms of b and f?

Rather than solving for a single variable, we're going to solve for an expression. Fortunately for us, the expression we're looking for is already in the equation, so we do *not* want to distribute. Instead, we're going to treat $c + 2$ as though it were a single variable and isolate it on its own side of the equation.

$$b + 3(c + 2) = f$$
$$3(c + 2) = f - b \quad \leftarrow \text{divide by } 3$$
$$c + 2 = \boxed{\frac{f-b}{3}}$$

Factoring from a Binomial

WHAT YOU NEED TO KNOW

A binomial is a 2-term addition or subtraction expression, like $2x + 3$ or $n + m$ or $k - 3$. Anything with 2 terms that can't be simplified is a binomial. For example, $2n + 3n$ is not a binomial: it simplifies to $5n$ because 2 n's plus 3 n's equals 5 n's.

Nevertheless, although binomials can't be simplified, some binomials can be factored. Factoring a binomial basically undoes distribution. For example, let's distribute something. For $3(2x + 5)$, if we distribute the 3 (multiply each term by 3) we end up with $6x + 15$.

However, if we had been given $6x + 15$ in the first place, we could undo the distribution—by seeing that all the terms are multiples of 3—and factor the binomial back to its original form. That's the goal here.

The basic idea of factoring a binomial is to find the greatest common factor (GCF) of all the terms of the binomial—that means not only finding the GCF of all the coefficients (the numbers in front of the variables), if there is a GCF, but also pulling out all the variables that the terms have in common.

For a refresher on GCF, see page 120).

Let's look back to our example ($6x + 15$). First, we look at the coefficients 6 and 15. The greatest common factor of 6 and 15 is 3, so we put the 3 out in front of the parentheses.

Technically what we're doing is dividing each term in the binomial by 3, putting 3 out in front of the parentheses, and leaving the dividends inside the parentheses.

factoring $6x + 15$

$$\underset{\text{GCF}}{\nearrow} 3 \underset{\underset{6x \div 3}{\uparrow}}{(2x} + \underset{\underset{15 \div 3}{\uparrow}}{5)}$$

Let's look at something more challenging about factoring. At this point we've factored out a variable but we haven't factored out a binomial itself, which is totally legal! Let's look at $ab - b$. You should see that you can factor b out of this: $b(a - 1)$. However, what if I showed you $a(a + b) - (a + b)$? You need to recognize that $(a + b)$ can be factored out of $a(a + b) - (a + b)$ leaving you with $(a + b)(a - 1)$, just like b can be factored out of $ab - b$. If you see that, you're golden.

Leaving a Placeholder

Now, sometimes the coefficients won't have a GCF, but some of the variables will, and sometimes both the coefficients and the variables will be factorable.

Here's a simpler but slightly trickier example: $6x + 6$. Notice that the GCF here, 6, happens to be identical to a term in the equation. That's fine! However, when you factor out the entire term, meaning, when you pull the whole term out of the parentheses, it doesn't just disappear—we have to hold its place.

$$6x + 6 \;\rightarrow\; 6(x + 1)$$

We place the 1 inside the parentheses to hold the place of the 6 we factored out. If we were going to distribute that 6 back out to the terms, we would do $6 \times x$ and 6×1. If that 1 weren't there, there wouldn't be anything holding the place of the term.

To factor $(4xy + 2x)$ we bring out the GCF of the coefficients, 2, but we also have the common factor x, so we pull it out, as well. Factoring this expression will give us $2x(2y + 1)$.

Factoring Binomials in Fractions

Factoring binomials is especially important when a fraction contains binomials in the numerator or denominator and you want to reduce the fraction. Individual terms of a binomial—things that are being added or subtracted—*cannot* cancel with the denominator! Don't be tempted!

We $\underline{\text{cannot}}$ cancel $\dfrac{8x + 5}{4}$ like this: $\dfrac{\cancel{8}x + 5}{\cancel{4}} \rightarrow \dfrac{2(x + 5)}{1}$

Canceling is legal only when *all* the terms in the numerator and denominator are being multiplied together. Fortunately, when we're only adding binomials, factoring allows us to create multiplication and often, especially on the SAT, an opportunity to cancel.

Again, no canceling individual terms with addition and subtraction in fractions—only cancel terms involved in multiplication.

HOW THEY ASK THE QUESTIONS

Basic Binomial Problems

Basic binomial problems generally require factoring to solve them as quickly as possible, from the easiest to the most challenging.

EXAMPLE 1: LEVEL 1
If $3x + 6 = 12$, then $x + 2 = ?$

Quickly factor that $3x + 6 = 12$, since they've made it clear that what they gave you, $3x + 6 = 12$, and $x + 2 =$ are related.

You always want to factor to try to find something you've already been given. Don't take a blind stab at it; try to create a relationship. If we factor 3 out of $3x + 6 = 12$, we find $3(x + 2) = 12$. Next, we divide both sides by 3, and end up with $x + 2 = \boxed{4}$. That's our answer.

EXAMPLE 2: LEVEL 5
If $a + b = 8$ and $ab = 5$, then $a^2b + ab^2 = ?$

This is hard because the only integers that multiply to equal 5 are 1 and 5, but those aren't possible values for a and b because they don't add up to 8, our second parameter. So what do we do? We have to use the binomial and factor it, trying to create something that looks more like what they gave us in the first place (that is, ab or $a + b$). We'll factor $a + b$ and ab out (because we can) and see what happens: we get $a^2b + ab^2 = ab(a + b)$. Go figure.

We can just pop the values we were given into $ab(a + b)$ and be done: $5 \times 8 = \boxed{40}$.

FOILing and Factoring

FOILing

Multiplying 2 binomials sounds fancy, but there's only 1 way to do it, and it's pretty straightforward. It's a 5-step process in which the first 4 steps create the acronym FOIL. Let's look at this example: $(x + 4)(x - 2)$

First: Multiply the first terms of each binomial together: x times x.

$$x^2$$

Outer: Multiply the outer terms together: x times -2.

$$x^2 - 2x$$

Inner: Multiply the inner terms together: 4 times x.

$$x^2 - 2x + 4x$$

Last: Multiply the last terms together: 4 times -2.

$$x^2 - 2x + 4x - 8$$

Then we combine like terms—in this case, $-2x$ and $4x$—and get, finally,

$$x^2 + 2x - 8$$

Which, by the way, is a trinomial.

Factoring Trinomials

So the basic idea is that we can go back and forth from 2 binomials to 1 trinomial and back to the 2 binomials. They're entirely interchangeable in meaning and value.

Let's say we had started with $x^2 + 2x - 8$ and hadn't seen the binomials it's made from. Factoring a trinomial is basically a way of finding the 2 binomials from which the trinomial came.

Again, we'll be undoing what has been done to the x, this time undoing the FOIL process. We'll start by putting down our parentheses and 4 placeholders, then we'll just fill them in: (_ _) (_ _).

First, because our trinomial starts with x^2, we know the first terms multiplied together must have been x and x, so we pop those into our parentheses: $(x \_)\, (x\_)$.

This is the tricky part: we now need to come up with 2 numbers that add to +2 (because it's the middle term of the trinomial that we know resulted from the Outer and Inner steps). Our 2 numbers must also multiply to –8 (the last term of the trinomial that we get from the last step). I'm going to go out on a limb and say that if you need a huge explanation of this, you should check in with your math teacher because it's probably not so efficient for us to get into it all here. The basic idea is this: find all the pairs of factors of 8 (that is, 1 and 8, 2 and 4), and, assigning negatives and positives to them as needed, choose the pair that add to 2 and multiply to –8.

We'll choose –2 and +4 and pop them into the slots. In this case, because the parentheses are otherwise identical, we can put –2 and +4 into either slot: $(x-2)(x+4)$ will produce the same trinomial as $(x+4)(x-2)$.

Voilà. We have factored the trinomial.

Factoring Trinomials to Solve for Variables

You may be wondering why we would want to factor a trinomial. Well, sometimes trinomials aren't free-floating expressions; often they're part of an equation. When those trinomials are in equations that equal 0, we can solve for the value of the variable in them. For example, what if the example we just worked through had been set like so: $x^2 + 2x - 8 = 0$? We still want to factor it into 2 binomials, just as we did before, but we're going to leave it equal to 0: $(x-2)(x+4) = 0$. Because we've created a multiplication problem—$x-2$ times $x+4$ equals 0—we know from number behavior that 1 of those binomials must be equal to 0 in order for the whole thing to be true. Either $x-2=0$ or $x+4=0$. We can solve these little equations and find the 2 possible values of x that make the equation true:

$$x - 2 = 0 \quad \text{or} \quad x + 4 = 0$$
$$\boxed{x = 2} \qquad\qquad \boxed{x = -4}$$

Difference of Squares

There is only 1 type of binomial that factors out into 2 binomials multiplied together: the difference of squares (that is, a perfect square minus another perfect square). Put simply,

$$a^2 - b^2 = (a+b)(a-b)$$

This makes sense because when we FOIL $(a + b)(a - b)$, the 2 middle terms, $-ab$ and $+ab$, cancel each other out when we simplify.

Beyond just memorizing this, every time you see $a^2 - b^2$ I want you to immediately expect $(a + b)(a - b)$ to come up, and vice versa.

The trap: $(x + 1)^2$

The expression $(x + 1)^2$ is *not* the same thing as the difference of squares. Don't overlook it; because we're squaring what's in parentheses, it actually means $(x + 1)(x + 1)$, which FOILs out to $x^2 + 2x + 1$.

HOW THEY ASK THE QUESTIONS

Distribution Using Binomials

EXAMPLE 1: LEVEL 2

If $a(n + p) = 75$ and $an = 25$, what is the value of ap?

Again, just as before we were factoring to create relevance between given elements of a problem, here we're going to distribute to see if we can create the variable combination an.

$$a(n + p) = 75 \rightarrow an + ap = 75$$

Because we were given that $an = 25$, we can just pop that 25 into our distributed equation: $25 + ap = 75$. Then we isolate the variable combination ap.

$$25 + ap = 75$$
$$ap = 50$$

Notice that we were never required to find the exact values of a, n, or p. Don't try to.

EXAMPLE 2: LEVEL 4

If $4a^2 + b^2 = 60$ and $ab = 40$, what is the value of $(2a + b)^2$?

You could spend all afternoon trying to come up with suitable numbers that fit the given parameters (that is, to find what integer combo multiplies to 40 and so on). *Or* you can distribute that squared binomial, $(2a + b)^2$, and compare with the given info. (Hint: Distribute the binomial. Always.)

$$\left(2a + b\right)^2 =$$
$$\left(2a + b\right)\left(2a + b\right)$$
$$4a^2 + 2ab + 2ab + b^2$$
$$4a^2 + 4ab + b^2$$

Let's look at what we ended up with—definitely elements of what we've been given. For starters, we can pull that $4a^2$ and b^2 out, since they fit the bill for $4a^2 + b^2 = 60$. That leaves us with $4ab$ to deal with. Now, if we were given that $ab = 40$, then $4ab$ must equal 4(40), or 160.

Put all that information together and you've got your answer:

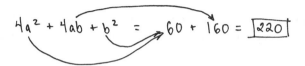

$$4a^2 + 4ab + b^2 = 60 + 160 = \boxed{220}$$

When Trinomials Are Set Equal to Zero

These problems don't require you to factor the trinomial; you just need to be able to find solutions for the variables within the problems.

EXAMPLE 1: LEVEL 3

If $(4x - 2)(x + 3) = 0$, what are all the possible values of x?

We know that when the product of a multiplication problem is 0, something within the problem must be equal to 0. Therefore, we know that either $4x - 2 = 0$ or $x + 3 = 0$, so we solve them to find out what values of x make those little equations true.

$$\left(4x - 2\right)\left(x + 3\right) = 0 \quad \text{so...}$$
$$4x - 2 = 0 \quad \text{or} \quad x + 3 = 0$$
$$4x = 2 \qquad \qquad \boxed{x = -3}$$
$$\boxed{x = \frac{1}{2}}$$

EXAMPLE 2: LEVEL 3

If $p(x - 2)(x - 4) = 0$ and $x > 4$, what is the value of p?

Again, this is the same issue—if everything is multiplying together to equal 0, either p, $x - 2$, or $x - 4$ must equal 0. However, because $x > 4$, there's no way that either $x - 2$ or $x - 4$ can be equal to 0. So we know that p must be the culprit. Therefore, $p = 0$.

Miscellaneous Trinomial/FOILing Problems

These problems follow less of a formulaic pattern than some of the other FOIL problems we've looked at, but you can take the keys to unlocking these problems with you and apply them to other problems of this genre.

EXAMPLE 1: LEVEL 3

Provided n is greater than 5, which of the following is equal to
$n - 5 = \sqrt{n + 4}$?

(A) $n^2 - 20 = 0$
(B) $n^2 - 20n = 0$
(C) $n^2 - 11n - 29 = 0$
(D) $n^2 - 11n = 0$
(E) $n^2 - 11n - 21 = 0$

Generally the first thing I point out on a problem like this is that there is no $\sqrt{}$ sign in our answer choices, so we should probably square both sides to get rid of it. That's usually the best bet. The rest of this should be a piece of cake.

$$n - 5 = \sqrt{n+4}$$
$$(n-5)^2 = \left(\sqrt{n+4}\right)^2$$
$$(n-5)(n-5) = n+4$$

I also like to write out squared binomials as I just did, actually writing out the $n - 5$ twice so I can be sure I won't forget what I'm doing. Because each of my answer choices includes n^2, I should go ahead and FOIL.

$$n^2 - 10n + 25 = n + 4$$

Getting warmer. All of my answer choices also equal 0, so I'm going to do some rearranging to see what I come up with.

$$n^2 - 10n - 21 = n$$
$$n^2 - 11n - 21 = 0$$

I've found the answer: E.

EXAMPLE 2: LEVEL 4

If n and p are constants and $x^2 + nx + 5$ is of the same value as $(x + p)(x + 1)$, what is the value of n?

Let's look at those 2 expressions right next to each other.

$$x^2 + nx + 5 = (x + p)(x + 1)$$

What you want to home in on here is that p and 1 must multiply together to make that 5 in the other expression. There's only 1 option for p, then: p must equal 5. Let's pop that in: $(x + 5)(x + 1)$. Suddenly we have something familiar and FOILable:

$$(x + 5)(x + 1) = x^2 + 5x + x + 5 = x^2 + \underline{6x} + 5$$

Because n is the coefficient of the middle term in $x^2 + nx + 5$, then n must equal 6.

Using the Difference of Perfect Squares

Recognizing the difference of perfect squares is pretty important to the College Board, so it's key for you to recognize this situation, too.

EXAMPLE 1: LEVEL 2
If $a^2 - b^2 = 20$ and $a + b = 10$, what is the value of $a - b$?

Remember, if you see $a^2 - b^2$, you factor:

$$(a + b)(a - b) = 20$$

. . . and then sub in what you've been given:

$$10(a - b) = 20 \quad \leftarrow \text{then divide by 10}$$
$$\boxed{a - b = 2}$$

EXAMPLE 2: LEVEL 5
$(a^2 + 2ab + b^2)^2 = \left(\dfrac{25}{(a - b)^2} \right)^2$ is equal to which of the following?

(A) $a - b = 0$
(B) $a^2 + b^2 = 25$
(C) $a^2 + b^2 = 5$
(D) $a^2 - b^2 = 5$
(E) $a + b = 0$

First of all, this is totally overblown (as most "hard" problems are), with both sides being squared, so let's just cancel that to begin with (technically, we're taking the square root of each side of the equation):

$$a^2 + 2ab + b^2 = \frac{25}{(a-b)^2}$$

Because, at this point, $a^2 + 2ab + b^2$ should be familiar, we should factor it to see if it's at all related to that $a - b$ buried in there:

$$(a+b)(a+b) = \frac{25}{(a-b)^2} \quad \text{OR} \quad (a+b)^2 = \frac{25}{(a-b)^2}$$

Now, none of those cancels, but we do seem to be on to something: we've got an $a + b$ and an $a - b$ in there. That should catch our attention and signal that we're probably moving toward an answer that will include a^2-b^2.

However, at this point everything in that problem is squared, so let's fix that:

$$\sqrt{(a+b)^2} = \sqrt{\frac{25}{(a-b)^2}} \quad \longrightarrow \quad (a+b) = \frac{5}{(a-b)}$$

Now things are starting to simplify. Since I have no fractions in my answer choices, I'm going to move that $a - b$ over to the numerator on the other side (by multiplying both sides by $a - b$):

$$(a+b)(a-b) = 5 \quad \rightarrow \quad a^2\text{-}b^2 = 5$$

We've found choice D.

Inequalities

WHAT YOU NEED TO KNOW

Inequalities operate very much like any other equation—in fact, they're almost exactly like equations, save for a few major details.

So the basic idea here is that, rather than both sides being equal to each other, which requires an equals sign, inequalities are not equal (go figure), meaning they use greater-than or less-than signs: $<$, $>$, $\leq$, and $\geq$. Nevertheless, we solve inequalities with almost the exact same "undoing what was done to the variable" method that we'd use with a regular algebraic equation.

The only difference appears when we multiply or divide each side of the inequality by a negative number: multiplying or dividing an inequality by a negative number requires reversing the direction of the sign in the same step.

For example, to solve $-3x > 6$, we divide both sides by -3 and flip the sign:

$$-3x > 6$$
$$\frac{-3x}{-3} < \frac{6}{-3}$$
$$x < -2$$

HOW THEY ASK THE QUESTIONS

EXAMPLE 1: LEVEL 2
If $4x + 3 > 8$, which of the following cannot be x?

(A) 1
(B) 2
(C) 3
(D) 4
(E) 5

First, you won't see many problems like this because it's difficult to come up with a selection of answer choices that isn't automatically the least or the greatest number available. A problem like this is an easy guess, which makes it unpopular with the test maker. However, I wanted to make sure we were all clear on how to do the math, so I've included it. Let's start solving.

$$4x + 3 > 8$$
$$4x > 5 \quad \leftarrow \text{divide by } 4$$
$$\boxed{x > \frac{5}{4}}$$

Because we get that $x > \frac{5}{4}$ (or $1\frac{1}{4}$), answer A, $x = 1$, is impossible.

Absolute Value

WHAT YOU NEED TO KNOW

Absolute value always measures a distance from a central point—usually 0—and uses tall vertical bars, that look like this, $|x|$, to enclose numbers or variables or expressions in much the same way that brackets or parentheses would. These bars aren't part of the PEMDAS order of operations, though; instead, they give directions about what do with whatever is between the absolute value bars.

If you're familiar with absolute value, it's likely you understand that the bars direct us to find the positive value of whatever is between them, whether an expression is between the bars or the bars are included in an equation or inequality. However, that's not the full story on absolute value. Absolute value was not invented by some mathematician sitting in an office somewhere who needed a way to "find the positive" of something. Absolute value goes a bit further. We agree that the absolute value of 3 is 3, right? It's is already positive, so we just drop the bars and use the 3. The absolute value of –3 is 3 as well; we just lose the negative sign. However, the reason the absolute values of –3 and 3 are both 3 is because they are each 3 away from 0.

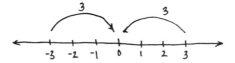

the absolute values of 3 and –3
are each 3 because they are 3 away
from 0.

Absolute Value Facts You Need to Know

When you see an absolute value sign buried in an expression:

> Use arithmetic (and PEMDAS) to find the value of whatever is between the absolute value bars. Once you've found that, make the value positive, lose the bars, and continue simplifying as usual.

When you see an absolute value sign buried in an equation:

> Do the same thing, as if the bars were in an expression: solve for what's inside, make it positive, and drop the bars. Solve.

When you see an absolute value sign encasing an entire expression that's equal to a single, positive value:

> Set up 2 equations. For starters, drop the bars and set the entire expression equal to the given positive value. Then, set the entire expression equal to the opposite of the given value.

When you see an absolute value signencasing an entire expression that is either < or > a given value:

> Set up 2 inequalities. First, drop the bars and simply rewrite the inequality. In the second equation, drop the bars, reverse the < or > sign, *and* make the given value negative. Your answer is true in the first case or the second case.

HOW THEY ASK THE QUESTIONS

Showing an Understanding of Basic Absolute Value Expressions

EXAMPLE 1: LEVEL 2

If $|3 - b| > 5$, which of the following could be the value of b?

- (A) –6
- (B) –2
- (C) 2
- (D) 4
- (E) 6

Rather than trying out answer choices, it's always in your best interest to quickly jot down the 2 forms of the inequality and work from there: $|3 - b| > 5$ becomes $3 - b < -5$ and $3 - b > 5$.

Solve each equation for b:

$$3 - b < -5 \qquad 3 - b > 5$$
$$-b < -8 \qquad\quad -b > 2$$
$$b > 8 \qquad\qquad b < -2$$

reminder –
we flipped signs here because we divided by a negative

The only option we have that satisfies those requirements (that b is either greater than 8 or less than –2) is answer A.

EXAMPLE 2: LEVEL 3

If $|12 - a| = 9$ and $|a - 4| = 17$, what value of a solves both equations?

This is solved the same way—no thinking. Just set up your 2 equations and solve:

$$12 - a = 9 \quad \text{or} \quad 12 - a = -9 \qquad \text{AND} \qquad a - 4 = 17 \quad \text{or} \quad a - 4 = -17$$

$$-a = -3 \qquad \qquad -a = -21 \qquad \qquad \boxed{a = 21} \quad \cdot \, a = -13$$

$$a = 3 \qquad \qquad \boxed{a = 21}$$

Obviously, the common answer is 21.

Combining Number Lines with Absolute Value Expressions

EXAMPLE 1: LEVEL 3

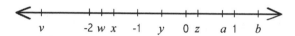

In this number line, which is closest to the value of $|xy|$?

- (A) a
- (B) b
- (C) x
- (D) y
- (E) z

> Every absolute value problem can be made more challenging by incorporating lots of changing signs in the original problem, particularly by using subtraction and negative numbers. Because these problems are fundamentally simple, be very careful about sign changes.

You'll always want to use fractions to represent your variables to keep things as simple as possible and to make sure you're not using your calculator when it's unnecessary. Naturally, these number lines must be to scale (or else how could you estimate a value?). That being the case, let's pick some values for x and y. Be very careful—don't drop negative signs, and remember that negative numbers get "bigger" as you move left.

I'm going to say that $x = -1\frac{1}{2}$ and $y = -\frac{1}{2}$. Because I'm multiplying those values, it makes sense to use $-\frac{3}{2}$ as the x value instead of the clunky mixed number.

Now I need to find $\left| -\frac{3}{2} \times -\frac{1}{2} \right|$, so I'll multiply and take the positive value of my answer:

$$\left| -\frac{3}{2} \cdot -\frac{1}{2} \right| = \left| \frac{3}{4} \right| = \frac{3}{4}$$

Referring back to my number line, it appears that the variable closest to $\frac{3}{4}$ is a.

When Your Absolute Is Not Zero

These problems are usually harder because they center absolute values around values other than zero.

EXAMPLE 1: LEVEL 5

At a certain greenhouse, pepper plants are only put up for sale when they are between 10 and 14 inches tall. Which of the following expressions represents those pepper plants that are put up for sale, where h is the height of a potentially salable pepper plant?

(A) $|h + 12| = 12$

(B) $|h - 12| = 0$

(C) $|h - 12| \leq 2$

(D) $|h - 12| < 2$

(E) $|h + 10| < 2$

What you need to understand here is that the ideal-sized pepper plant is 12 inches tall. The greenhouse will not sell peppers that are more than 2 inches smaller than the ideal (10 inches) or more than 2 inches larger than the ideal (14 inches). This absolute value problem is centered around 12 and the distance we're measuring is 2 inches away from that 12 on either side.

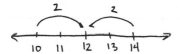

This tells us that we're going to have an equation that says that *the distance we're willing to travel from 12 is less than 2:* $| \underline{\quad} | < 2$.

Now we need to decide what belongs within those bars. Think of it this way: if we were centered around 0 (rather than 12), we'd be going −2 or +2 away from it. Instead, we're going −2 or +2 away from 12. That's the trick—our plant height distance needs to be less than 2 away from 12 in either direction, represented by $|h - 12| < 2$.

Graphing Inequalities

Representing an inequality on the number line is pretty simple. If your inequality uses a plain > or < sign that does not have a little line underneath it, use an open point, and shade in the number line accordingly. *Greater-than* or *less-than* signs are not "inclusive," a math term that means your answer does not include that exact number, but it does include everything just a smidge greater than (or less than) it is.

$-1 < x < 7$

If the inequality uses *greater than or equal* signs, like this, $\geq$, you use a closed dot on the number line and then shade. Coloring in the dot is the element of your graph that denotes that the answer includes the point.

$$-1 \leq x \leq 7$$

HOW THEY ASK THE QUESTIONS

Understanding How to Graph Inequalities

EXAMPLE 1: LEVEL 1

Which of the following graphs represents the solution set of $x + 3 < 4$?

Rather than give you answer choices, let's just draw our own graph first, by simply solving for the value of x.

$$x + 3 < 4$$
$$x < 1$$

Because this inequality uses a *less-than* sign, we use an open dot to graph the solution.

EXAMPLE 2: LEVEL 3

Which of the following graphs illustrates the solution set of the inequality $|x + 3| < 4$?

This time we'll use a single line graph, but we'll have 2 expressions of x because of the absolute value sign. First let's solve for the values of x:

$$x + 3 < 4 \qquad x + 3 > -4$$
$$x < 1 \qquad x > -7$$

The x values we solved for actually limit the graph: x has to be less than 1 to make this inequality true, but it also must be greater than –7. Because of this, our graph will stop at endpoints –7 and 1, it will include open points (because they're *less-than* and *greater-than* signs), and it will be shaded between those 2 values.

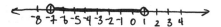

Distance, Rate, and Time: *d = rt*

Let's cut to the chase: Distance = Rate × Time. Distance is how far you go (obviously), rate is your speed, and time is how long it'll take you. I think it was my fourth grade teacher who helped me remember the formula using the mnemonic "dirt" (that is, $d = rt$). It works for me.

This is the key here: the distance in these problems is not always how far you drove to work or ran down the street. Sometimes the distance is something that's *accomplished*, like 1 room cleaned or 1 bathtub filled. The amount of time that it takes to accomplish 1 unit of *anything* can also be expressed with the $d = rt$ equation.

The other secret is that when 2 people are doing the same thing, you can *add their individual rates* to find a joint rate. That means that if Jack and Joe are both painters who paint 1 room at individual rates, you can add their rates per hour to find out how long it will take them to paint 1 room together. If Jack paints 2 rooms in an hour and Joe paints 3 rooms in an hour, their joint rate is 5 rooms per hour.

Calculating Distances or Rates
When All of the Information Is Given

EXAMPLE 1: LEVEL 2

If one flock of geese travels 40 miles in 2 hours and a second flock of geese travels 80 miles in half the time, at what rate is the second flock of geese traveling?

Let's see, half of 2 hours is 1 hour, so we'll use that time and solve for the second flock. We're going to simply write out $d = rt$ and solve:

$$d = rt$$
$$80 \text{ miles} = r \times 1 \text{ hour}$$
$$80 \frac{\text{miles}}{\text{hour}} = r$$

Finding Missing Values Needed
to Calculate Distance or Rates

EXAMPLE 1: LEVEL 5

Lee drove to work at a rate of 50 mph. She drove home at a rate of 45 mph. If her total travel time was 2 hours, how far did she drive to work?

Believe it or not, this is actually a midyear Algebra I problem; you may have worked on material like this as early as the seventh grade. That being the case, it can still seem terribly challenging, particularly because we've been given so little information. However, if you understand how the problem works, you can most likely complete it in about a minute.

What we're going to do is quickly set up a chart that represents Lee's trips to and from work:

$d \neq r$	r	t
d	50	t_1
d	45	t_2

Notice that we've got 2 variables here, d and t. Every time you're faced with a problem like this you'll have 2 variables—1 will stay the same and 1 will be changing. In this case, Lee drives the same distance to and from work, but the time in which she does it changes (obviously, if she's driving at different rates). Because of that, I've labeled the time variables t_1 and t_2. Now, if this were all the information we'd been given, we'd be pretty stuck; however, you will *always* receive additional information about the variable that changes. In this case, we're told that Lee's total trip took 2 hours: $t_1 + t_2 = 2$. What we're going to do is find the values of t_1 and t_2 in terms of d. We can use our chart to find the 2 little equations $d = 50t_1$ and $d = 45t_2$. To find just t_1 and t_2, we divide both sides by their rates: $\frac{d}{50} = t_1$ and $\frac{d}{45} = t_2$. Now we pop those values for t_1 and t_2 into the $t_1 + t_2 = 2$ hours equation and solve:

$$\frac{d}{45} + \frac{d}{50} = 2$$

Sometimes common denominators are easy to see; sometimes not so much. I'm just going to multiply 45 and 50 to find the denominator and then put *every* element of the equation over it:

$$\frac{50d}{2250} + \frac{45d}{2250} = \frac{4500}{2250}$$

Now that I've put everything over the common denominator, I can multiply both sides by its reciprocal so the denominators cancel, which lets me focus on the numerators:

$$50d + 45d = 4500$$
$$95d = 4500 \quad \leftarrow \text{divide by 95}$$
$$d = \frac{4500}{95} \quad \leftarrow \text{simplify}$$
$$\boxed{d = \frac{900}{19} \ \left(\text{or } 47.37\right) \text{ miles}}$$

Graphs: The Coordinate Plane and Ordered Pairs

The *coordinate plane* is the official name for a graph with 2 axes on which you can plot points. The 2 axes are called x and y; the x-axis is the horizontal axis (the flat axis), and the y-axis is vertical. Every point on your graph will be labeled in relation to these x- and y-axes.

Now, each point on the graph has 2 elements, an x- and a y-coordinate. The x-coordinate directs you to move left or right on the graph and the y-coordinate tells you to move up or down. Each little pair of instructions is called a "coordinate pair" and it will always be listed with the x-coordinate first and the y-coordinate second, like so: (x, y).

The most important coordinate pair you need to know is called the *origin*. The origin is the dead center of the graph, the point $(0, 0)$. Each of those 0's gives us a specific direction: the first 0 says "move 0 spaces along the x-axis" and the second 0 says "move 0 spaces along the y-axis." Whenever you come across the phrase "the origin" in a word problem, always write down $(0, 0)$ somewhere on your paper. It's going to come in handy.

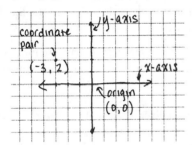

All other coordinate pairs work as sets of directions, too. While the origin point's 0's say "stay right here," every other coordinate pair says "move it." To plot any point, start at the origin and, depending on the sign of the x-coordinate, move along the x-axis just like you would on a number line. Then use the y-coordinate to direct you to move up or down. Count up or down that amount and you've found your point.

Midpoint

Finding the midpoint between 2 points on a graph is actually pretty easy and very logical, even though the formula looks a little weird. But knowing why the midpoint is what it is will help you find any midpoint quickly even without the formula.

The midpoint can also be understood as the halfway point when traveling from a given point to another—just stop exactly halfway between the points. If you're traveling from $(2, 3)$ over to $(6, 9)$, to find the midpoint we look at the x's and y's separately. Here's what you'd do to find this in your head: In the x direction, we're going from 2 to 6; halfway between 2 and 6 is 4, so we'd stop there. In the y direction, we're moving from 3 to 9; 6 is halfway between 3 and 9, so that's our y value. The midpoint is those 2 points combined: (4, 6).

It works just the same when the points are both negative numbers or even if they're mixed. The idea is to think like you're traveling on a number line from a given point to another—split that distance in half, and your stopping point is the midpoint. Doing this for both gives you the official midpoint.

The midpoint formula says just that:

The Midpoint Formula

$$\left(\frac{x_2 - x_1}{2} , \frac{y_2 - y_1}{2} \right)$$

The Distance Formula

The distance formula is a twisted version of the Pythagorean Theorem that calculates the distance—the length of a straight line—between 2 points. Here's what you need to know about it:

- *When not to use the distance formula:* when you're finding the distance between 2 points with an x- or y-coordinate in common, such as (3, 6) and (3, 11). You're only moving 5 spaces in the y direction, so the line is 5 units long. Spare yourself the trouble.

- *When to use the distance formula:* when the distance that you're measuring is not parallel to either axis (when you'd draw a diagonal line between them on the coordinate plane).

I personally never use the distance formula. Ever. Because I'm obsessed with knowing *why* everything works the way it does in math. And because the distance formula is unnecessarily complicated and is a breeding ground for mistakes, I have my own ad hoc method for calculating distance. Nevertheless, here's the distance formula, in case you want to use it: $d = \sqrt{(x_2 - x_1)^2 + (y_2 - y_1)^2}$, where the 2 points are labeled (x_1, y_1) and (x_2, y_2). The distance formula is not given to you at the beginning of the math section, so if you're planning to use it, make sure you have it totally, unmistakably memorized.

How I Find the Distance

Because the distance formula is so tricky, I've developed my own way of finding distances that I always use. It results from my belief that the *best way* we can find the length of a diagonal line—*any* diagonal line—on the SAT is by making it the hypotenuse of a triangle.

Step 1: Plot the 2 points and connect them. Let's use (–2, 6) and (6, –2) as an example.

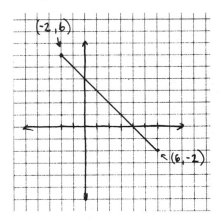

Step 2: Create a triangle on your graph, making a side parallel to the *x*-axis and a side parallel to the *y*-axis. This will give you a right triangle. Bingo, instant hypotenuse.

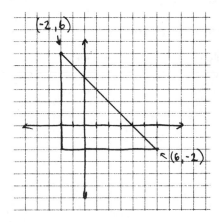

Step 3: Label each of those new sides with their lengths. You can find each length by calculating how far the point was shifted along each axis.

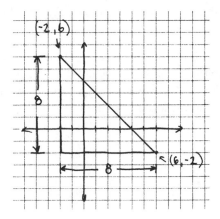

Step 4: Use the Pythagorean Theorem to find the length of the line (the hypotenuse of your new triangle), which also happens to be the distance between your original 2 points.

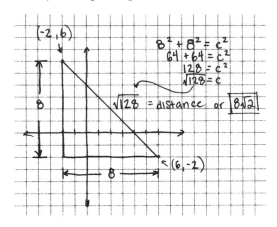

HOW THEY ASK THE QUESTIONS

Identifying and Using Coordinate Pairs

Because it's fairly simple to identify a coordinate pair, these questions use irritating distracters to increase difficulty.

EXAMPLE 1: LEVEL 3

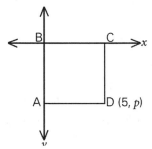

In the figure above, $\overline{BC} = \overline{CD}$. If the coordinate of point D is (5, p), what is the value of p?

You should probably be able to see this is a square (these are all right angles because we're on the coordinate plane). It's likely that you'll think, "Oh, all 4 sides must be length 5, so p's gotta be 5." However, this isn't a question about the length of the side; we're asked to find the location of the y point, which is down at (5, –5), so the answer is $\boxed{-5}$.

EXAMPLE 2: LEVEL 3

For which of the following coordinate pairs is it true that $|x| + |y| = 6$?

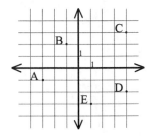

- (A) A
- (B) B
- (C) C
- (D) D
- (E) E

This is only as tricky as you allow it to be: ultimately, we're just looking for 2 numbers (ignoring their signs) that add to 6. You could have a combination of 1 and 5, 2 and 4, or 3 and 3. Of the given points, only 1 of the coordinate pairs is made up of a combination that equals 6, and that's D.

Understanding and Using Midpoint

EXAMPLE 1: LEVEL 1

In the figure below, if C is the midpoint of $\overline{AB}$, what is the value of p?

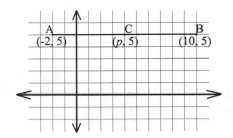

As you can see, the y values across this line are all 5. Because each of our points are the same distance from the y-axis, we can ignore the y value (which is why it's already labeled 5 in the figure) and simply calculate the midpoint between the 2 x values, –2 and 10. The distance between –2 and 10 is 12. Without turning this into a complex absolute value issue, think of the distance between those 2 points as a distance traveled on a map. For example, if I travel from –2 over to 10, I've traveled a distance of 12 units. If our total travel distance is 12, half of that travel distance is 6. So I add 6 to my starting point, –2, and I find that $p = \boxed{4}$.

EXAMPLE 2: LEVEL 3

What is the midpoint between (–4, –3) and (7, 3)?

You may want to jot a quick graph of these 2 points—I always do. It helps me keep track of those positive and negative values and visualize the distances between them.

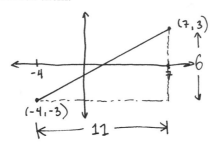

Be aware that calculating a midpoint cannot be made more difficult. Therefore, to complicate matters, the endpoints may be placed in visually intimidating situations, like at the top of a triangle or at the center of a circle. A problem may require you to find the endpoints by using geometric formulas. It's most important that you understand how moving up, down, left, and right on a graph affects a coordinate pair.

Let's focus on the x values first: if we're traveling from –4 over to 7, our total trip is 11 units, which we need to split in half: $\frac{11}{2}$. Add that to the starting place on our x trip, –4, and we have the x value of the midpoint:

$$-\frac{4}{1} + \frac{11}{2}$$

$$-\frac{8}{2} + \frac{11}{2} = \boxed{\frac{3}{2}}$$

So far so good. Now we need to calculate half of the y trip. Be careful here—traveling from –3 to 3 is not a trip of 0—it's a distance of 6. Splitting that total trip in half gives us 3, and then adding it to our y starting place, –3, gives us the y value of the midpoint: 0. The final midpoint is $\boxed{\left(\frac{3}{2}, 0\right)}$.

Calculating Distances between Points

The distance formula does not pop up on the SAT very often, and it's rarely asked about with a straightforward "find the distance between these 2 points." Remember—the distance is always a hypotenuse of a triangle. If you need more info on how to find the length of a triangle's hypotenuse, check out page 237.

EXAMPLE 1: LEVEL 1

Which of the following points is furthest from the origin?

(A) (0, 1)
(B) (1, 0)
(C) (–1, –1)
(D) $\left(\frac{1}{2}, -\frac{3}{2}\right)$
(E) $\left(\frac{1}{2}, 1\right)$

It's in your best interest to quickly graph these points so that you can see what they're doing:

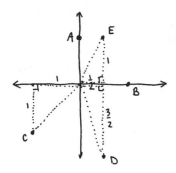

We're really dealing with line segments and right triangles here. Each triangle's hypotenuse measures the distance from the origin $(0, 0)$ out to the points. The negative signs are in there just to freak you out—because we're looking at the absolute value of the distances, it doesn't matter where the points are on the graph.

For those segments that lie on an axis, the lengths are easy to calculate. For those not on an axis, we use the Pythagorean Theorem.

A) length 1

B) length 1

C) $(-1)^2 + (-1)^2 = c^2$

$1 + 1 = c^2$

$\sqrt{2} = c$

D) $\left(\frac{1}{2}\right)^2 + \left(-\frac{3}{2}\right)^2 = c^2$

$\frac{1}{4} + \frac{9}{4} = c^2$

$\sqrt{\frac{10}{4}} = c^2$ $\left(\text{or } c = \sqrt{2.5}\right)$

E) length $\frac{3}{2}$

Compare—answer D is the longest length. Some students may be confused because choice C uses 1 and 1, and D uses $\frac{1}{2}$ and $-\frac{3}{2}$. It seems counterintuitive that, despite the absolute values of both coordinates adding up to 2 in both cases, choice D is actually longer. That's why it's so important not to skip steps and to carefully (but quickly) do the work.

EXAMPLE 2: LEVEL 3

The coordinates of points A, B, and C are (2, 3), (2, 6), and (6, 3) respectively. What is the perimeter of $\triangle ABC$?

Again, quickly and carefully plot it out. Because we're on the coordinate plane, we know that we can create a right triangle to find the distance between points.

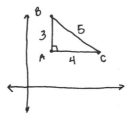

As you plot the points and calculate the lengths of the sides, you may see that this is a 3-4-5 triangle. It's a special triangle that we'll look at again in the Geometry section. For now, if you stop to use the Pythagorean Theorem for the lengths 3 and 4, fine, but it's a timesaver if you memorize the 3-4-5. Sometimes every second counts. To find the perimeter, add the lengths of the sides: $3 + 4 + 5 = \boxed{12}$.

EXAMPLE 3: LEVEL 5

In the xy-coordinate plane, the distance between points (–5, 6) and (10, p) is 17. What is one possible value of p?

Feel free to use the distance formula here. Personally, I like to plot these points by more or less eyeballing them. Estimation won't mess up the numerical calculations; it'll just help you keep track of things. Just plot (–5, 6) and then move over and put (10, p) higher or lower. I'm going with higher, for no particular reason.

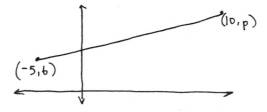

Now, because every distance is really the hypotenuse of a triangle, I'm going to connect those 2 points and label it length 17. Then, I'm going to draw in a triangle that maps out the change in x and change in y values, like so:

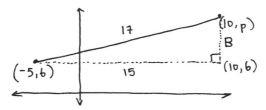

Because the coordinate plane is made up entirely of right angles, we've actually created a right triangle perfect for using the Pythagorean Theorem. We've been given both x values, so we can label a side of the triangle 15 (because we traveled from –5 to 10 on the x-axis). Now we can use $a^2 + b^2 = c^2$ to solve for the length of the other side of the triangle (the side for which we're missing some information).

$$15^2 + b^2 = 17^2$$
$$225 + b^2 = 289$$
$$b^2 = 64$$
$$b = \pm 8$$

Be really careful at this point—we haven't finished the problem! We just solved for b, *not* the value of p, the y-coordinate in the second coordinate pair. To find the possible value of p, we need to either add or subtract 8 from 6 (the height of the bottom triangle): p could equal either $\boxed{-2 \text{ or } 14}$.

EXAMPLE 4: LEVEL 5

In the figure below, how much shorter would a direct route between points A and D (not shown) be than the trip along the streets shown if each street runs directly north-south or east-west?

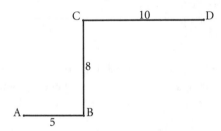

First, let's quickly add up the distance traveled if we follow the map given: $5 + 8 + 10 = 23$. Now, let's draw in the direct route as a straight line between points A and D. At this point, most students will start looking at that diagonal as 2 hypotenuses, 1 tiny triangle up top and 1 larger triangle below. Forget it! There's not enough information to solve that way. However, because this map is ordinal (meaning it only runs north-south/east-west), we know that all these streets are perpendicular to each other. Everything is at a right angle, which means we can draw lines outside the map to make the direct route the hypotenuse of a large right triangle.

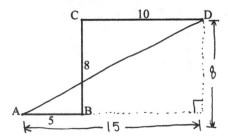

The total east-west distance between A and D is 15, and the total north-south distance between A and D is 8. The Pythagorean Theorem tells us that:

$$8^2 + 15^2 = c^2$$
$$64 + 225 = c^2$$
$$289 = c^2$$
$$17 = c$$

. . . so the direct route would be 17 units long. Don't stop there, though—this question wants to know how much shorter the direct route is: $23 - 17 = \boxed{6}$.

Linear Equations and $y = mx + b$

On the SAT, we're constantly graphing lines, analyzing lines, and making statements about what they would look like if we did any number of things to them. Fortunately there's only 1 basic equation you need to understand, and everything else line-related plays off of it.

The basic formula for a line on the coordinate plane (aptly called a *linear equation*) is $y = mx + b$. Each variable has a specific role and gives us a particular piece of information. Let's talk about each element.

The Ordered Pair

The x and y in this equation represent any point (x, y) that is on the line. If you plug in a specific x value, multiply it by m and then add b, you'll end up with that x's corresponding y value on the graph.

m, the Slope

The m value indicates the slope of the line—it expresses how steep the line is and in what direction it moves, uphill or downhill. Slope is very often a fraction, and we explain it by saying that slope $= \frac{\text{rise}}{\text{run}}$. Really, that's just a set of directions. For example, if our slope were $\frac{2}{3}$, that tells us that from anywhere on the line, if we move up 2 units in the numerator and move right 3 units in the denominator, we will always land directly on the line. Slope is what keeps our line straight, consistent, and predictable everywhere on the graph.

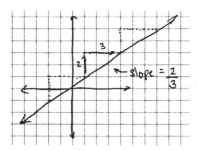

Slope Facts You Need to Know

○ A slope written as a whole number can be set over 1 to get the $\frac{\text{rise}}{\text{run}}$ directions (i.e., $m = 2$ becomes rise 2, run 1, or $\frac{2}{1}$)

○ The larger the slope is, the *steeper* it becomes, meaning the closer it gets to the *y*-axis.

○ A slope less than 1 is a flatter slope—it stays closer to the *x*-axis.

○ Because slopes act like fractions, if your slope is positive, it's also legal to both rise negatively and run negatively to create a line.

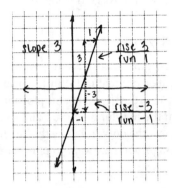

○ If a given slope is negative, you can rise positively and run negatively *or* rise negatively and run positively. You'll end up on the line either way.

○ No matter how far away your 2 points on a line are, the slope will always be consistent.

○ A slope of 0 means a line is flat, running parallel to the x-axis; its equation will just be $y = b$.

○ A line that is completely vertical has an "undefined" slope. Because slopes are rise-over-run directions, if we go up, up, up and never "run," the denominator of our slope fraction would be 0. Denominators can never be equal to 0. Ever.

○ Lines are parallel when they have identical slopes but different *b* values (*y*-intercepts).

○ To find a slope perpendicular to a given line, take the *m* value and find its reciprocal, then change its sign. Again: a perpendicular slope is the negative reciprocal of the original.

Calculating the Slope between Two Points

The slope formula is very easy, but it's also easy to mess up. It uses variables for the *x*'s and *y*'s of 2 different points, so let's be clear on what's what. Take the time to actually label the 2 points you're using to find the slope as (x_1, y_1) and (x_2, y_2). Then, plug the values into this formula:

$$\text{slope} = \frac{(y_2 - y_1)}{(x_2 - x_1)}$$

When calculating slope, it doesn't matter which point you call (x_1, y_1) and which you call (x_2, y_2); it's just imperative that once you decide which is which, you keep them straight throughout the problem.

Note: you can always find the slope of any line that intersects the origin by using any point on the line and $(0, 0)$. Don't forget to reduce the resulting fraction!

b, the *y*-intercept

The *b* value in the $y = mx + b$ equation is the *y*-intercept of the equation. That means that without any additional number crunching on your part, you can use that *b* value (taking its sign along with it) and plot it directly on the *y*-axis. It's the point $(0, b)$. The equation of the line will always go through that point.

Graphing Lines Using Slope and *y*-intercept

Graphs of linear equations can be sketched quickly and accurately without doing much math at all. Rather than number crunching to find coordinate pairs, a graph can be created by drawing a coordinate plane and plotting the *y*-intercept. Using the slope directions from the *m* value, count up and over to plot another point on the line. You can connect the dots and draw the line from just these 2 points, although for accuracy's sake, you may want to plot a couple of points and then connect them.

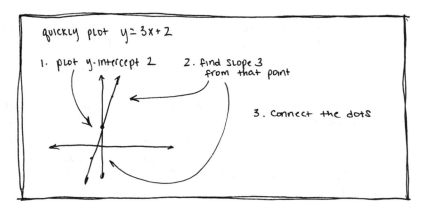

Provided you're accurate, this the fastest method of sketching line equations.

HOW THEY ASK THE QUESTIONS

Basic Line Questions

The most basic questions revolve around simply proving that you know the basics about slope, *y*-intercept, how a coordinate pair fits into the equation of the line, and what graphs should generally look like.

EXAMPLE 1: LEVEL 2
Point Q lies on a line with the equation $y - 4 = 2(x - 3)$. If the *y*-coordinate of point Q is 8, what is the *x*-coordinate of point Q?

This is just a plug-and-play equation. If we're given the value of y, we just pop it in and solve for x.

$$8-4 = 2(x-3)$$
$$4 = 2(x-3)$$
$$2 = x-3$$
$$\boxed{5 = x}$$

Using and Understanding Slope

Slope can be tested in simple ways, like calculating it or analyzing how changing a slope can affect a line. More challenging questions require you to identify a line with a particular group or assign slopes to new lines, given specific parameters.

EXAMPLE 1: LEVEL 4

On the graph below, line p (not shown) passes through the origin and intersects $\overline{MN}$ between point M and point N. Find the value of a possible slope for line p.

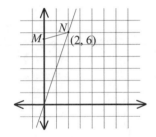

Remember how we said you can find the slope of any line, provided that it passes through the origin and 1 of the points along the line is labeled? Well, let's go ahead and use that $(0,0)$ and $(2,6)$ to find the slope of the existing line:

$$\frac{y_2-y_1}{x_2-x_1} = \frac{6-0}{2-0} = \frac{6}{2} = 3 \leftarrow \text{slope}$$

Now, because $\overline{MN}$ is above that existing line, we're going to need a line that's even steeper than 3. We can actually choose any number under the sun for our new slope, provided it's greater than 3. I'm going to choose 24 just for fun.

Understanding and Using Rules of Perpendicular Lines

EXAMPLE 1: LEVEL 2

If line l passes through the origin and has a negative slope and line m is perpendicular to line l, which of the following must be true about line m?

> Whenever you see the words *the origin* spelled out in a problem, jot down the point $(0, 0)$. It's simple to overlook the word; it's much more difficult to ignore the numbers.

(A)   Its slope is negative.

(B)   It has a positive y-intercept.

(C)   Is has a negative y-intercept.

(D)   Its slope is positive.

(E)   It goes through the origin.

The stipulation that a line is perpendicular to another tells us 1 specific thing: the signs of the 2 slopes are opposite each other. Since this line l has a negative slope, no matter what, the slope of line m must be positive, answer D. We can't prove anything else about it.

EXAMPLE 2: LEVEL 3

If line k passes through point (4, –6) and is perpendicular to the x-axis, which of the following must be the equation for line k?

(A) $y = 4$

(B) $y = 4x$

(C) $y = x + 4$

(D) $x = 0$

(E) $x = 4$

Let's zero in on the fact that line k is perpendicular to the x-axis. That tells us that the line is straight up and down—that no matter where we are on the line, our point will always need to have the same x value. If line k intersects the point (4, –6), that means we must always be at $x = 4$ for all our stipulations to be true. That's the answer: $x = 4$.

EXAMPLE 3: LEVEL 4

Square RSTU lies on a graph such that point R lies on the line $x = 3$ and point S lies on the line $x = 4$. What is the product of the slopes of each of the four sides of square RSTU?

You can sketch this out any way you like—it doesn't matter how long you make each side of the square.

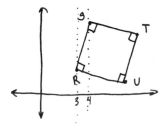

The tricky part here is that (as you should see) the sides of the square are not parallel to either of the axes. So what do we do? Well, because this a square we're working with, we know that each of the interior angles of the square are equal to 90°, meaning they're perpendicular to each other. If they're perpendicular, no matter what slope you assign to the first side, the other slope will be the *negative inverse* of that slope. That means that when you multiply them, you'll just end up with 1.

Let's say we choose to assign these sides slopes 1, −1, 1, and −1. Multiply those together and we get 1. If we got fancy (or thought the problem demanded more) and assigned each side slopes $\frac{3}{4}, -\frac{4}{3}, \frac{3}{4}$, and $-\frac{4}{3}$, we'd still get a slope of *positive 1*.

Using Slope to Find Missing Values in Charts of (*x, y*) pairs

These types of questions usually pop up in the function section as lists of domains and their ranges, but because they must be linear equations (in $y = mx + b$ format) to be solvable, it makes sense to put them here. The important thing to know about these problems is that all of the points on the line of a single linear equation are related by slope: you can always set the slope between any 2 points on the line equal to the slope of any other 2 points on the line.

EXAMPLE 1: LEVEL 4

The following coordinate pairs are all values found by using linear equation *R* (not shown). Using the values in the chart below, find the value of *n*.

x	5	9	17	n	33
$f(x)$	17	29	51	72	101

Again, because we know that all of these points lie on the same line (because they're all answers to the same equation), we can set their slopes equal to each other. In other words, I'm going to choose 2 points for which I have the coordinates, find the slope between them, then set that slope equal to the slope between another complete point and the point that includes the variable. In short, I'll find the slope between (5, 17) and (9, 29) and set that equal to the slope between (17, 51) and (*n*, 72) and solve for *n*.

$$\frac{y_2 - y_1}{x_2 - x_1} = \frac{y_4 - y_3}{x_4 - x_3}$$

$$\frac{29 - 17}{9 - 5} = \frac{72 - 51}{n - 17}$$

$$\frac{12}{4} = \frac{21}{n - 17}$$

$$12(n - 17) = 84 \quad \leftarrow \text{divide by } 12$$

$$n - 17 = 7$$

$$\boxed{n = 24}$$

EXAMPLE 2: LEVEL 5

Function $h(x)$ is a linear function, and some of its points appear in the chart below. What is the value of $w + z$?

x	0	1	2
$h(x)$	w	36	z

Again, we are not given the equation for $h(x)$, so we have no idea if the line intercepts the origin or what. It's just sort of out there somewhere on the coordinate plane. Because we don't know if the line goes through the origin, we really only have 1 point given to us. That's not going to be enough to say specifically w equals *this* and z equals *that*. But, using the same comparative slope stuff that we used above, we can build a slope relationship between the points and use algebra to say that $w + z$ equals *something*, which is all the question asks for.

We'll say the slope between $(0, w)$ and $(1, 36)$ is equal to the slope between $(1, 36)$ and $(2, z)$. It's ok to use $(1, 36)$ twice.

$$\frac{36 - w}{1 - 0} = \frac{z - 36}{2 - 1}$$

$$\frac{36 - w}{1} = \frac{z - 36}{1}$$

$$36 - w = z - 36$$

$$72 - w = z$$

$$\boxed{72 = w + z}$$

Linear Equations That Intersect an Axis or Each Other

WHAT YOU NEED TO KNOW

Let's first look at individual linear equations that intersect the x-axis. In the following image, it's important to recognize that all of the points where those lines intersect the x-axis have a big thing in common: their y value is 0.

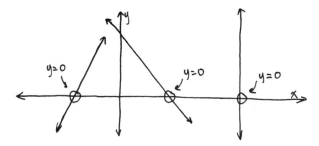

We can rely on this consistency, and when we're asked to find the x-intercept of any linear equation, we can simply pop in 0 for the value of y and solve for x.

The same goes for finding the y-intercept of any equation (if it's not already in $y = mx + b$ form)—pop 0 into the equation for x and solve.

Linear equations that intersect are just 2 lines that intersect somewhere on a graph. All intersecting lines share an important characteristic: they intersect at 1 specific point, and that point is a coordinate pair (x, y) that solves both equations.

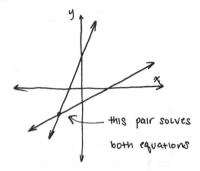

As far as I'm concerned, the easiest and fastest way to find the point of intersection for 2 equations written in $y = mx + b$ form is just to set them equal to each other. That means that if we're looking for the point of intersection of $y = 2x + 4$ and $y = 3x - 2$, I would set up and solve the equation $2x + 4 = 3x - 2$. Why? Because that equation says: "When I put a specific x value into the first equation, I get the same y value as when I put that specific x into the second equation."

In other words, by setting those 2 recipes for y equal to each other, we guarantee we'll get the single x value that gives us y both times. Once I set the equations equal to each other, I solve for x, find its value, and then sub the x value back into either of my original equations to get the corresponding y.

HOW THEY ASK THE QUESTIONS

Lines That Intersect an Axis

Because it's not so tricky to find the y-intercept of a line (as it's the b in the equation of a line), you can expect to be asked about the x-intercept.

EXAMPLE 1: LEVEL 2
If the line $y = 4x + 7$ intersects the x-axis at point (m, n) in the xy-coordinate plane, what is the value of m?

The m value in the coordinate pair is the x value in the equation. All we need to do is pop in 0 for y (because we're intersecting the x-axis) and solve for x.

$$y = 4x + 7$$
$$0 = 4x + 7$$
$$-7 = 4x$$
$$\boxed{\dfrac{-7}{4} = x}$$

Lines That Intersect Each Other

These questions usually involve $y = x^2$, but don't let that make you nervous. Because these are amped-up plug-and-play questions, they are designed to look like rocket science. More challenging problems of this type will include constants—you'll find an (x, y) pair and then pop it back into the equation to find the value of the constant.

EXAMPLE 2: LEVEL 3

Point $(l, 0)$ is one of the points of intersection in the xy-coordinate plane of the graphs of $y = -x^2 + 16$ and $y = x^2 - 16$. If l is negative, what is the value of l?

In this problem those squares are in there because the square roots provide us with 2 possible values of x. We need to find the value of x that makes both equations true, just as if we were solving a pair of absolute value problems. Because the point of intersection *must* solve both equations, we know that we can use the 0 from $(l, 0)$ to start. Let's put 0 into both those equations and solve for l:

$$y = -x^2 + 16 \qquad \ldots or \ldots \qquad y = x^2 - 16$$
$$0 = -l^2 + 16 \qquad\qquad\qquad 0 = l^2 - 16$$
$$-16 = -l^2 \qquad\qquad\qquad\quad 16 = l^2$$
$$16 = l^2 \qquad\qquad\qquad\qquad \pm 4 = l$$
$$\pm 4 = l$$

Because we need the negative value of l, our answer is $l = \boxed{-4}$.

EXAMPLE 2: LEVEL 4

The graphs of $y = x^2 - 11$ and $y = -x^2 + q$, where q is a constant, intersect at point $(\sqrt{8}, r)$. What is the value of q?

The $\sqrt{8}$ is there only to make you nervous—as soon as you put it into the equation, it's cancelled out by the squared sign. Now, because that second equation has 3 variables in it $(y, x,$ and $q)$, we can't solve for q until we've found values of x and y.

Let's go back and plug $(\sqrt{8}, r)$ into the first equation to find the value of r.

$$r = \left(\sqrt{8}\right)^2 - 11$$
$$r = 8 - 11$$
$$r = -3$$

Now that we know the value of r, we know that the coordinate pair that solves both equations is $(\sqrt{8}, -3)$. We can use those values for x and y in the second equation and solve for q, the constant.

$$-3 = -\left(\sqrt{8}\right)^2 + q$$
$$-3 = -8 + q$$
$$5 = q$$

EXAMPLE 3: LEVEL 5

Line r passes through the origin and is perpendicular to the line $y = \frac{1}{3}x + j$, where j is a constant. The two lines intersect at the point $(z, z + 2)$. What is the value of z?

It feels like there are a million variables in this problem, right? That's part of the point; the test maker wants to overwhelm you. Because we know that we're not given extra info in SAT questions, let's take a look at this line r and work on finding its equation. We know we need to get something in the form $y = mx + b$, and we've got 2 key pieces of information: line r passes through the origin, and its slope is perpendicular to $\frac{1}{3}$.

If the slope of line r is perpendicular to $\frac{1}{3}$, line r's slope must be -3. That gives us 1 part of line r: $y = -3x + b$. The next part is not so much difficult as it is just tricky: We're told line r passes through the origin, so its y-intercept must be 0. We can just drop the b and keep the final equation for line r: $y = -3x$.

What's so great about the equation we've found? Well, it only has an x and a y, so we can put the $(z, z + 2)$ right in there and solve! This is thrilling stuff, I know. Let's pop that point into $y = -3x$: we get $z + 2 = -3z$. See what I've done? I've subbed $z + 2$ in for y and z in for x. Now we solve.

$$\left(z + 2\right) = -3z$$
$$2 = -4z$$
$$-\frac{2}{4} = z$$
$$\boxed{-\frac{1}{2} = z}$$

Simultaneous Equations

WHAT YOU NEED TO KNOW

You'll recognize simultaneous equations when you're given multiple sources of information about the same few variables, like $2a + 3b = 17$ and $a + 5b = 19$. If we were given only the first equation, we could never find the values of a and b. We might be able to conjure up some numbers that *work*, but we couldn't be really sure we had the right numbers until we had another equation to work with. Sometimes pairs of equations (and occasionally on the SAT, a set of 3 equations) will contain different information about the same variables. It's impossible to find the value of 2 separate but related variables if you don't have 2 separate equations.

There are 2 ways to solve simultaneous equations. The first is *exactly* like the method for solving for the point of intersection of intersecting equations. Suppose we were given the equations $a = 2b + 6$ and $a = 4b$. Since both equations are equal to a, we can set the other sides equal to each other, $2b + 6 = 4b$, and solve for b. Once we find the value of b, we just pop it right back into either equation (whichever seems easier) and solve for a.

Similarly, if we were given the equations $a - 6 = 2b$ and $a = 4b$, it's completely legal to add 6 to both sides of the first equation to force both sides to equal a. All is fair if you're using algebra.

The short rule: 2 variables require 2 equations to confidently identify the values of each of the variables. Likewise, 3 variables require 3 equations to solve.

Stacking Simultaneous Equations

An alternative method for solving simultaneous equations is to stack them up and add. Let's go back to that first pair that used a and b: $2a + 3b = 17$ and $a + 5b = 19$. It's easy to see that trying to get both equations to equal a or b could get messy. In these instances you'll want to "solve them simultaneously." We're going to add the equations an columns and manipulate 1 (or sometimes both) of the equations so that when we add them together a variable will cancel.

$$\begin{cases} 2a + 3b = 17 \\ a + 5b = 19 \end{cases}$$

$$\begin{cases} 2a + 3b = 17 \\ -2a - 10b = -38 \end{cases}$$
$$0 - 7b = -21$$

$$-7b = -21$$
$$b = 3$$

What I think is best for this pair of equations (and what I think will ultimately give me the least amount of work) is to multiply the *entire bottom equation* by –2. Put another way, I'm going to distribute a –2 to each element of the bottom equation. If this is new to you and you're not sure why I'm doing that, check out what happens.

When I add straight through those columns I find that $-7b = -21$, so $b = 3$. If my question had asked for the value of b, I'd be done. If it had asked for the value of a, I could pop b back into either of the equations and solve for it:

$$2a + 3b = 17$$
$$2a + 3(3) = 17$$
$$2a + 9 = 17$$
$$2a = 8$$
$$a = 4$$

This stacking trick is easy once you've practiced it—just be very careful and make sure that you distribute to *both sides* of the equation. If I hadn't multiplied the 19 by –2 in the first place, the whole problem would have been wrong.

HOW THEY ASK THE QUESTIONS

Using Substitution to Solve Multiple Related Equations

EXAMPLE 1: LEVEL 1
If $6x = 48$ and $xy = 2$, $y = ?$

It makes the most sense to solve for x and then plug that value of x into the next equation:

$6x = 48$

$x = 8$

$8y = 2$

$y = \dfrac{2}{8} \rightarrow \dfrac{1}{4}$

However, you could also substitute in this question. If $xy = 2$, then $x = \frac{2}{y}$. You may substitute $\frac{2}{y}$ for x in the other equation:

$6 \cdot \dfrac{2}{y} = 48$

$\dfrac{6}{1} \cdot \dfrac{2}{y} = 48$

$\dfrac{12}{y} = \dfrac{48}{1}$

$12 = 48y$

$\dfrac{1}{4} = y$

Again, when an equation uses the variable x, you're better off using a • to indicate multiplication so things don't get confusing.

That's (obviously) a much longer route to the correct solution, but it's important that you understand that either method will reliably get you to the same answer.

EXAMPLE 2: LEVEL 2
If $4p + 7q = 62$ and $q - p = 1$, what is the value of p?

Substitution is a particularly good option for this problem because solving the second equation for q gives us a simple binomial, $q = p + 1$, to pop into the first equation:

$$q - p = 1 \quad \leftarrow \text{Isolate } q \text{ and plug in}$$
$$q = 1 + p$$
$$4p + 7q = 62$$
$$4p + 7(1+p) = 62$$
$$4p + 7 + 7p = 62$$
$$11p + 7 = 62$$
$$11p = 55$$
$$p = 5$$

Using Stacking to Solve Multiple Related Equations

EXAMPLE 1: LEVEL 4
If $3a + c = 3b$ and $3a + 3b + c = 54$, what is the value of b?

You may be inclined to think we can't solve this problem because I keep harping about how 3 variables require 3 equations. However, there are 2 ways to solve this problem. Admittedly, because I always do things the same way, I often overlook the quick method to attack these problems. As you're liable to do the same thing, let's look at the long way first, reorganizing and stacking. The second equation is already pretty well organized, so I'm going to line up my first equation to look like it:

$$\begin{cases} 3a + c = 3b \\ 3a + 3b + c = 54 \end{cases} \quad \leftarrow \text{rearrange the top equation so that everything aligns}$$

$$\begin{aligned} \begin{cases} 3a - 3b + c = 0 \\ -(\underline{3a + 3b + c = 54}) \end{cases} \quad &\leftarrow \text{now I subtract the bottom equation from the top} \\ 0 - 6b + 0 = -54 \\ -6b = -54 \\ b = 9 \end{aligned}$$

Now, the second and faster way of solving this is actually using substitution: we're given $3a + c = 3b$ and $3a$ and c are *right in* that second equation. If you want to, you can just pop out the $3a$ and the c and pop in the $3b$:

$$3a + 3b + c = 54$$
$$3b + 3b = 54$$
$$6b = 54$$
$$b = 9$$

The fastest way to solve a problem like this is usually the first way *you* see how to work it out.

EXAMPLE 2: LEVEL 3

Three students took quizzes worth 50 points. Alice and Bob earned a combined 85 points, Alice and Cameron earned a combined 95 points, and Bob and Cameron earned a combined 90 points. What was Bob's score on the test?

This problem is considered more challenging because it involves 3 variables. (I'll use *a*, *b*, and *c* to represent Alice, Bob, and Cameron.) Now, although I know you could probably sit down and figure this out just by messing around with different numbers, the quickest way to do this problem is to solve simultaneously. You'll find that these problems are usually arranged so that you can easily manipulate them to cancel out everything you don't need. In this problem, we're going to add everything together and then use our original information to cancel:

$$+ \begin{cases} a + b = 85 \\ a + c = 95 \\ \underline{b + c = 90} \end{cases}$$

$2a + 2b + 2c = 270$ ← now we'll factor out the 2 and divide.

$2(a + b + c) = 270$

$a + b + c = 135$ ← since we're looking for b, we replace $a + c$ with 95, which was given

$95 + b = 135$

$$\boxed{b = 40}$$

So we find that Bob scored 40 points.

Direct and Indirect Variation or Directly and Indirectly Proportional

WHAT YOU NEED TO KNOW

When 2 variables *vary directly*, or are *directly proportional*, that means that the first variable is always multiplied by the same constant to get the other. The equation to use for direct variation is $y = dx$, where d is a constant and x and y are a typical coordinate pair.

Likewise, if variables *vary indirectly*, or are *indirectly proportional* to each other, the constant is divided by the x value to get the y, that is, $y = \frac{d}{x}$

Although you may be tempted to solve problems involving these concepts in several different ways, consistently and immediately resorting to a formula is always the safest bet.

Finding a Direct Relationship Between Pairs or Points

Like many SAT questions, this type of question is designed specifically to see if you know a term or understand a concept—in this case, how a directly varying relationship affects pairs of points.

EXAMPLE 1: LEVEL 3

In which of the following pairs does p have a direct relationship with t?

(A)

p	4	5	6
t	6	7	8

(B)

p	4	5	6
t	16	25	36

(C)

p	4	5	6
t	14	15	16

(D)

p	4	5	6
t	4	10	18

(E)

p	4	5	6
t	20	25	30

A directly varying relationship is, by definition, a relationship in which the first term is repeatedly multiplied by the *same* number to produce the second term (x is multiplied by the same number to create y). Choice E is the only option in which this takes place—each p term is multiplied by 5 to create the t term.

Finding the Constant

A common way the SAT adds difficulty to direct and indirect variation problems is by giving you a pair of values and asking you to find a new pair of values without giving you the constant in the problem. The question involves more steps, so it's "harder."

EXAMPLE 1: LEVEL 3

If y varies indirectly with x, and $x = 3$ when $y = 12$, what is the value of y when $x = 20$?

Now, these problems are easier to get wrong because you may feel compelled to do them in your head. The most important rule of solving SAT math problems is to write your work down, *particularly* if you think you know where the problem is headed.

Remember that the formula for indirect variation is $y = \frac{d}{x}$. We're going to plug in our first *xy* pair to find *d*:

$$12 = \frac{d}{3}$$

$36 = d$ ← take the constant and plug it

into the indirect variation formula

$y = \frac{36}{20}$ ⟵ along with the new *x* value

to get *y*

$$\boxed{y = \frac{9}{5}}$$

Again, this will always be the same process: pop in the first pair to find the constant and then use the constant in a new equation to find the missing *x* or *y*.

Reflections

Reflections move linear equations in the coordinate plane as though they are being reflected in a mirror—not a mirror held up to the page, but a mirror that we pretend is lying along the *x*- or the *y*-axis. Now, before I show you how I do this, I'll admit that there *is* a pattern between the original equation and what the new equation will look like, based on whether it's reflected in the *x*- or the *y*-axis. I imagine you can memorize it, but I never have. I'm always against memorizing potentially confusing things that can be easily figured out, so I'll just show you the simple way to quickly draw the original line, find its reflection, and then find the new equation of the reflected line.

Let's find the reflection of $y = 3x + 4$ in the *x*-axis. The trick here is in the sketch, so it's in your best interest to be a little uptight and sketch the line as carefully as possible.

Now, this is a 3-step process. First, it matters that we're reflecting in the *x*-axis. I want you to think about an actual mirror. Just as it looks like you're touching your own finger when you touch a mirror, the reflection of the line we'll draw will look like it's touching itself (the old line) in the *x*-axis, the mirror axis. So the first step is to mark the point where the line crosses the *x*-axis.

Then we flip the point on the *y*-axis over the *x*-axis, as though we were folding the page in half with the crease right on the *x*-axis. Again, we're flipping over the *x*-axis because it's the axis in which we're reflecting.

Once we have a point marked on the x-axis and y-axis, we connect those 2 points to create our new line.

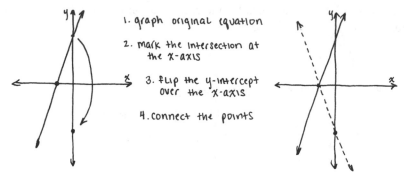

1. graph original equation

2. mark the intersection at the x-axis

3. flip the y-intercept over the x-axis

4. connect the points

Gathering the equation of our new line from our drawing is the most important part of the process, which is why it's so important to make your sketch as accurate as possible. You'll need to accurately find the y-intercept and the slope; be particularly careful to make sure the signs are correct.

If the instructions had been to find a reflection over the y-axis, the process would have been the same but all in reference to the y-axis rather than the x-axis. This means that we would pinpoint where our line crosses the y-axis, label it, and then flip the x-intercept across the y-axis. Again, connecting those points yields the reflected line, and finding its slope and y-intercept (which, incidentally, stays the same) will give us the equation of the reflection of the line.

HOW THEY ASK THE QUESTIONS

Identifying the Equation of the Reflection

EXAMPLE 1: LEVEL 3

In the xy-plane, the equation of line m is $y = 3x + 6$. If line j is the equation of the reflection of line m in the y-axis, what is the equation of line j?

- (A) $x = 3y + 6$
- (B) $y = \frac{1}{3}x + 6$
- (C) $y = -3x + 6$
- (D) $y = -3x - 6$
- (E) $y = 4x + 3$

OK, I'd like you to quickly sketch out a graph of the original equation. This time we're reflecting the y-axis, so we first touch the y-axis where our original line crosses it, at $(0, 6)$. You'll probably notice that when you're reflecting over the y-axis, your y-intercept is the same for both the original equation and its reflection. At this step alone we can eliminate answers D and E.

Next, we flip the point where the line intercepts the x-axis *over* the y-axis; here we go from $(-2, 0)$ over to $(2, 0)$.

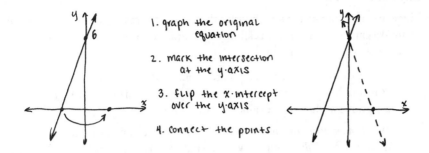

1. graph the original equation
2. mark the intersection at the y-axis
3. flip the x-intercept over the y-axis
4. connect the points

Our new line has a *y*-intercept of 6 and a negative slope. Of our answer choices, C is the only possible option. However, what if we'd needed to choose between $y = -3x + 6$ and $y = -\frac{1}{3}x + 6$? In that case, the accuracy of our drawing would have mattered even more—we would have needed to observe not only that our new slope was negative, but also that it was a slope that travels down 3 steps and over 1, rather than down 1 and over 3 (which would be a slope of $-\frac{1}{3}$).

Functions

WHAT YOU NEED TO KNOW

Functions are a special variety of equations that you can consider a step up from a basic linear equation ($y = mx + b$). The whole idea behind a function is that we plug a value into an equation, crunch the numbers, and get a new value, sort of like when we plug *x* into an equation and get *y*.

In fact, with any linear equation we could simply rewrite $y = mx + b$ as $f(x) = mx + b$ and call it a function.

(*x, y*) Is the Same as (*x, f(x)*)

Again, in a function, the relationship between (x, y) is the same as ($x, f(x)$). This $f(x)$ term is read as "*f* of *x*." It is a term, its own single variable; it *does not* mean "*f* times *x*." I cannot stress this too much:

$f(x)$ stands for a specific number, <u>not</u> multiplication.

So what? Well, what's cool about $f(x)$ (or at the very least, useful), is that $f(x)$ gives you more information about what happened in the equation than *y* alone could. Basically, if I tell you that $y = 3$, that's a single piece of info, but if I tell you $f(2) = 3$, then I'm telling you that I put 2 into a function and got 3 out of that function. That's 2 pieces of information, and they're related: they create an ordered pair (2, 3).

Key Function Facts

There are a couple of facts and terms that make functions special and define them. We can't just run around calling every equation under the sun a function. Here's what you need to know:

- ○ *The vertical line test.* When you're looking at a graph of an equation, if you can draw a vertical line through any part of the graph that intersects 2 *y* points at the same *x* value, it's not a function.

- ○ *What the vertical line test means.* For each *x* value entered into a function, there can be *only a single y* value. That means that when you're solving equations, any equation for which you find 2 *y* values with 1 *x* value—for example, $(2, 6)$, $(2, -3)$, or ($y = \pm 2$)—that equation cannot be a function. However, having 2 *x* values for 1 *y* value—such as $(2, 5)$ or $(4, 5)$—is fine; that can be a function.

- ○ *Domain and range. Domain* is the term for all of the possible *x* values of a function. *Range* is the term for all of the possible *y* values of a function.

Some problems use notation that asks you to multiply the whole function by some number. If a problem reads $3f(g)$, all you need to do is put parentheses around the function and multiply the whole thing by 3. So if I tell you that $f(g) = 2x + 2$ and ask about $3f(g)$, you would write $3(2x + 2)$ and go from there. It's just that easy.

HOW THEY ASK THE QUESTIONS

There are 3 basic types of function problems on the SAT: there are problems that use equations, problems with graphs, and charts of ordered pairs.

Type One: Using Equations

These basic problems use a given function equation to get you to your answer; the function will be spelled out for you right on the page.

EXAMPLE 1: LEVEL 2
If $f(x) = \frac{5 - 2x^2}{2}$, then $f(2) = ?$

When we are asked to find *f* of anything (such as the value of $f(2)$), all we are being asked to do is plug the number in parenthesis into every *x* value in the given function and solve.

$$f(x) = \frac{5 - 2x^2}{2}$$

$$f(2) = \frac{5 - 2(2)^2}{2}$$

$$f(2) = \frac{5 - 8}{2}$$

$$f(2) = \boxed{\frac{-3}{2}}$$

EXAMPLE 2: LEVEL 3

Let the function g be defined by $g(x) = 12 + \frac{x^2}{16}$. If $g(4n) = 7n$, what is one possible value of n?

This time, we are given a value to plug into the function for x and we are told the function's output once that x value is plugged in. For example, this problem says that when we plug $4n$ into the function, the whole thing gives us $7n$. We can set it up like a simple equation.

$$7n = 12 + \frac{(4n)^2}{16}$$

$$7n = 12 + \frac{16n^2}{16} \leftarrow \text{the 16's cancel}$$

$$7n = 12 + n^2$$

$$0 = n^2 - 7n + 12$$

$$0 = (n-3)(n-4)$$

$$n - 3 = 0 \quad \text{or} \quad n - 4 = 0$$

$$n = 3 \quad \text{or} \quad n = 4$$

Either $\boxed{3 \text{ or } 4}$ would be a correct answer for the value of n.

EXAMPLE 3: LEVEL 3

Let the function f be defined by $f(x) = x + 4$. If $3f(q) = 36$, what is the value of $f(2q)$?

This question incorporates the element of multiplying the entire equation (which is really just distribution).

$$3(q+4) = 36 \qquad \rightarrow f(2q) = ? \quad \text{find } f(2 \cdot 8), \ f(16)$$
$$q + 4 = 12 \qquad\qquad\qquad\qquad f(16) = 16 + 4$$
$$q = 8 \quad \text{so} \qquad\qquad\qquad f(16) = 20$$

EXAMPLE 4: LEVEL 4

Let the function f be defined by $f(x) = 3x - 2$. If $\frac{1}{2}f(\sqrt{r}) = 5$, what is the value of r?

This problem is exactly like the example before it, in which the whole function is being multiplied by some amount; this problem just looks harder. Rather than have you multiply by something not-so-intimidating, like 2, they throw in a fraction and a square root to freak you out. It's messy, but really not that hard:

$$f(x) = 3x - 2 \text{ and } \tfrac{1}{2}f(\sqrt{r}) = 5$$

$$\tfrac{1}{2}(3\sqrt{r} - 2) = 5 \quad \leftarrow \text{multiply by 2 to get rid of the } \tfrac{1}{2}$$

$$3\sqrt{r} - 2 = 10$$

$$3\sqrt{r} = 12 \quad \leftarrow \text{divide by 3}$$

$$\sqrt{r} = 4 \quad \leftarrow \text{square both sides}$$

$$\boxed{r = 16}$$

More Type One: Word Problems with Functions

Word problems built around functions will always have you plug in either a value of x or a value of $f(x)$ and find the other. They won't always be written with f's and x's, but each term will be defined right within the problem.

EXAMPLE 1: LEVEL 1

A group of students held a bake sale to raise money. The net amount M, in dollars, raised by selling c cupcakes is given by the function $M(c) = 2c - 45$. If the students sold 220 cupcakes, how much money did they raise?

All we do is pop 220 for c into the given function and solve.

$$M(c) = 2c - 45$$

$$= 2(220) - 45$$

$$= 440 - 45$$

$$= \boxed{\$ 395}$$

EXAMPLE 2: LEVEL 1

The final count C of a certain toy produced by x pounds of plastic is given by the function $C(x) = \dfrac{7x + 5}{2}$. How many pounds of plastic are required to produce 643 toys?

This the same problem as earlier, but we are given $f(x)$ and we need to find x.

$$C(x) = \frac{7x + 5}{2}$$

$$643 = \frac{7x + 5}{2}$$

$$1286 = 7x + 5$$

$$1281 = 7x$$

$$\boxed{183 = x}$$

EXAMPLE 3: LEVEL 3

The weekly profit p from selling g units of a certain product is given by the function $p(g) = 16g - (10g + k)$. If 200 units were produced and sold last week for a total profit of $1,100, what is the value of k?

This question is a step up on the difficulty chart because it includes a constant in the function. These word problems set up a scenario and give you values for both x and $f(x)$ and ask you to solve for an additional constant buried in the equation. The constant will always be just another variable already in the function, and just to be even more clear, the problem will always say "where k [or whatever variable they picked] is a constant." Once you fill in x and $f(x)$, the constant will be the only variable in the equation and you can just isolate it like you would in any other algebra problem.

$$p(g) = 16g - (10g + k)$$
$$1100 = 16g - 10g - k \quad \leftarrow \text{I just distributed}$$
$$1100 = 16(200) - 10(200) - k$$
$$1100 = 6(200) - k \quad \leftarrow \text{fancy factoring}$$
$$1100 = 1200 - k$$
$$-100 = -k$$
$$100 = k$$

By the way, I got that 6(200) by factoring the 200 out of 16(200) − 10(200). If that's not clear, working it out the long way will still get you the right answer. I just wanted to show you the fancy short cut.

EXAMPLE 4: LEVEL 2

For which of the following functions is $f(-3) > f(3)$?

(A) $f(x) = 3x^2$
(B) $f(x) = 3$
(C) $f(x) = \dfrac{3}{x}$
(D) $f(x) = 3 - x^3$
(E) $f(x) = x^4 + 4$

Sometimes you'll have to compare outputs of different functions—what you're going to need to do here is plug in −3 and 3 for each value of x and find $f(x)$.

A) $f(x) = 3x^2$

$3(-3)^2 \overset{?}{>} 3(3)^2$

$3 \cdot 9 \overset{?}{>} 3 \cdot 9$ No.

B) $f(x) = 3$

$3 \overset{?}{>} 3$ No.

C) $f(x) = \dfrac{3}{x}$

$\dfrac{3}{-3} \overset{?}{>} \dfrac{3}{3}$ No.

D) $f(x) = 3 - x^3$

$3 - (-3)^3 \overset{?}{>} 3 - (3)^3$

$3 - {}^-27 \overset{?}{>} 3 - 27$

$30 \overset{?}{>} -24$ ✓

E) $f(x) = x^4 + 4$

$(-3)^4 + 4 \overset{?}{>} (3)^4 + 4$

$81 + 4 \overset{?}{>} 81 + 4$ No.

Tip: Whenever a negative input makes a function's output bigger, always try out the options with odd exponents first.

Last of Type One: Increases over Time and Depreciation

The most difficult function questions often include the concepts of increasing costs over time and depreciation (in which something like a car predictably loses value over the course of several years). These problems also give you a function in which $f(x)$ stands for the total value of the car and the x value will be an exponent representing the amount of time the car has left to depreciate. These can look scary and are often some of the very last problems in a section, but relax. The work is just as simple as any other function problem: pop in the given information and solve using algebra. You won't need to pull out logarithms or do any advanced math. For more info on exponent rules, see page 142.

These problems are made more challenging by put ting exponents in them. Don't be intimidated—just use PEMDAS (see page 109). No problem.

EXAMPLE 1: LEVEL 5
The cost of maintenance on a boat increases each year by 10 percent, and Mark paid $500 this year for maintenance on his boat. If the cost C for maintenance on Mark's boat n years from now is given by the function, $C(n) = 500x^n$ what is the value of x?

Now, if I'm going to find x, I'm going to need values of n and $C(n)$ to plug in.

$C(n) = 500x^n$

$550 = 500x^1$ ← that's 1 yr in the exponent

$\dfrac{550}{500} = x^1$

$\boxed{\dfrac{11}{10} = x \ (\text{or } 1.1)}$

This is just a question of logic: if we're told that it goes up by 10 percent every year, in 1 year ($n = 1$) the cost of maintenance will be $550 because $C(n) = 550$. (That's percent increase in action.)

EXAMPLE 2: LEVEL 5

Bernie purchased an engagement ring for $12,500, the value of which depreciates by 60 percent a year. The value in dollars of the ring after n years is given by the function V, where $V(n) = 12,500\left(\frac{3}{5}\right)^n$. How many years from the ring's purchase will the ring have a resale value of $2,700?

$$V(n) = 12500\left(\frac{3}{5}\right)^n$$

$$2700 = 12500\left(\frac{3}{5}\right)^n \quad \leftarrow \text{divide by } 12500$$
$$\text{and reduce the fraction}$$

$$\frac{27}{125} = \left(\frac{3}{5}\right)^n \quad \leftarrow \frac{3}{5} \text{ to what power equals } \frac{27}{125}?$$

$$\frac{27}{125} = \frac{3}{5} \cdot \frac{3}{5} \cdot \frac{3}{5} \quad \ldots \text{so} \quad \boxed{n = 3}$$

There we have it: 3 years.

Type Two: Using Graphs

Sometimes the SAT presents function problems in which the actual function equation isn't given and we need to use graphs to get answers. Rather than spelling out some crazy function for us, the SAT provides only a graph of $g(x)$ with no explanation, just "$y = g(x)$." What that means is that we can get on the graph, choose a given x value, and then go up and find its corresponding y value on the graph. That y value will be the same number as $g(x)$. (Remember how I couldn't stress too much that $f(x)$ represents a number? This is why.)

EXAMPLE 1: LEVEL 2

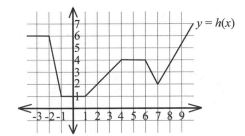

In the graph of $h(x)$ above, which of the following is equal to $h(3)$?

(A) 5
(B) 8
(C) 3
(D) 1
(E) 6

This basic function graph problem is just to see if you can get from an x to an $f(x)$ value and vice versa.

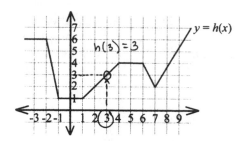

Just plug in 3 for x on the graph and find the corresponding y value. We can see the $h(3) = \boxed{3}$.

EXAMPLE 2: LEVEL 3

Name a possible value of k if $g(k) = 1$.

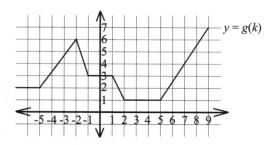

Any value between 2 and 5 will score you a point for a question like this. The y value is the same everywhere on the graph between 2 and 5.

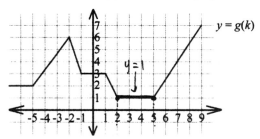

EXAMPLE 3: LEVEL 3

This figure shows the graph of $j(x)$. If the function $r(x) = j(-2x) + 4$, what is the value of $r(2)$?

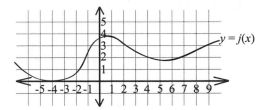

Here you're being given both a graph of a function and the mathematical formula for another. In these problems you need to get information from the graph to insert into the other function to solve it.

$$r(x) = j(-2x) + 4$$
$$r(2) = j(-2 \cdot 2) + 4$$
$$r(2) = j(-4) + 4 \quad \leftarrow \text{plug } -4 \text{ into the } j(x) \text{ graph}$$
$$r(2) = 0 + 4$$
$$\boxed{r(2) = 4}$$

When I got to the third line that said $j(-4)$, that's when I used the graph: I plugged in -4 for x and got a y value of 0.

> Rather than asking you to choose a single point on the graph, sometimes an SAT problem will ask about a range of points on the graph, like finding all of the x values for which $f(x)$ is negative. The answers will usually be written with greater-than or less-than expressions.

Type Three: Using Charts of Ordered Pairs

For these function problems you'll need to determine the function that explains how the ordered pairs are related. The pairs come in a chart, and they will not always be labeled x and $f(x)$; instead, they may be some crazy pair like q and $r(q)$. This is supposed to freak you out—really, you just need to treat them like x and y.

EXAMPLE 1: LEVEL 3

The following table gives values of the linear function r for selected values of q. Which of the following defines q?

q	0	1	2	3
$r(q)$	−2	0	2	4

- (A) $r(q) = q + 1$
- (B) $r(q) = 2q + 2$
- (C) $r(q) = 2$
- (D) $r(q) = \frac{q}{2} + 2$
- (E) $r(q) = 2q - 2$

This question is just a basic example of a set of inputs and outputs for a particular function. It's really most efficient to guess and check your way to the solution: plug the given q values into the function and see if you get the corresponding $r(q)$ values. Plugging in the pair 0 and -2 doesn't check out until we get to E.

$$E) \quad r(q) = 2q - 2$$
$$-2 = 0 - 2 \ ?$$
$$-2 = -2 \ \checkmark$$

Remember to always check answers A and E first!

Because both sides of the equation are equal, E defines the function.

EXAMPLE 2: LEVEL 3

The function $f(x)$ is linear in x. Using the following chart, what is the value of z?

x	0	1	2	3	4
$f(x)$	2	5	z	11	14

Instead of being asked to find the function from a chart of points, here you're given an incomplete chart of pairs of points from a linear equation and asked to fill in the missing pair. The really important thing to take from this is that all the points on a line from a single linear equation are related by slope: you can always set the slope between any 2 points on a line equal to the slope of any other 2 points on a line. For efficiency's sake, you should check out the last problems in the slope section (page 187) for more info on that. Please go look at it—they're important.

For this problem, you'll most likely see that $f(x)$ increases by 3 with every single increase of x, so we can safely say that $z = 8$, because that's 3 more than 5.

Parabola

WHAT YOU NEED TO KNOW

You're going to run into graphs of parabolas and their equations in a couple of different forms: standard form and general form. If you haven't seen this before, relax. The test doesn't delve too deeply into the topic.

The Standard Equation

If you were going to learn only 1 thing about the formula for a parabola, I would want you to learn its *standard form equation* and the information that equation gives you about the graph.

The standard equation for a parabola is

$$y = \pm a(x - h)^2 + k$$

The x and y in this equation are just like the (x, y) coordinate pair in a $y = mx + b$ equation. Everything else in the equation makes the line curvy.

First, the + or − in front of the line tells you whether the parabola faces up or down. Positive is up, negative means flip it.

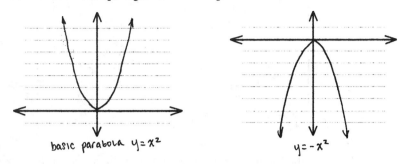

The *a* value tells you how tall and skinny or flat and wide the parabola is. If *a* is greater than 1, your parabola pulls in toward its axis of symmetry; if *a* is less than 1 (usually in fractional form), it tells you that the parabola is flattened out and looks more like a deep bowl.

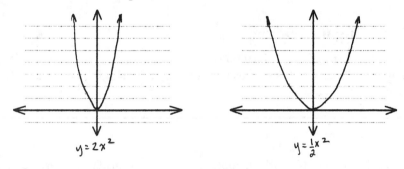

The *h* value directs the horizontal shift of the graph—the entire parabola moves to the left or right of the *y*-axis based on the value inside the parentheses. *But be careful!* If *h* is positive, the parabola shifts left (in the negative direction); if *h* is negative, it moves the parabola right (in the positive direction). This is totally counterintuitive, so watch out!

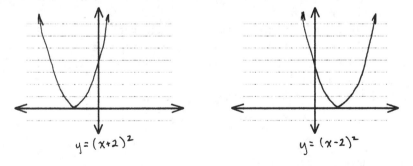

Finally, the *k* value shifts the graph up or down from the *x*-axis, but at least this shift is with the sign. If *k* is positive, the parabola moves up; if *k* is negative, the parabola moves down.

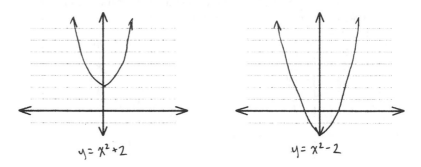

$y = x^2 + 2$ $y = x^2 - 2$

In fact, the coordinate pair (h, k) is the (x, y) pair for the vertex of the parabola. Now, what's important to get here is that because the formula for the graph is x *minus* h, you have to flip h's sign in the given equation to get the x value of the vertex. For example, if the equation reads $(x - 2)^2$, your h value is *positive* 2, not negative.

The General Equation

The other format for the equation of a parabola is the *general equation*. (You don't actually need to known the name of either; you simply need to get information out of each of them.)

The general equation looks like this:

$$y = ax^2 + bx + c$$

Just like in the standard equation, the x and y in this formula are holding the place of an (x, y) pair from a graph. In fact, you may recognize it as a good old quadratic equation from Algebra I. For a refresher on the quadratic, check out page 159. However, for our purposes here, the a, b, and c give us all the info we need.

The a in this equation is the same a that appears in the standard equation. If it were negative, it would flip the graph, and its magnitude tells us whether the parabola is skinny or fat.

The b here is a little trickier. It's very unlikely that you'll need to use this so specifically on the SAT, but stranger things have happened. Arranging what you've been given so you have $\frac{-b}{2a}$ will give you the axis of symmetry for the parabola. That means if $\frac{-b}{2a} = 4$, then $x = 4$ is your axis of symmetry, the invisible line that splits the parabola straight up the center.

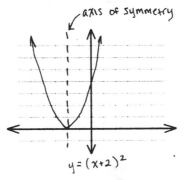

axis of symmetry

$y = (x + 2)^2$

The c value is actually much closer to what we grew accustomed to in the Algebra I lesson; c is just the y-intercept of the parabola—the point $(0, c)$ on the graph.

Understanding the Two Forms of Parabolic Equations and Their Graphs

The truth is that you really only need to be comfortable with these formulas to the point that you don't get scared of them and skip the question when you come across it. This is not a huge test of Algebra II skills; it's all very basic.

EXAMPLE 1: LEVEL 4
Which of the following could be the graph of $p(x)$ when $p(x)=ax^2 + bx + c$ and a is a positive constant and c is a positive constant?

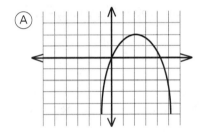

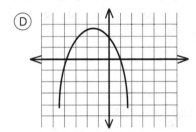

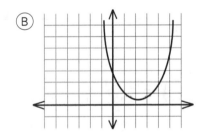

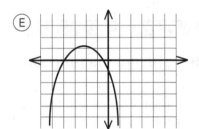

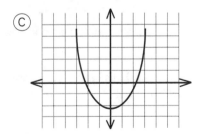

Your best bet is to eliminate systematically. If a is positive, that means our parabola needs to face up; that eliminates A, D, and E right off the bat.

Remember how we said c in this formula is just like the y-intercept in a linear equation? We need to find the parabola that intercepts the y-axis in a positive place—above the x-axis. There's only 1 parabola that does that: B.

Dingbat Math

A math problem that involves some sort of dingbat—a heart or star or half moon or some other funny little symbol—is designed specifically to be distracting. However, these dingbat problems are really just plug-and-play pattern problems. The pattern is defined at the outset using variables and a dingbat. Then the variables and the dingbat are said to equal some expression that uses the variables around the dingbat. For example: $r \odot s = \frac{r+s}{s-2}$.

Again, on the left we are given 2 variables centered on the dingbat; on the right we are given an expression that uses those variables. Now, all of this stuff is just a set of instructions. All it tells me is that if I am given [anything] $\odot$ [anything], I'm going to use that pattern to create an expression and then simplify it.

For our example, if I'm given $4 \odot 2$, I simply take everything to the left of the dingbat and plug it in everywhere I see r. Then I take everything to the right of the dingbat and plug it in everywhere I see s. This will give me $\frac{4+2}{6-2}$.

Then, I just simplify

$$\frac{4+2}{6-2} \rightarrow \frac{6}{4} \rightarrow \frac{3}{2}$$

No matter what dingbat the problem uses, or what the expression after it says, all you ever need to do is take the values on either side of the dingbat and plug them into the appropriate spots in the expression.

Simplifying the Dingbat

These just check to see if you can get past your initial, "What the . . . ?" reaction when presented with a nontraditional math problem. With these, you'll primarily need to plug in and simplify.

EXAMPLE 1: LEVEL 3

Let $a \, R \, b \, R \, c$ be defined as $a \, R \, b \, R \, c = a^c + b^c$ when a, b, and c are integers. What is the value of $10 \, R \, 6 \, R \, 2$?

Again, all we're going to do here is take the stuff that's been placed between those R-things and put it into the expression. If $a \, R \, b \, R \, c = a^c + b^c$, then

$$10 \; R \; 6 \; R \; 2 \rightarrow 10^2 + 6^2$$

plug in   simplify: $10^2 + 6^2 = 100 + 36 = \boxed{136}$

EXAMPLE 2: LEVEL 3

For integers n, p, and q, let $n \propto (p, q)$ be false if $\frac{nq}{p} < 1$. If $2 \propto (p, 6)$ is false, what is one possible value of p?

First, let's arrange what we have to see what we'd need to make sure we can choose a proper value of p:

$$\frac{2 \times 6}{p} < 1 \ \rightarrow \ \frac{12}{p} < 1$$

Now, the definition says that the expression given to us is *false*. That doesn't mean "make the following mathematical statement false"; it's simply a characterization that the test writer is using to trip you up. You could think of it this way: the question could have been: "Let $n \propto (p, q)$ be *blue* if $\frac{nq}{p} < 1$. If $2 \propto (p, 6)$ is *blue*, what is one possible value of p?" The point is, we want $\frac{12}{p} < 1$ to be a true statement, which means we need any value for p that is either larger than 12 (because that would give us a fraction less than 1) or any negative number (because then the entire fraction becomes negative). Remember, 0 is not an option, because 0 cannot be the denominator of a fraction.

Creating Equations with Dingbats

Dingbat problems are made more challenging by setting 1 dingbat expression to equal another. It's just another way of adding more steps and possible confusion.

EXAMPLE 1: LEVEL 4

If $x \star y = x - 3y$ and $x \blacktriangle y = x + 6y$ for all real numbers x and y, and $3 \star 2b = 4b \blacktriangle 6$, what is the value of b?

This time we've got 2 different dingbat expressions to create and set equal to each other. Once we've done that, we'll be using algebra to get to the value of b. Let's start with the left side of the equation, $3 \star 2b$. We need to use the star expression for this side:

$$3 \star 2b \ \text{becomes} \ 3 - 3(2b)$$

Now let's do the triangle expression:

$$4b \blacktriangle 6 \ \text{becomes} \ 4b + 6(6)$$

Then we set what we've found equal to each other and solve for b:

$$3 - 3(2b) = 4b + 6(6)$$
$$3 - 6b = 4b + 36$$
$$-10b = 33$$
$$b = \frac{33}{-10} \ \text{or} \ -3.3$$

By the way, real numbers are every number— positive, negative, and zero; that doesn't include i, which is the symbol for the impossible "square root of −1." *Imaginary* numbers— represented by i—never appear on the SAT.

EXAMPLE 2: LEVEL 5

If βp represents the set of all multiples of p, which of the following includes the sets β3, β4, and β5?

(A) β12
(B) β18
(C) β40
(D) β50
(E) β60

There's nothing tricky going on here conceptually, but it is an example of the hardest of the dingbat problems: those that include the dingbat process in the answer choices. That means that you have to *solve the answer choice* in addition to doing the work in the problem. In this particular problem, it's not so difficult—those β's just represent sets of multiples; you can read them as "all the multiples of 12, all the multiples of 18, all the multiples of 40," and so on. Of all our answer choices, the only answer choice that contains each of the 3 smaller number sets (the multiples of 3, 4, and 5) is 60.

Word Problems

WHAT YOU NEED TO KNOW

The issue with word problems is not the level of math involved—it's usually algebra or simple geometry. Instead, the challenge is getting the right information out of the problem and organizing it correctly. Fortunately, the SAT does not include any extraneous information in word problems, so you can be sure you'll use every detail given.

Break up a word problem sentence by sentence; if those sentences are punctuated with commas that break up different phrases, break down each sentence phrase by phrase. Write down each element of information you are given—once it's written in note form on the page, you're much more likely to see where to go with the problem.

English to Math: Word Problems with No Scenario

Some word problems forgo a story or a scenario entirely and simply use algebraic terms or geometric measurements as the prompt for the work. Translating the English into algebra is the most challenging element of the problem. There are usually a few tricky elements thrown into these problem, so it is important to understand how to interpret them.

For example, the phrase *4 less than a number n* means $n - 4$. You'll also need to make sure you remember that *of* means *multiplication*, as does *their product*. Some problems incorporate several steps; it is most important to continually add parentheses to these problems to make sure your order of operations is consistent with the English.

HOW THEY ASK THE QUESTIONS

Translating English into Math

Sometimes you'll need to find the value of a particular number; other times they just want to make sure that you can get complex English translated into an equation effectively.

EXAMPLE 1: LEVEL 2

The sum of three times a number and 20 is 290. What is the number?

Remember, *sum* means addition. Here we're adding *three times a number* ($3n$) and *20*, and *is* means *equals*.

$$3n + 20 = 290 \leftarrow \text{once it's written out,}$$
$$\qquad\qquad\qquad \text{solving is easy}$$
$$3n = 270$$
$$n = 90$$

EXAMPLE 2: LEVEL 3

Twenty less than 5 times a number is 180. What is the number?

This example is more challenging for 2 reasons: the word *twenty* is spelled out, which means you're more likely to overlook it, and *less than a number* can be harder to understand.

Realize that *20 less than 5 times a number* means ($5n$) *minus* 20:

$$5n - 20 = 180$$
$$5n = 200$$
$$\boxed{n = 40}$$

> Whenever a word is spelled out on the test, write down the number in numerals on top of it.

EXAMPLE 3: LEVEL 3

Which of the following equations illustrates the following relationship: the product of z and 6 is equal to the sum of $5z$ and p?

Rather than give you options, I just want to make sure you can write out the work. First, *the product of z and 6*—*product* means *multiply*, so we can write this as $6z$. Next, *the sum of 5z and p*—*sum* means *addition*, so this is $5z + p$. These are evidently equal to each other, so we're left with $6z = 5z + p$.

Real-Life Applications

Word problems are all about understanding what the heck is going on when you're faced with real-life applications of arithmetic and algebra. Word problems, as opposed to curveball problems (which we'll cover next), ask you to solve for some value, like a measurement; they're far more concrete than what we'll tackle in the next lesson.

EXAMPLE 1: LEVEL 2

Lee eats x pieces of fresh asparagus on Monday, 5 times as many pieces of asparagus on Tuesday, and 5 more pieces of asparagus on Wednesday than she did on Monday. In terms of x, what is the average number pieces of asparagus she ate over 3 days?

(A) $\frac{7x + 5}{3}$

(B) $\frac{x + 5}{3}$

(C) $7x + 5$

(D) $7x + 3$

(E) $5x + 5$

This problem is all about keeping things organized and expressing information as related to a single piece of info. If on Monday, Lee ate x pieces and on Tuesday she ate 5 times as many, that means she ate $5x$ pieces on Tuesday. *Five more* pieces on Wednesday means she ate $x + 5$ pieces. To find the average, we just add up those 3 values and divide by 3:

$$\frac{x + 5x + (x + 5)}{3} \quad \leftarrow \text{combine like terms}$$

$$\frac{7x + 5}{3}$$

EXAMPLE 2: LEVEL 3

If Ron earns \$25 for each television (t) he sells at Television Barn on top of a weekly base salary s, which is \$400, which of the following expressions represents Ron's weekly pay?

(A) $25t + 400$

(B) $t + s$

(C) $400t + 25s$

(D) $25t + 400s$

(E) $25t + s$

No matter what happens, Ron earns a weekly base salary—that's s, not \$400 times s. Then he earns \$25 for *each* television he sells; that's $25t$. Add them together and we get E, $25t + s$.

EXAMPLE 3: LEVEL 4

Arthur and Bob are digging ditches with different-sized shovels. Each man removes 15 shovelfuls of dirt from a ditch. Next, Bob uses his shovel to completely refill each of the ditches; it takes him 27 shovelfuls to do so. What is the ratio of the size of Bob's shovel to Arthur's shovel?

It sounds so simple and yet—ugh! The first thing I do when I know I'm going to have to do a little figuring is to write the end goal at the bottom corner of the problem. If we're looking for the ratio of Bob's shovel to Arthur's shovel, we're looking for $\frac{b}{a}$ (using b to represent Bob's shovel and a to represent Arthur's). Sticking that down in the corner of the workspace can keep you on track.

Now for solving the problem: your best bet here is to draw something.

$$\boxed{15\ a} \ + \boxed{15\ b} \ = \ \boxed{27\ b}$$

My little picture here shows that Arthur's ditch of 15 shovels and Bob's ditch of 15 shovels are, combined, the same as 27 shovels of just Bob's shovel. Conveniently, that's also an equation we can work with: $15a + 15b = 27b$. I'm just going to solve what I have, using algebra to make it look like the goal I set in the beginning, $\frac{b}{a}$:

$$15a + 15b = 27b$$
$$15a = 12b \quad \leftarrow \text{divide by } a$$
$$15 = \frac{12b}{a} \quad \leftarrow \text{divide by } 12$$
$$\frac{15}{12} = \frac{b}{a}$$
$$\boxed{\frac{5}{4} = \frac{b}{a}}$$

Converting Measurements

A typical word problem will require conversion between gallons and quarts, feet and inches, or yards and feet. You'll always be given the conversion ratio, so the trickiness is in simply remembering to convert the stuff! There's no reason to give too many examples, as the problems consistently cover the same concepts.

EXAMPLE 1: LEVEL 3

How many square yards of Astroturf are needed to cover an outdoor play area that is 18 feet by 33 feet? (1 yard = 3 feet)

The first thing I'll always do is draw the area first:

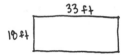

Whenever it's possible to
draw a picture of what's
going on in the problem,
do so.

It makes the most sense to me to divide up those lengths into yards before multiplying; it keeps the numbers smaller and, in fact, makes the problem simpler. We divide the number of feet by 3 to find the number of yards.

Now we find the area by multiplying length by width: $11 \times 6 = \boxed{66 \text{ yards}^2}$.

Curveball Problems

WHAT YOU NEED TO KNOW

If I had to choose the most universally annoying, frustrating, and irritating problem type on the SAT, curveball problems would have to win the prize. These problems, rather than using numbers and variables to ask for a specific value, use only variables and ask for an expression using those variables that represents what is going on in the problem (for example, how much Doug saves in a week or the price of a bunch of shirts or the cost of a single paper plate in a pack that's shipped in boxes of multipacks). They're frustrating and sometimes counterintuitive and, come to think of it, most like the algebra you may actually have to use in real life.

And therein lies the secret.

Your best shot at figuring out curveball problems is by using your real-life knowledge and developing the ability to analyze the math that you do reflexively in your head every day. What I mean is, you know you can figure out how much you're going to spend at the grocery store or the mall or on your lunch. You can figure out how long it's going to take you to save $500 if you're saving $10 a day. You know the price of a single pencil in a pack of 20. These are the skills that are used in curveball problems; you just need to keep them organized.

Now, if you're struggling to keep the variables organized, what you can do is assign values *that make sense* to all the variables and then do the math that you'd do in real life to find what the problem is directing you to. Once you find that value, like *1 balloon would cost $.07*, use the values you chose and test out each of the given answer choice expressions to find which yields $.07, the value that you found using your real-life numbers. The reason I emphasize "values that make sense" is that your numbers have to be related properly; some variables in problems will be related, in their definitions, to other variables in the problem. You have to make sure your chosen values represent those values.

The $n - 1$ Problems

EXAMPLE 1: LEVEL 3

A music supply shop wants to attract shoppers to its store. During a weekend sale, the store advertises that it will sell a certain microphone for s dollars. However, they limit this price to one per customer. Each additional microphone a customer buys is sold at the original price, $s + p$. Which expression represents the total cost of n microphones?

- (A) $s + s(n - 1)$
- (B) $(n - 1)(s + p)$
- (C) $n(s + p)$
- (D) $s + n(s + p)$
- (E) $s + (n - 1)(s + p)$

OK, let's talk about what's going on here. Let's say we're going to buy 5 microphones. We're going to buy 1 at the sale price and then we're going to buy 4 more at the original price (that's the total number minus 1). Now that we've mapped out what's going on with the problem conceptually, let's plug in values from the problem:

$$(1 \times \text{sale price}) + (4 \times \text{original price})$$
$$(1 \times s) + ((n-1) \times (s+p)) \leftarrow \text{simplify}$$
$$s + (n-1)(s+p)$$

So answer E is correct.

Now, pay attention: the most important part of this kind of problem, the element that shows up over and over again, is the $n - 1$. Sometimes the context is shopping: we pay the original price and then we buy $n - 1$ more of something at a lower price. Sometimes the context is the phone company: we pay 50 cents for the first minute and some other value for the $n - 1$ remaining minutes. No matter what the situation is, if you can piece together an equation that represents the total price, you can always rearrange that equation after the fact to solve for any of the variables in terms of the others.

Arranging Variables Twenty Ways to Tuesday

EXAMPLE 1: LEVEL 5

At a particular public high school, a total scholarship of s dollars is awarded to n students annually, provided those students go on to a public university. In 2006, three of the recipients decided to go on to private universities, thereby forfeiting their share of the scholarship award. The total dollars are then redistributed among the remaining scholarship winners. In terms of s and n, how much more money did each of the remaining awarded students receive?

Let's look at this in bits. First, let's look at how much the students were going to get in the first place. That would be the total scholarship money divided up among them: $\frac{s}{n}$.

Now that 3 students have dropped out, though, we're dividing the scholarship money up among the total minus the 3: $\frac{s}{n-3}$.

You should know which of those fractions represents more money: the fraction where we're splitting up the same amount of money among fewer people!

Imagine that before the students forfeited, everyone got $7,000; now, perhaps everyone gets $10,000. This problem is looking for how much *more* money everyone received; that would be the extra $3,000. Just like we get $3,000 from $10,000 minus $7,000, we're going to use those fractions to find an expression that represents the difference:

$$\frac{s}{n-3} - \frac{s}{n} \quad \leftarrow \text{bigger} - \text{smaller}$$

Find the common denominators and simplify:

$$\frac{sn}{n(n-3)} - \frac{s(n-3)}{n(n-3)}$$

$$\frac{sn-sn+3s}{n(n-3)}$$

$$\boxed{\frac{3s}{n(n-3)}}$$

You'll find that the denominators usually aren't distributed in these types of questions.

An Alternative Way to Solve Curveball Problems

In keeping with the idea that curveball problems are usually examples of real-life situations, some students find it useful to plug in a value for each variable in the problem and then use those numbers to solve for a real numerical value of "total cost" (or whatever the problem is looking for). Then they keep those values and work through the answer choices, looking for the answer with a value that matches their found value.

EXAMPLE 1: LEVEL 4
The price of a case of pencils is d dollars for p packages. If each package contains n pencils, what is the dollar cost of one pencil in terms of d, p, and n?

(A) $\dfrac{dn}{p}$

(B) dnp

(C) $\dfrac{d}{pn}$

(D) $\dfrac{1}{dnp}$

(E) $(dp)^n$

Let's just pop in numbers that make sense to us:

d: $ 100 dollars

p: 10 packages

n: 30 pencils

So if we're trying to find the price of a pencil, we have to break it down. A case is $100 for 10 packages. That means that each package costs $10. If there are 30 pencils in a pack, we just divide $10 by 30 to find the price of each pencil: $0.33.

I hope you're seeing the point that these problems are not so fundamentally hard; they just become really challenging in all the translation between math and English. Now then: let's check which answer choice equals 0.33 when we sub in our assigned value. This becomes a plug-and-play question. Let's look at how we worked through the answer choices:

> Avoid choosing 1 to pop in to a problem like this because it doesn't behave like other numbers when multiplied.

A) $\dfrac{dn}{p} = \dfrac{100 \cdot 30}{10} = \dfrac{3000}{10} = 300$

B) $dnp = 100 \cdot 30 \cdot 10 = \cancel{30000}$

C) $\dfrac{d}{pn} = \dfrac{100}{10 \cdot 30} = \dfrac{100}{300} = .33$

D) $\dfrac{1}{dnp} = \dfrac{1}{100 \cdot 30 \cdot 10} = \dfrac{1}{30000}$

E) $(dp)^n = (100 \cdot 10)^{30} = (1000)^{30}$

Only answer C will give us the 0.33 value.

Just as the details are most important in the Numbers and Operations section, using consistent problem-solving methods will help you conquer the algebra-based questions. Every time you are given an equation (or you can create an equation) take the time to write it down and solve it step-by-step. Never try to anticipate answers, which can be especially tempting with problems that seem straightforward. These questions demand discipline! Remember, the SAT isn't a test of your math prowess; it's a test of your ability to arrive at the correct answer.

geometry

Perhaps you're a student for whom learning Geometry was a lost cause. Maybe you struggled to remember the difference between complementary and supplementary angles and hid behind your book when it was time to construct proofs in class. Well, let me be the first to tell you that you can relax; SAT geometry never requires you to know terminology or complete a proof. Furthermore, most of the geometry you'll be responsible for fits into neat chunks of information. We'll start by talking about angle measurements in the most basic situations and work our way up to exploring how to solve the most outlandish scenarios you may encounter.

Basic Lines and Enclosed Forms

Before we get into more complicated stuff, let's review some line basics.

Angles on a Line

All of the angles on a line add up to 180°.

Granted, there aren't any angles to see in a drawing of a single line. Sometimes it's easier to see with another line thrown into the mix.

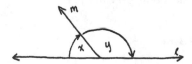

Here, you can probably imagine yourself getting out your protractor and measuring the number of degrees from line *l* up to line *m* (and getting *x*°) and then measuring from *m* back down to *l* (and getting *y*°). Your protractor will tell you that you've traveled 180°, and that's how we know that in this diagram, $x + y = 180°$, because, again, they are the sum of the angles on a line.

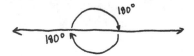

When we travel across the top of line *l* and then travel underneath it, we measure 180° twice. Basically, we've gone 360° and measured a circle.

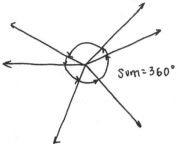

I don't necessarily have to have a straight line to measure "around," specifically. However, as I measure from angle to angle, I get the same circle as I did when I just measured across the top of the line and then across the bottom.

Another thing you need to know about simple line drawings is the concept of vertical angles. For starters, any time 2 lines intersect in a big X, the angles that lie directly opposite each other are equal. You'll find a pair on the top and bottom and a pair that lie left and right of each other. This is true for any intersecting lines, even if there are 5 or 6 lines that intersect to form a circle. Provided you know that they're complete lines, the opposite angles are always equal.

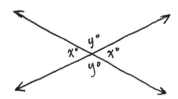

By the way, just like in these line drawings, $x + y = 180°$ because they are angles on a line. Again, $x + x + y + y = 360°$ because we're measuring a circle, just as we did when we only had a single line on the previous page.

Bisecting and Perpendicular Lines

You'll also need to know 2 terms: *bisect* and *perpendicular*.

Bisecting Lines

When a line *bisects* an angle, it splits that angle into 2 equal sections.

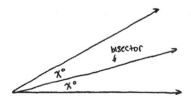

You can identify a bisected angle 2 ways: either the angles will already be labeled equal to each other or the word part of the problem will read "segment

LM bisects angle C" (or whatever variables the problem uses). If it's not spelled out for you, you may see something like "$\overline{LM}$ bisects $\angle$ C".

Perpendicular Lines

When 2 lines are *perpendicular* to each other, they intersect at a 90° angle to each other.

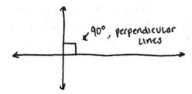

Again, you'll either be told that 1 segment is perpendicular to another or you'll see the following symbol: $\perp$ (that is, $\overline{LM} \perp \overline{XZ}$). The next section takes a closer look at perpendicular lines' cousins, parallel lines.

Parallel Lines

Parallel lines never intersect and are always the same distance apart from each other. The symbol for parallel lines is $\parallel$. Let's take a look at how to label the angles on a typical parallel line drawing.

Even if you remember terms like *alternate interior* from your geometry class, the SAT never tests students on the names of theorems or other rules—they just want to make sure you know how to implement them. Because the SAT doesn't require them, I proceed as though they don't exist. Instead, I just use vertical angles to label these things every time. That being said, let's look at my first step in labeling this drawing.

Say we start with the *x* on the left. We label the second angle *x* because it is vertical to the *x* that we were given.

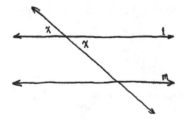

Next, let me show you something about the ways parallel line drawings "match." Basically, if we put a picture frame around our given *x* and its vertical angle and then slide it down to frame the intersection below it, we create matching pictures:

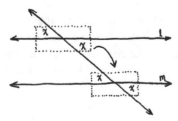

Because we create matching pictures, we can label the angles in a "matching" pattern. This matching happens with every pair of parallel lines. We're halfway there and so far we've used only 2 rules: (1) Vertical angles are equal to each other. (2) Parallel lines contain matching minipictures.

To label the other 4 angles in our drawing, let's remember that angles on a line add up to 180°. Sure, we could label the other angle *y* and put 4 of them into our drawing, but it's always a good idea to use the variables you already have rather than bring new things into the mix. This way, you keep all elements in relation to each other. When labeling the supplementary angles on any figure, it is always a better idea to call it "180 minus the first variable" rather than making up a new label.

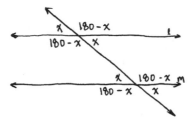

Just like that, the whole drawing has been labeled and we only had to use 1 more fact: (3) Angles on a line add up to 180°.

Transversal Line

In the parallel lines example we saw a transversal (a line that crosses 2 parallels) that was extended beyond those 2 parallel lines.

You'll see this in plenty of problems. Sometimes the transversal looks cut off and can be confusing, but rest assured that the angles inside can be labeled just as if the lines were extended. Sometimes I extend the ends of the line on the drawing in my test booklet so it looks like the figures we labeled above—just to make it easier.

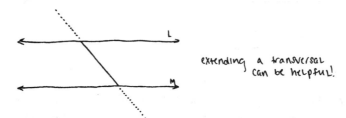

extending a transversal can be helpful!

Multiple Intersections

So far we've looked at plain line drawings and lines that are parallel to each other. Another style of SAT problem uses an arrangement of a bunch of lines that intersect in multiple places. It's just another labeling challenge, but these intersections often start to form closed figures, and the enclosures will always be the key to the problem.

To label this drawing, you don't need any more information than you used to label the parallels.

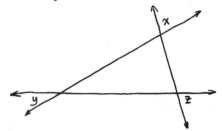

If you're given x, y, and z, you can label the rest of the drawing using vertical angles and the tip about defining supplementary angles as 180° minus the first angle $(180 - x)$.

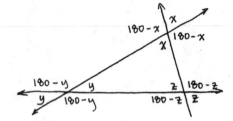

The other thing that's important about this drawing is that the lines create a triangle, so 9 times out of 10 the key to the answer will be in setting the sum of those angles to 180°. (For more info on that, check out the triangle section.) In this drawing, $x + y + z = 180°$.

Enclosed Forms

It may not look like it, but this next form is just a souped-up multiple intersection image.

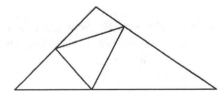

However, rather than having all those lines extending infinitely, this form is entirely enclosed. Rest assured that you'll be using triangles and polygons to get to your answer. It's pretty easy to find the 5 triangles in the drawing, so the test maker will challenge you and ask you something that demands finding and using the angles in a polygon within the figure.

If you can find the following quadrilaterals in the preceding figure, you're in good shape. Just remember to look for them when you see problems with drawings like this!

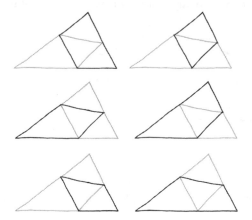

 HOW THEY ASK THE QUESTIONS

Line Questions

EXAMPLE 1: LEVEL 2

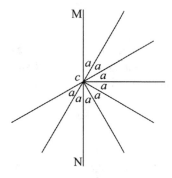

In the figure above, what is the value of c?

What's key in this problem is the segment labeled $\overline{\text{MN}}$. We're going to zero in particularly on that piece of info particularly (remember, the SAT never gives you any unnecessary info). To the right of line $\overline{\text{MN}}$ are 6 $\angle a$'s. Because these are "angles on a line," we know that those 6 a's add up to 180°.

$$6a = 180$$

$$a = 30$$

Now that we know that $a = 30°$, we can look to the left of line $\overline{\text{MN}}$ and see that 2 a's and 1 c add up to 180°. Well, if $a = 30°$, we can do quick algebra again:

$$2(30) + c = 180$$

$$60 + c = 180$$

$$c = \boxed{120°}$$

EXAMPLE 2: LEVEL 3

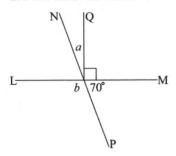

The figure above shows $\overline{LM}$ intersecting $\overline{NP}$ and perpendicular to the segment containing point Q. What is the value of $a + b$?

Well, let's start by labeling what we know: if the stuff on the right is perpendicular, the stuff on the left must be perpendicular. Also, because of the vertical angle rule, we know that angle opposite the 70° must also be 70°.

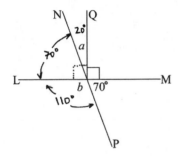

Super. The reason they didn't just label that 70° in the first place is because they wanted you to *figure it out*. (These problems are so straightforward that they need all the jazzing up they can get.) Let's figure out the value of a first: if it's part of the 90° angle and the rest of the angle is 70° . . . bingo, $a = 20°$. Now, you should also notice that b and that 70° on the bottom are *angles on a line*, so they must add up to 180°. Quick algebra: $b + 70° = 180°$ so $b = 110°$. If the question wants to know the value of $a + b$, we just add 'em up: $20° + 110° = \boxed{130°}$.

EXAMPLE 3: LEVEL 3

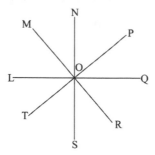

Note: figure not drawn to scale.

In the figure above, $\overline{LQ}, \overline{MR}, \overline{NS}$, and $\overline{PT}$ intersect at point O. If $\angle LOT$ and $\angle QOR$ are each equal to 40° and $\overline{NS}$ bisects $\angle MOP$, what is the value of $\angle MOS$?

Again, the first thing we do is label:

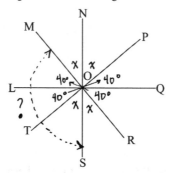

Once we've labeled, we can rely on all these intersecting lines to quickly lead us to our answer. Remember, what we're looking for is $\angle MOS$, so we'll have 2 40°s and 1 of the unknowns. If you want, you can label each of those unknown angles *x*. I'm going to focus on line LQ, knowing—again—that all the angles on a line add up to 180°. That means that

$$40 + x + x + 40 = 180$$
$$2x + 80 = 180$$
$$2x = 100$$
$$x = 50$$

Now then, if $\angle MOS$ is made up of 2 40°s and an *x*, then we know that

$$\angle MOS = 40 + 40 + 50 \rightarrow \boxed{\angle MOS = 130°}$$

EXAMPLE 4: LEVEL 3

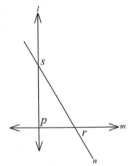

Note: figure not drawn to scale.

In the figure above, if $p = 70°$, what is the value of $s - r$?

The first thing you should notice here is that triangle in the middle—it's there for a reason. Right now the s, p, and r have nothing in common, but we can relate them by that triangle easily (all the angles inside a triangle add up to 180°). Let's label the interior angles of the triangle. Because I need my answers in terms of s and r, it makes the most sense to just use them:

> Be careful with problems like these: sometimes they're labeled right on the drawing, and sometimes values are given in the text of the problem. You *must* read!

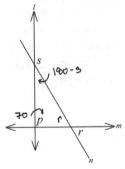

Because all those angles in there add up to 180°, I'm not going to overthink things; I'm just going to add 'em up and solve for $s - r$.

$$70 + (180 - s) + r = 180$$
$$70 + 180 - s + r = 180$$
$$250 - s + r = 180$$
$$-s + r = -70$$
$$-1(-s + r = -70)$$
$$s - r = \boxed{70}$$

EXAMPLE 5: LEVEL 4

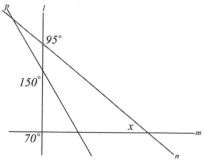

Note: figure not drawn to scale.

In the figure above, what is the value of x?

This enclosure problem was made more challenging by adding 1 more line that encloses 2 more spaces: an additional triangle and a 4-sided figure. Again, the entire thing can be labeled using vertical angle rules and those interior shapes—the triangle and the 4-sided polygon (anything enclosed that has 4 sides). All 4-sided figures' interior angles add up to 360°.

For more on 4-sided fig-

ures, check out page 268.

As usual, because we have to work toward the x, we may as well start labeling everything we can that will get us into that 4-sided figure. Just labeling vertical angles and angles on the line isn't going to cut it here, though. We need to find the values of the angles in the triangle so we can work over to the 4-sided figure. First I'll label the top angle in the triangle 30°, because it's on the same line as the 150°, and then I'll add the 30° and 70° to find the remaining 80° angle in the lower right, because there are 180° in a triangle.

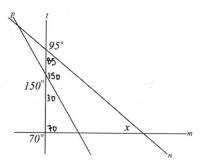
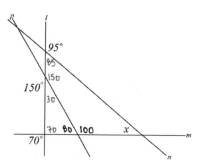

Once I've got that, I use the 80° and angles on a line rule to find that lower left angle in the 4-sided figure, 100°. Finally, because we've got a 4-sided figure in there, all those angles must add up to 360°.

$$85 + 150 + 100 + x = 360$$
$$335 + x = 360$$
$$x = \boxed{25°}$$

Using Parallel Lines to Find Other Information

EXAMPLE 1: LEVEL 2

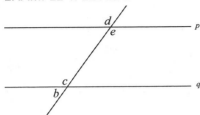

In the figure above $p \parallel q$ and $\angle b = 40°$. What is the value of $b + c + e$?

I'd like you to treat this like a no-brainer labeling problem. If we're given that 40°, we can label everything from there and add:

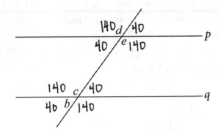

$$b + c + e = 40 + 140 + 140 = \boxed{320}$$

EXAMPLE 2: LEVEL 3

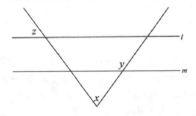

In the figure above, lines l and m are parallel. In terms of y and x, what is the value of angle z?

Again, it's the triangle in this problem that's the important element (because of the sum of its angles), so let's label the drawing so everything relates to the triangle. Once we've done that, we can sum all those values to 180° and solve for z:

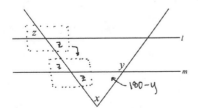

$$x + z + 180 - y = 180$$
$$z + x - y = 0$$
$$\boxed{z = y - x}$$

EXAMPLE 3: LEVEL 4

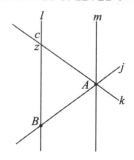

In the figure above, $l \parallel m$ and j bisects $\angle$MAK. If the value of angle z is between 112° and 129°, what is one possible value of $\angle$JAK?

First, let's zero in on line k. It's often really helpful when we have 2 transversals to completely ignore 1 of them as we begin labeling. Because our given info includes an our-choice value of z, I chose to focus first on line k because it's clearly related to z. Let's label all the angles that are the same size as z. We'll also label the angle inside $\angle$MAK as bisected, meaning we'll label angles $\angle$MAJ and $\angle$JAK as equal to each other and $\frac{1}{2}$ the value of z.

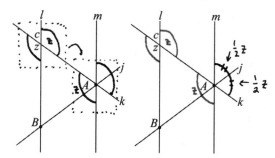

From here it's easy. As we get to choose any value of z between 112° and 129°, we may as well choose a value that divides easily in half. I'm going to go with 126°. We know that 1 of those smaller hashed angles has to be half the size of z, so we just divide 126° by 2 and, voilà! A possible value of z is 63°.

Enclosed Forms and Polygons

Although we've already seen some enclosed forms that included parallel lines, some problems use only enclosures.

EXAMPLE 1: LEVEL 5

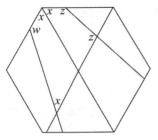

Note: *figure not drawn to scale.*

In the figure above, what is the value of *w* in terms of *x* and *z*?

Stop! Do not do this

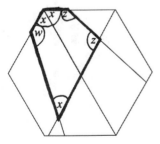
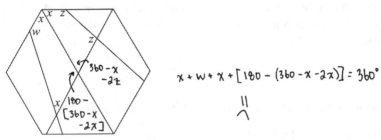

then add up all the angles in the left trapezoid. If you drop a single sign, your answer will be wrong, if you even get that far. Plus it's time-consuming and ugly. Instead, focus on *this* shape:

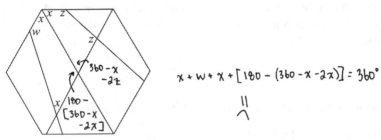

It's a 5-sided figure, which means its interior angles add up to 540°. As a short rule of thumb, the way I figure that out is that if all 4-sided figures have 360°, adding another side adds an additional 180° interior degrees. (There'll be more on that in later lessons.) Anyway, here we've got a 5-sided figure, and all of the angles are already labeled! Easy:

$$w + x + x + z + z + x = 540$$
$$w + 3x + 2z = 540$$
$$w = 540 - 3x + 2z$$

. . . and *that* would be among the hardest problems on the test.

Triangles

WHAT YOU NEED TO KNOW

I just want to remind you that this list of triangles is totally inclusive: the following info is All You Need to Solve Every Triangle Problem on the SAT. Sometimes using trigonometry works, but in all honesty, if you're using trig you're probably overlooking something really obvious. I'd avoid it.

Sum of Interior Angles

The measures of the 3 angles inside a triangle always add up to 180°. It doesn't matter if the triangle is short, fat, skinny, or spiky—the angles inside total 180°. Always.

Area

To find the area of a triangle, multiply $\frac{1}{2}$ times the base times the height.

$$Area = \frac{1}{2} \cdot base \cdot height$$

Depending on your triangle, the location of the base and the height can vary. For example, in a typical right triangle, the base and the height are exactly what they seem to be: the base is the bottom of the triangle and the height measures how tall the triangle is.

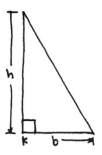

The base and the height of a triangle are always related to each other by a 90° angle.

In this triangle the 90° is built right into the shape. However, not all triangles have 90° angles built into them, and those 90°'s are critical to getting the height and base correct.

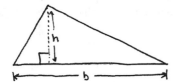

This triangle is shaped more like a mountain than anything else. You can imagine that if you were standing on top of a mountain like this and if you wanted to know how high above sea level you were, you would want to measure straight down through the mountain, not measure how long the hike was to get to the top. To find the height, you'll want to drop a line straight down from the top of the mountain (the vertex) to the base, creating the 90° angle. It's really important to understand that the height of the triangle is not the length of a side in this case.

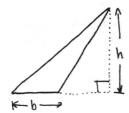

This triangle looks especially difficult, as you can't even measure "down through the middle of the mountain" to create your 90° angle. Nevertheless, if you were standing out on the tip of this thing and wanted to measure your height, you'd extend your measuring tape straight down from where you were standing. So to find the height of this triangle you'll need to go outside the shape. Don't worry. It's a totally legal move.

The bottom line is that for any triangle, the base and the height are both related to a 90° angle. If you don't have a 90° angle, make a 90° angle.

Perimeter and the Pythagorean Theorem

As it's likely that you have area and perimeter filed away in your head in relation to each other, let's talk about the perimeter of a triangle. Just like any other geometric figure, the perimeter of a triangle is just the sum of the lengths of all of its sides. Sometimes it's pretty easy to find; all the sides are labeled and you can just add 'em up. Usually you'll need to find side lengths, though, so here's how to find them when they're not given.

The most frequent solution for finding lengths of sides is to use the Pythagorean Theorem. You may recall learning the Pythagorean back in geometry—it usually feels like a big deal because it's generally the first time we learn something with a fancy name that appears to do complex things. Fortunately for us, it's not so fancy, not so complex, and we never need to identify its name.

Now, the Pythagorean only helps us find the lengths of the sides of right triangles—that is, triangles that include a right, or 90°, angle.

If you've got a right triangle, here's the rule: label the sides of the triangle (the ones that touch the 90° angle) *a* and *b*. Label the hypotenuse (the part of the triangle directly across from the 90° angle) *c*. Just so you know, *a* and *b* are totally interchangeable—the only thing that matters is that *c* is always the hypotenuse.

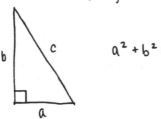

The Pythagorean Theorem

$$a^2 + b^2 = c^2$$

Once you've labeled, pop the lengths into the formula $a^2 + b^2 = c^2$. You can solve for any of the sides with it. Make sure, though, that you square *a* and *b* separately and *then* add them—remember PEMDAS?—otherwise you'll get an incorrect answer.

There are several other ways to find the lengths of the sides of a triangle without using the Pythagorean. First let's cover the different triangles we may come across; then we'll get into how to mine them for info.

Types of Triangles

There are 2 types of triangles that are really important to know: isosceles and equilateral.

Isosceles

An *isosceles* triangle has 2 sides of equal length and 2 angles of equal measure adjacent to those sides. There are no rules about how long the sides must be or what the angles are. Occasionally a problem will use the term *isosceles*; more often, you'll be shown 2 angles labeled with the same variable in the figure or be told, for example, that $\overline{AB} = \overline{BC}$. Either way, stop reading the question and get in there and label the triangle isosceles with both hatch marks on the sides and little arcs on the angles.

Equilateral

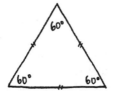

The term *equilateral triangle* has the word *equal* buried in it, so it's pretty simple to figure out what it is: all of the sides are equal to each other, and all of the angles are each 60° (180° divided by 3). The moment you are told a triangle is equilateral, stop what you're doing, label the lengths of the sides, and write 60° in each of its angles.

Terms: Congruent and Similar

When triangles (or any figure for that matter) are *congruent,* all of the sides and the angles are equal to each other. They're identical figures, as though they'd been punched with a cookie cutter.

Similar triangles are triangles that have the same degrees in each angle, so they're the same shape, so to speak, but the lengths of the sides are different. Similar triangles are directly proportional to each other, meaning each side of the smaller triangle has been multiplied by the same number to create the new, bigger, corresponding sides.

Special Triangles

There are 3 "special" triangles you need to know: the 30-60-90, the 45-45-90, and the 3-4-5.

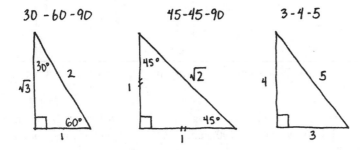

These triangles are special because they always maintain a proportional relationship between their angles and the lengths of their sides. Any 30-60-90 triangle will always be similar to every other 30-60-90, and you will have memorized the relationships between the lengths of the sides.

Memorize these special triangles and be able to label the drawings. We'll use them in sample problems later.

Exterior Angle Theorem

Last thing—the exterior angle theorem. This is optional to learn, as you can solve all the problems on the SAT without knowing it. Nevertheless, if you do know it, it'll save you a ton of time and make things simple. I always want to save you time when I can; that buys you time to wrestle with problems that are more challenging for you.

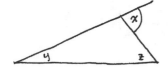

The Exterior Angle Theorem

$$x = y + z$$

Say you've got a triangle with a side extended out beyond the triangle itself (in tutoring sessions this side is commonly referred to as the *stickie-outie side*). Conveniently, the measure of the angle between that extended side and the triangle itself is equal to the sum of the angles opposite it inside the triangle. This is a great shortcut—learn it.

HOW THEY ASK THE QUESTIONS

Questions All About Degrees

These questions just test to see if you know that triangles have 180 interior degrees—very plain and simple.

EXAMPLE 1: LEVEL 2

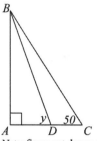

Note: figure not drawn to scale.

In the figure above, $\overline{BD}$ bisects angle b and angle $c = 50°$. What is the value of y?

What we have here are 2 embedded right triangles: $\triangle ABC$ and $\triangle ABD$. Let's look at $\triangle ABC$ first. We've got $\angle A$ (90°) and $\angle C$ (50°), which means angle $\angle B$ must equal 40°.

$$90 + 50 + b = 180 \rightarrow 140 + b = 180 \rightarrow \boxed{b = 40}$$

We know that segment $\overline{BD}$ bisects $\angle B$; that means the angles on either side of the bisector must be half of that 40°, so they're 20° each.

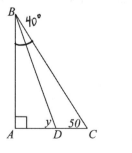
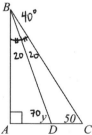

Now we can solve for y:

$$90 + 20 + y = 180 \rightarrow 110 + y = 180 \rightarrow \boxed{y = 70}$$

Understanding the Use of the Area Formula

EXAMPLE 1: LEVEL 4

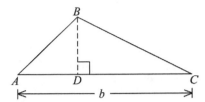

In the figure above, $\overline{BD}$ is $\frac{4}{9}$ of b. What is the area of $\triangle ABC$ in terms of b?

Let's start by simply remembering that the formula for the area of a triangle is $A = \frac{1}{2}bh$. We've got a base b here; no problem. The first thing we need to do, then, is label the height of the triangle in terms of b, as that's all the info we've been given. If the height is $\frac{4}{9}$ of b, we label the height $\frac{4}{9}b$, or $\frac{4b}{9}$, like so:

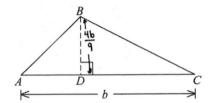

We'll be calling the height $\frac{4b}{9}$, so we now we just pop it into our original area equation. Be sure to notice that I've put that b on top of the fraction. I know this came up a lot in the fraction section, but I cannot overemphasize how important it is to place your numerators and denominators very specifically and to write your fractions vertically, not like this: $4b/9$.

Let's get back to simplifying our area formula with its new values:

$$A = \frac{1}{2} \cdot \frac{b}{1} \cdot \frac{4b}{9}$$

$$A = \frac{4b^2}{18} \quad \leftarrow \text{simplify} \rightarrow \quad \boxed{\frac{2b^2}{9}}$$

EXAMPLE 2: LEVEL 5

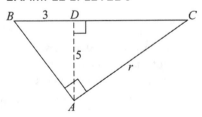

In the figure above, if the length of $\overline{BD}$ is 3 and if the area of $\triangle ABC$ is $\frac{5\sqrt{34}}{2}$, what is the value of r?

The way to start here is to figure out what you're going to need to find the components of the area formula for $\triangle ABC$. You need a base measurement and a height measurement. Base and height are always related by a 90° angle, so I say we assign $\overline{AB}$ as the height and r as the base.

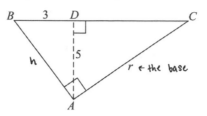

This is all very well and good, except that we don't have a value for either h or r. That's why the 3 and the 5 are in the problem: $\overline{AB}$ happens to be the hypotenuse of the right triangle that they form.

We're going to start by using the Pythagorean Theorem to find the length of $\overline{AB}$, or h, and we'll go from there:

$$3^2 + 5^2 = h^2$$
$$9 + 25 = h^2$$
$$34 = h^2$$
$$\sqrt{34} = h$$

This is a good sign, as what we've found is part of the given information. We're clearly on the right track. *However*, knowing you're on the right track is not an excuse to jump to conclusions and say: "Oh well, it's obviously answer D." Students do this all the time, and I'm telling you, you're going to guess incorrectly. Take the time to finish the problem.

Now then, we can use the height of the triangle we just found in our area formula to find the length of segment r. (Keep it organized!)

$$A = \frac{1}{2} \cdot b \cdot h \;\rightarrow\; \frac{5\sqrt{34}}{2} = \frac{1}{2} \cdot \frac{b}{1} \cdot \frac{\sqrt{34}}{1}$$
$$\frac{5\sqrt{34}}{2} = \frac{b\sqrt{34}}{2}$$
$$\boxed{5 = b}$$

> This type of problem, in which the area is given and the lengths of the sides must be found, is a classically difficult area problem. Whenever you see triangle drawings like this that include multiple 90° angles, consider rotating the test booklet. It can help you see the problem entirely differently.

Pythagorean Theorem Problems

We've already used the Pythagorean Theorem in 1 of the area questions; they often go hand in hand. There's not a whole lot that can be done to make the Pythagorean Theorem more difficult, so count on these problems to usually include a good dose of tedium. If you're careful, you'll get the point—no problem.

EXAMPLE 1: LEVEL 1

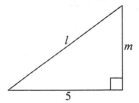

In the figure above, $m = 3$. What is the value of of l?

Just because 3 and 5 are lengths of the sides of this triangle, you can't just assume that the other side length is 4 because of the 3-4-5 special triangle. That's what they're after in this problem: the knee-jerk reaction. You can only rely on the 3-4-5 rule when 5 is the length of the hypotenuse. In this case, it's not. We'll have to quickly do the Pythagorean, assigning 3 for the value of m.

$$3^2 + 5^2 = l^2$$
$$9 + 25 = l^2$$
$$34 = l^2$$
$$\sqrt{34} = l$$

EXAMPLE 2: LEVEL 3

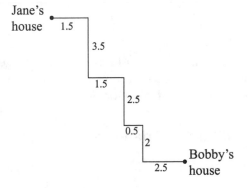

Note: *figure not drawn to scale.*

Some trickier problems involving the Pythagorean Theorem will include binomials (like $x - 8$ or $b + 2$) as the sides or hypotenuse of the triangle. Don't sweat this; it's obviously included just to mess you up. Just remember that if your problem says something like, $(b^2 + 2)^2 + 6^2 = 10^2$ the next step will look like this: $b^2 + 2b + 2b + 4 + 6^2 = 10^2$, because you've squared the binomial. It's messy, but completely doable.

Sara and Annie are walking from their friend Bobby's house over to Jane's house. Because of the layout of their neighborhood they must walk due north and due west repeatedly; their distance (in city blocks) is as shown. How much longer is Sara and Annie's real trip than the direct route to Jane's house?

Why don't we first calculate how many blocks they walk if they walk if they walk the route shown?

$$1.5 + 3.5 + 1.5 + 2.5 + .5 + 2 + 2.5 = 14 \text{ blocks}$$

Now we need to find the length of the direct route. Naturally, the first thing we should do is draw in the direct route we're looking for. Remember: On the SAT, any diagonal line is, in and of itself, a hypotenuse of a triangle. Well, if that's the rule, then this straight line showing the direct route must be the hypotenuse—and it is.

We're going to add up the short distances that Sara and Annie walk north and the short distances they walk west and call those total distances, 6 and 8, the lengths of the sides of our new big triangle:

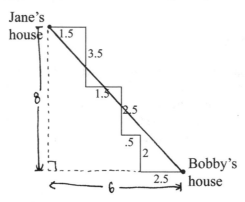

Then we use the Pythagorean to solve for the distance of the direct route:

$$6^2 + 8^2 = d^2$$

$$36 + 64 = d^2$$

$$100 = d^2$$

$$10 = d$$

There's just 1 more thing, though! The question asks us how much longer the real trip is than the direct trip, so we have to subtract: $14 - 10 = 4$ blocks. It's that last step that increases the difficulty level of this question.

Isosceles, Equilateral, and Similar Triangles

EXAMPLE 1: LEVEL 3

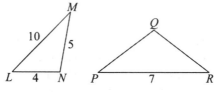

Note: figure not drawn to scale

In the figures above, $\overline{PQ} = \overline{RQ}$. If the perimeter of $\triangle LMN$ is equal to the perimeter of $\triangle PQR$, what is the length of $\overline{PQ}$?

Before you do anything, I always want you to mark any geometric drawings with the information that you're given—in this case, that $\overline{PQ}$ and $\overline{RQ}$ are equal. And, for the sake of consistency, even though angle measurements do not come into play in this problem, I want you to mark the angles that are equal to each other as well.

As the perimeters here are equal, let's find out the perimeter of △LMN: $10 + 5 + 4 = 19$. We know that the bottom side of △PQR is equal to 7 and its perimeter must also equal 19; that leaves 12 to split between $\overline{PQ}$ and $\overline{RQ}$. So $\overline{PQ}$ must equal 6.

EXAMPLE 2: LEVEL 3

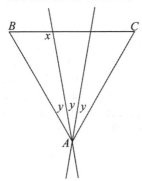

Triangle ABC is an equilateral triangle; what is the value of *x*?

In the right margin:

> In multistep problems, if you don't remember to *answer the question*, you'll likely be wrong. Always make sure the number you've arrived at is the answer to the question!

As always, as soon as a triangle is delineated as equilateral, we label angles before doing anything else. Let's also focus in on those *y*'s: if there are 3 of them and they add up to 60°, how much is each of them worth? Right: 20°. Let's label that too:

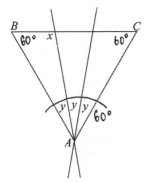 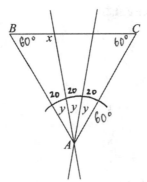

Now we can look at the far-left interior triangle. If its bottom angle is 20° and its top left angle is 60°, we can easily solve for the value of *x*:

$$20 + 60 + x = 180 \rightarrow 80 + x = 180 \rightarrow \boxed{x = 100}$$

In the right margin:

> Any time you're given an equilateral triangle, you must *always* mark *all* of the 3 side lengths and angles as equal to each other.

EXAMPLE 3: LEVEL 3

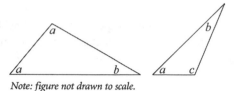

Note: figure not drawn to scale.

If $a = 60°$, what is the value of c?

First things first. I know we've seen this several times already, but this is a reminder: the words *figure not drawn to scale* means *ignore how this drawing looks and use math to solve this problem*. Obviously, I'm saying that now because things in this problem are not as they seem. Let's start labeling. Once you've labeled the a's, you should see those 60's are screaming something at us: equilateral triangle! If we've got 2 60°s, the third angle (b) *must* equal 60°. I'm going to label $\angle b$ 60° in this drawing and, more important, in the drawing on the right.

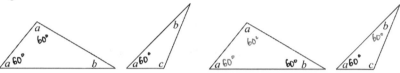

Again, if I know that 2 angles in the triangle on the right are equal to 60°, the third angle, c, must equal 60° as well. So $c = \boxed{60°}$.

EXAMPLE 4: LEVEL 3

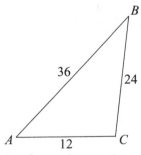

Note: figure not drawn to scale.

If $\triangle LMN$, not shown, is similar to $\triangle ABC$, and $\triangle LMN$'s perimeter is an integer and does not exceed $\triangle ABC$'s, what is one possible value of the perimeter of $\triangle LMN$?

In the grid-in section, it's likely you'll come across questions that have multiple correct answers. Regarding the triangle we're looking at here, we're going to treat the 36, 24, and 12 sort of like we'd treat numbers for which we needed a common denominator. However, rather than finding their least common multiple, we're interested in finding *any* common divisor. You'll notice (I hope) that in this problem there are a few possible common divisors: we can use 2, 3, 4, 6, or 12.

I'm going to choose 3, just for the heck of it. All we do is divide each of the sides by 3 and total up the result:

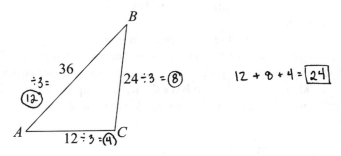

EXAMPLE 5: LEVEL 4

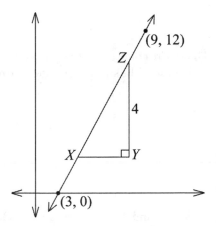

Note: *figure not drawn to scale.*

In the figure above, $\overline{YZ}$ = 4. What is the perimeter of △XYZ?

It appears that what we have here is a triangle not totally floating in space, but attached to a line. The only thing we know about the triangle's location is that it's somewhere between (3, 0) and (9, 12). What it may be difficult to see, though, is that △XYZ is similar to a triangle that's not shown—this triangle:

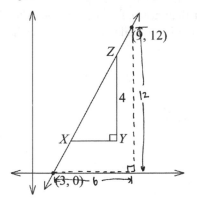

We can use the points we've been given to label the lengths of the sides and then set the bigger triangle similar to it. For starters, how far do we travel along the x-axis to get from $(3, 0)$ to $(9, 12)$? It's 6 units. How far do we travel in the y direction? From 0 to 12: 12 units.

At this point I'm not going to do the Pythagorean to find the length of the hypotenuse of the big triangle; I'd rather just focus on finding the length of $\overline{XY}$. I'm going to do that by setting up a proportion that relates the 2 longer sides to the 2 shorter sides. My math says that we *know* the relationship is 6 to 12, so a similar relationship would be *a to* 4. OK, so we quickly cross-multiply and find the value of *a*:

$$\text{big } \Delta \searrow \quad \frac{6}{12} = \frac{a}{4} \quad \leftarrow \text{xyz } \Delta$$

$$24 = 12a$$

$$2 = a$$

Now we know that $\overline{XY}$ is 2 units long. Then we're going to use the Pythagorean to find the length of $\overline{XZ}$, which is the hypotenuse of the smaller triangle! (We're almost finished. . . .)

$$2^2 + 4^2 = c^2$$

$$4 + 16 = c^2$$

$$20 = c^2$$

$$\sqrt{20} = c \quad \leftarrow \text{simplify} \rightarrow \quad c = 2\sqrt{5}$$

Now we know the lengths of all 3 sides: 2, 4, and $2\sqrt{5}$, so we can just add 'em up to get the perimeter.

$$2 + 4 + 2\sqrt{5} = \boxed{6 + 2\sqrt{5}}$$

Enough steps for you?

Using Special Triangles

These problems are either much shorter than normal triangle problems or, in some cases, can only be solved if you recognize special triangles and use them.

EXAMPLE 1: LEVEL 4

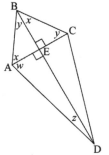

Note: figure not drawn to scale.

In the figure above, $x = y$, $\overline{EC}$ is length 1, and $\overline{AD}$ is length 2. What is the value of z?

We have to label. But I'm going to kill 2 birds with 1 stone: because I know that $x = y$, I know that these are 45-45-90 triangles, which means I also know the lengths of several segments right off the bat.

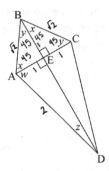

Because we're looking for the value of z, we should focus on △AED, the lower-left triangle. If you were unsure of your special triangles (which by the time you take the test, you shouldn't be), you could use the Pythagorean Theorem to find the length of $\overline{ED}$. However, because we *know* special triangles, we can be sure we've got a 30-60-90 triangle. Just remember that the 30° angle is always opposite the shortest side, the 1:

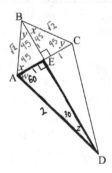

The answer sort of falls into our laps: $z = 30°$.

EXAMPLE 2: LEVEL 4

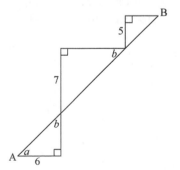

Note: figure not drawn to scale.

To get from town A to town B one can either hike or take a helicopter. If Chris chooses to walk, he must walk along a 5-sided north and west route. If Chris flies, he can travel directly along path $\overline{AB}$. If $a = b$, what expression represents the distance saved if Chris takes a helicopter?

First, let's not forget what we're looking for here: longer trip minus shorter trip. Now we need to label our drawing. I'm going to fill in 3 things here: angles, side lengths, and hypotenuse lengths. This is super easy to do because when you're dealing with the sides of a 45-45-90 triangle, you can simply multiply the length of the side by $\sqrt{2}$ to find the length of the hypotenuse. Because of that key ingredient, $a = b$, we know we're dealing with 45-45-90 triangles across the board:

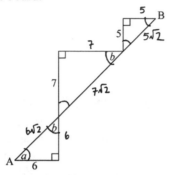

Let's use what we've found to add up the distances of the 2 trips. First, we can just add the lengths of the sides of the triangles together to find the longer trip: $6 + 6 + 7 + 7 + 5 + 5 = 36$. Now we can add those 3 hypotenuses: $6\sqrt{2} + 7\sqrt{2} + 5\sqrt{2} = 18\sqrt{2}$.

If you're confused about that, you can say that problem to yourself as "6 root-twos plus 7 root-twos plus 5 root-twos equals 18 root-twos." You can treat those roots-twos just like you'd treat an x—but only because they are identical. The same would not work if all the roots did not match.

At any rate, now that we've found the length of the 2 trips, we subtract the shorter from the longer to find the distance saved: $\boxed{36 - 18\sqrt{2}}$.

Understanding the Exterior Angle Theorem

Again, you don't need to know the exterior angle theorem, but if you do familiarize yourself with it, it'll likely save you some time on a more complex problem. The more time you save, the more you have to spend on problems that are stumping you.

EXAMPLE 1: LEVEL 3

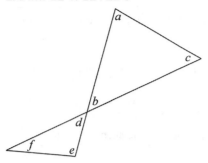

Note: figure not drawn to scale.

Which of the following is equal to the value of $a + c$?

(A) $b + d$
(B) $d + e$
(C) $b + c$
(D) $180 - f$
(E) $180 - d$

There is no sensible way of solving this problem other than labeling the angles where these 2 triangles meet. Let's look at the exterior angles as they relate to a and c. We're going to ignore the bottom triangle and look at the drawing this way:

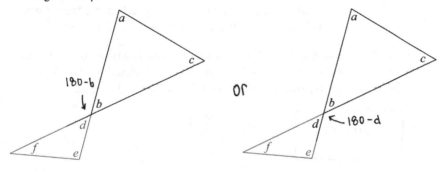

Now, the exterior angle theorem tells us that the angle between that extended side and the outside of the triangle is *equal to the sum of the 2 opposite interior angles*. In this case, that means that $180 - b = a + c$ and $180 - d = a + c$. So choice E, $180 - d$, is correct.

Squares and Rectangles

WHAT YOU NEED TO KNOW

Our basic 4-sided figure is a rectangle. All rectangles have 4 sides that meet at 4 vertexes. (A *vertex* is always the point where 2 lines, as in this case, or line segments meet.) Every angle in a rectangle is a right angle; they are all 90°.

Basic Rectangle Facts

The sum of the angles in a rectangle is 360°. In fact, in every 4-sided figure, the angles always total 360°.

○ *Area*: The *area* of a rectangle is found by multiplying its length by its width.

$A = l \times w$

○ *Perimeter*: The *perimeter* of a rectangle is the sum of the lengths of its sides.

$P = 2l + 2w$

"A square is a rectangle, but a rectangle is not always a square." This catchy grade school phrase couldn't be more true—or helpful. All rectangle formulas are true for squares as well. However, it will help if you change your formulas just a bit for squares. Rather than $A = l \times w$, use $A = s^2$. As the length and width are equal in a square, you're likely to get to the answer more quickly if you assign the same variable to both sides.

HOW THEY ASK THE QUESTIONS

Calculating Perimeter and Area

EXAMPLE 1: LEVEL 2
The area of the Walkers' rectangular back yard is 168 square feet. If one end of the yard is 7 feet long, what is the perimeter of the yard?

Even for simple questions, I think it makes sense to make a quick sketch of what you've been given. The likelihood of getting confused on the SAT is high just because it's a stressful situation, so be disciplined and careful.

Area = 168

Now, because area equals length times width, we can solve for the length of the rectangle by plugging in and dividing, then label all 4 sides of the rectangle:

$A = L \cdot W$
$168 = L \cdot 7$
$24 = L$

24
7 | Area = 168 | 7
24

Now we can add to find the perimeter:

$7 + 7 + 24 + 24 = \boxed{62 \text{ feet}}$

EXAMPLE 2: LEVEL 2

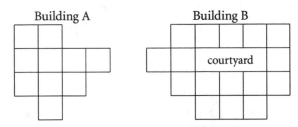

Building A   Building B

courtyard

Each of the smallest rectangles in the figure above represents 1 motel room, each of equal square footage. If the total square footage in Building A is 1,450 square feet, what is the total square footage of Building B, not including the courtyard?

This is all about working with units; we first need to find the size of 1 room (which we'll do using the info about Building A). If Building A's total number of square feet is 1,450, we have to divide that 1,450 by the number of rooms within the building. Count carefully!

1450 ÷ 10 = 145

Each room is 145 square feet. Now we need to count up the number of rooms in Building B: 16. Multiply 145 by 16 and you've got your answer:

145 × 16 = 2,320 ft²

EXAMPLE 3: LEVEL 3

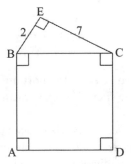

Note: *figure not drawn to scale.*

In the figure above, what is the area of the square ABCD?

There's not much to this problem; there's just a dicey element that sometimes causes panic among students who are a little less geometry-savvy. It's no big deal. Let's look.

First, we need to find the length of 1 of the sides of the square so that we can find its area. I imagine you already know that we need to use the Pythagorean Theorem to find the length of the hypotenuse of the top-right triangle, which also happens to be a side of the square. Let's go ahead and do that:

Another typical problem
will bury a square entirely
within another, like this:

The problem will ask
about lengths of triangle
sides, areas of triangles,
or the area of either of the
squares. The bottom line is
this: because both figures
are squares, all of the
triangles within the figure
must be congruent.

$$2^2 + 7^2 = c^2$$
$$4 + 49 = c^2$$
$$53 = c^2$$
$$\sqrt{53} = c$$

So the top side of the square is $\sqrt{53}$. Well, we find the area of the square using the formula Area $= s^2$. We just pop that $\sqrt{53}$ right in there: Area $= \sqrt{53}^2$ so the area of square ABCD is 53.

I think there is general confusion with this because it seems so easy. Also, because some students use length times width to find the area of a square, they write $\sqrt{53} \times \sqrt{53}$ and stumble a bit. Just remember that $\sqrt{53} \times \sqrt{53}$ and $\sqrt{53}^2$ are the same thing, and they both simplify to 53.

EXAMPLE 4: LEVEL 5

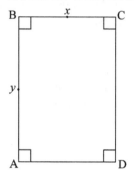

Note: figure not drawn to scale.

The owner of property ABCD has decided to sell one of the corners of his land, △YBX, where x and y are the midpoints of $\overline{AB}$ and $\overline{BC}$, respectively. If the area of polygon AYXCD is $\frac{5}{7}$ of a mile, what is the area of △YBX?

First of all, $\frac{2}{7}$ is *NOT* the correct answer; the given $\frac{5}{7}$ is *not* the portion of the rectangle we have, it's the measurement of its area. They give you a fraction like that to confuse you. Don't get sucked in.

Now, what we need to do is figure out how much of the rectangle is taken up by the polygon; in other words, what fraction of that rectangle is the polygon? To do this reliably (and not in your head), you'll want to divide the rectangle up into equal-sized triangles. Draw right on it:

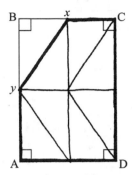

I split the rectangle up into 8 smaller triangles, purposely making them the same size as $\triangle$ YBX. So now we know 2 things: the *area* of AYXCD is $\frac{5}{7}$, and it takes up $\frac{7}{8}$ of the whole rectangle. To find the whole area (let's call it *w*), we write out what we know in math:

$$\frac{5}{7} = \frac{7}{8} \cdot w \quad \leftarrow \text{"five sevenths is seven eighths of w"}$$

Now solve for the area, *w*.

$$\frac{5}{7} = \frac{7w}{8}$$

$$40 = 49w$$

$$\frac{40}{49} = w$$

Ignore the weird fractions; they're there only to stress you out. Now we want to find $\frac{1}{8}$ of our total area. Don't think about it; do it.

$$\frac{1}{8} \cdot \frac{40}{49} = \text{area of } \triangle YBX$$

$$\frac{1}{1} \cdot \frac{5}{49} \quad \leftarrow \text{I cancelled the 8 and 40}$$

$$\boxed{\frac{5}{49} = \text{area of } \triangle YBX}$$

Circles

WHAT YOU NEED TO KNOW

Basic Circle Facts

Well, obviously, the big difference with circles is that they're round. (OK, that's dumb.) However, because circles have neither sides nor vertices, everything *is* a bit different with them.

First, here are some measurements in the circle:

○ *Radius:* The distance from the center of the circle out to its edge—it's the line that looks like the hand of a clock.

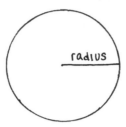

○ *Diameter:* the *diameter* is the distance from 1 edge of the circle through the center to the other edge of the circle.

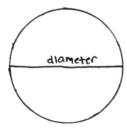

○ *Degrees:* Now, you've probably heard that circles have 360°. When I ask a student, "So, where are all those degrees in my drawing?" more often than not I'm met with a blank stare or an, "Um, in there somewhere?" The degrees in a circle are found at the center of the figure; they are seen most easily in reference to a radius. If you sweep a radius around the circle like the hand of a clock, the radius will sweep a full 360° from its starting place.

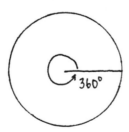

○ *Circumference:* The circumference of the circle is like the perimeter, only it's just 1 line, not a bunch of stuff added together. Basically, if you made a circle out of string, clipped it, and straightened it out to measure its length, you'd have the circumference. The formula for circumference is $C = 2\pi r$.

○ *Area:* The area of a circle is found using the formula $A = \pi r^2$. These 2 formulas look very much alike, so don't get them confused.

The Circle Formulas

Circumference = $2\pi r$ Area = πr^2

where r is the radius.

○ *Tangent lines:* As you may recall, *tangent lines* are lines that intersect a circle at a single spot—they nudge up to the edge of the circle. In addition, tangent lines are always at a right angle to the radius of the circle they touch.

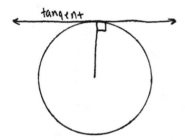

HOW THEY ASK THE QUESTIONS

Degrees

The key to solving these problems is to have an understanding of degrees and how circles are divided up.

EXAMPLE 1: LEVEL 3
When monster truck tires are discarded, they are sliced into wedges from the center of the tire to the edge. If each wedge is 20° and weighs 47 pounds, what is the total weight of a tire?

Let's draw this so we can see what we're doing:

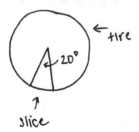

To figure out how much the whole tire weighs, we need to know how may slices can be cut from each tire. That's where the degrees come in. Granted, you can simply divide the 360° into 20° slices, but I'd like to consistently solve problems like this in ratio format. It will save you time and steps almost 100 percent of the time.

Because there are only so many ways to see if you know about the degrees in a circle, wedge-cutting problems come up pretty frequently. Sometimes you'll be given the total weight and will need to divide it up to find the number of degrees; sometimes you'll be given a range of acceptable weights per slice and you'll need to find degrees. Remember, you can only have a whole slice of something! These questions should never have an answer like "there are $16\frac{1}{5}$ slices;" either something is a slice or it's not.

Here's how you set it up:

$$\text{part} \rightarrow \frac{20°}{360°} = \frac{47 \leftarrow \text{part}}{x} \leftarrow \text{whole (total weight)}$$
$$\text{whole} \nearrow$$

Then we cross-multiply and solve for the total weight of the tire:

$$20x = 16920$$
$$x = 846 \text{ pounds}$$

EXAMPLE 2: LEVEL 4

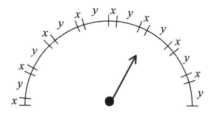

On the semi-circular speedometer above, each value of x is $\frac{1}{3}$ the size of y. What is the degree measurement of one segment of y?

OK, we've got a speedometer that's split up into segments of length x and length y. At this point we know only the relationship of their sizes compared to each other: y is 3 times the size of x. It's most important that we find a way to "measure" the semicircle as it is now. One way of doing that is to assign a measurement: we could think of it as x being 1 unit and y being 3 units and then find out how many units we have in total by counting up the segments.

According to my drawing, I have 8 of each: 8 1-unit x's and 8 3-unit y's.

$$(8 \times 1) + (8 \times 3) \rightarrow 8 + 24 = \underline{32 \text{ units total}}$$

Now we have something we can work with: we're going to find the degree value of a single unit by using a proportion:

$$\frac{1}{32} = \frac{x}{180}$$
$$180 = 32x$$
$$\frac{180}{32} = x \rightarrow \text{reduce} \quad \frac{45}{8} = x$$

So each x unit is $\frac{45}{8}$ degrees. The question asks us about y, which is $3x$ units, so we simply multiply $\frac{45}{8} \times 3 = \boxed{\frac{135}{8}}$.

EXAMPLE 3: LEVEL 4

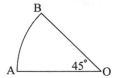

The area of the pie wedge above is 18π. What is the length of arc AB?

Here's a quick intro: an excellent way to make circle problems more labor intensive (and therefore "harder") is to introduce the relationship between area and circumference. Let's quickly compare their formulas: $A = \pi r^2$ and $C = 2\pi r$. It should be easy to see that if you have the radius of a circle you can quickly calculate either the circumference or the area. These problems tie up that radius by giving you the area of the entire circle, the circumference of the entire circle, or, worse, a portion of the circumference or area. That's exactly what's happened here.

We've got the area of the wedge, but we need the area of the whole circle to get to that radius (which will lead us over to the circumference and back to the arc).

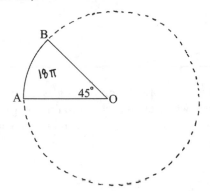

To find the area of the entire circle, we're going to set up, again, a proportion:

$$\frac{45}{360} = \frac{18\pi}{A}$$

$$45A = 6480\pi$$

$$A = 144\pi$$

OK! So the area is 144π. Notice how I left the π sign in the problem? That's because 99.9 percent of the time, answer choices retain the pi sign rather than asking you to multiply by 3.14. I'm going to carry that pi sign through the whole time, even if it ends up in my final answer.

Let's solve for the radius now using the area formula:

$$A = \pi r^2$$
$$144\pi = \pi r^2 \quad \leftarrow \pi\text{'s cancel}$$
$$144 = r^2$$
$$12 = r$$

Now bear with me: this is just a bunch of *steps*, not hard work. Keep going! We take the radius we just found and put it into the circumference formula. Why? Because an arc (what we're looking for) is just a piece of a circumference.

$$C = 2\pi r$$
$$C = 2\pi \cdot 12$$
$$C = 24\pi$$

Now we use that same proportion from the beginning to find the part of the whole, still using the degrees we were given:

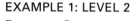

$$\frac{45°}{360°} = \frac{C}{24\pi} \quad \leftarrow \text{Length of the arc}$$
$$1080\pi = 360C$$
$$\boxed{3\pi = c}$$

So the length of AB is 3π. My final word on a problem like this is that you have to at least give it a shot. There's not a whole lot of tricky thinking going on here; it's just time-consuming. This is a very earnable raw point, and I want you to know that you can do problems like this.

Tangency

These problems are all about your understanding that a line that's tangent to a circle is at a right angle to the radius, meaning you can measure various figures using radii.

EXAMPLE 1: LEVEL 2

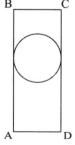

In the figure above the circle is tangent to $\overline{AB}$ and $\overline{CD}$. Rectangle ABCD measures 6 by 14. What is the circumference of the circle?

Because the drawing is not labeled "Figure not drawn to scale," we can safely say that the short side of the rectangle is 6 and the long side is 14.

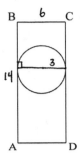

Because the circle is tangent, we can see that the diameter of the circle is 6. The radius, always half the diameter, is 3. We take the radius, pop it into the circumference formula, and we're done:

$$C = 2\pi r \quad r = 3$$

$$C = 2\pi 6$$

$$\boxed{C = 6\pi}$$

EXAMPLE 2: LEVEL 4

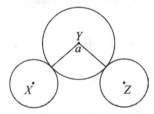

Note: figure not drawn to scale.

In the figure above the three circles are tangent to each other. The radii of circles X and Z are each 1 and the radius of circle Y is 2. The measure of angle *a* is 90°. What is the area of △XYZ ?

I'm going to go ahead and label this with all the info we've been given, including the 90° angle at *a*, and put in the triangle so we can see what we're doing.

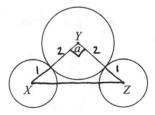

Because the circles are tangent to each other, we can treat segments XY and YZ as continuous, straight lines; in fact, what we're looking at here is an isosceles right triangle whose side lengths are 3. We're looking for the area of the triangle, so we're going to call those 2 sides the base and the height. Remember, as long as a triangle's measurements are connected by a right angle they can be the base and height.

$A = \frac{1}{2} \cdot b \cdot h$

$A = \frac{1}{2} \cdot 3 \cdot 3$

$A = \boxed{\frac{9}{2}}$

Radius and Diameter

These problems focus on knowing what the radius and diameter are and how to measure with them. As that can only go so far, you'll find a lot of other geometric concepts and shapes thrown into these problems. Be on the lookout.

EXAMPLE 1: LEVEL 2

In the figure above angle b equals 90° and $\overline{OP}$ is length 1. What is the length of segment $\overline{PJ}$ (not shown)?

The first thing to do, other than draw in $\overline{PJ}$, is to mark $\overline{OP}$ and $\overline{OJ}$ equal—they are both radii.

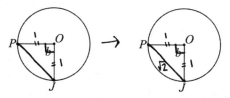

You should already see what we've got there—a 45-45-90 triangle. If the sides are each length 1, we know that the hypotenuse, $\overline{PJ}$, is $\sqrt{2}$. If you needed to, you could do the Pythagorean, but *please* just take the time to memorize them.

Even if the angle at the center hadn't been 90°, connecting any 2 radii in a circle at least will always create an isosceles triangle.

EXAMPLE 3: LEVEL 5

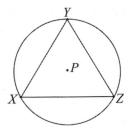

In the figure above, equilateral triangle XYZ is inside circle P, such that each vertex of △XYZ touches the circumference of the circle. If $\overline{XZ}$ equals 8, what is the circumference of circle P?

First, while you're reading a problem like this, you should stop after the first sentence and label. This will ensure that you don't drop valuable details.

Obviously, if we don't know the radius we can't find the circumference, so getting a radius is our first objective. Whenever figures are set inside each other like this, always draw lines that measure from a point to another, not *through* interior figures. I'm going to draw radii that connect the center of the circle with the vertices of the triangle. Now, there's no rule about a 30-30 isosceles triangle, which is what we have 3 of inside the big equilateral. I'm going to add 1 more line:

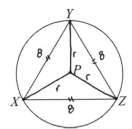
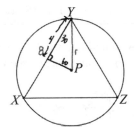

I've just created a little 30-60-90 triangle. I split $\overline{XY}$ in half, so the side that sits on that segment is now length 4.

Let's focus in on that little triangle so you can see how we're going to find the length of the radius. We set up a proportion between our triangle and the 30-60-90:

30-60-90 rule

$$\frac{\sqrt{3}}{2} = \frac{4}{r}$$

$$\sqrt{3}\,r = 8$$

$$r = \frac{8}{\sqrt{3}} \quad \leftarrow \text{simplify the radical!}$$

$$r = \frac{8}{\sqrt{3}} \cdot \frac{\sqrt{3}}{\sqrt{3}}$$

$$r = \frac{8\sqrt{3}}{3}$$

This is the kind of situation in which you don't want to think too much about how tricky the math is that you're doing—you just want to follow procedure and arrive at a value. It doesn't matter whether you understand how much $\frac{8\sqrt{3}}{3}$ actually is; it's our job to just pop that number into the circumference formula:

$$C = 2\pi r$$

$$C = 2\pi \frac{8\sqrt{3}}{3}$$

$$\boxed{C = \frac{16\sqrt{3}\,\pi}{3}}$$

The Coordinate Plane

When a circle is on the coordinate plane, you can be sure that questions will be all about measuring distances from 1 point to another. Sometimes these measurements will be endpoint to endpoint, sometimes between points that are equidistant along the circumference, and sometimes from the center to the circumference.

EXAMPLE 1: LEVEL 3
In the coordinate plane, circle J is centered at (–3, –8) and touches the x-axis at one point. What is the diameter of the circle?

Whenever we can draw something, we do. Now, the circle touches the x-axis at only 1 point, which means it can't reach beyond it.

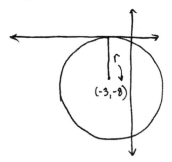

In these problems, the radius will always be parallel and perpendicular to the axes. Here, the radius is 8 long. But wait! The question asks about the *diameter*. Multiply the radius by 2. Diameter = 16.

EXAMPLE 2: LEVEL 3
In the xy-coordinate plane, the center of a circle lies at (–6, 3) and its radius is length 6. At what point on the coordinate plane is the circumference farthest from the y-axis?

If you're not already completely sure where this is going, let's look at the 2 directions in which we can move from that center point, right or left:

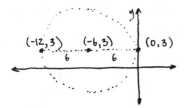

Obviously, the point (−12, 3) is farthest from the *y*-axis. What's important to know, though, is that the diameter will always be parallel and perpendicular to the axes, which means that along the *x*-axis, like in this case, the *y* value of the point will remain the same; only the *x* changes.

EXAMPLE 3: LEVEL 3

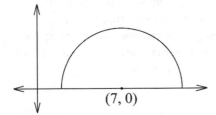

What is the *x*-coordinate of the point on the semicircle that shares a *y*-coordinate with the point (4, 4)?

What we're looking for is the point on the semicircle that has the same *y*-coordinate as the point we've been given:

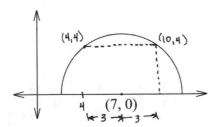

Don't feel like you have to find the radius of this circle, though; instead, you can focus on moving out, in steps, in either direction from the center out to the left and right. To get to (4, 4) we move 3 spaces to the left. To find the other point we move 3 spaces to the right of the center to (10, 4). The *x*-coordinate we're looking for is 10.

EXAMPLE 4: LEVEL 4

Circle O is centered at the origin with radius 10. Which of the following points does not lie on the edge of the circle?

- (A) (0, 10)
- (B) (−8, 6)
- (C) (−7, $\sqrt{51}$)
- (D) (6, 8)
- (E) (−5, −5)

Don't jump to conclusions and assume that it's not C simply because you've never seen something like that before. Instead, we need to go back to the idea that we can measure a radius really easily by making it the hypotenuse of a triangle. In this case, the value of each of these points is going to act as the length of a side of a triangle, and we'll see if the hypotenuse equals radius 10.

It's not so hard. First of all, it's pretty safe to say that (0, 10) is on the circumference. However, let's look at something a little trickier: (−8, 6). We're going to use the Pythagorean Theorem to see if it's true that the radius would fit into the drawing like this:

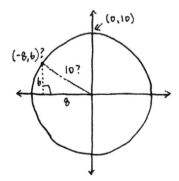

B.

$$(-8)^2 + 6^2 \overset{?}{=} r^2$$
$$64 + 36 = r^2$$
$$100 = r^2$$
$$\pm 10 = r \checkmark$$

Turns out that (−8, 6) works. If that's true, (6, 8) must be true too. That leaves us with C and E. Rather than drawing these points, it makes the most sense to just toss their values into the Pythagorean Theorem and see which doesn't equal 10:

C.

$$(-7)^2 + (\sqrt{51})^2 \stackrel{?}{=} 10^2$$

$$49 + 51 = 100$$

$$100 = 100 \checkmark$$

E.

$$(-5)^2 + (-5)^2 \stackrel{?}{=} 10^2$$

$$25 + 25 = 100$$

$$50 = 100 \; \times$$

So we choose answer E.

Just a repeat reminder: always try answer choices A and E first.

The Curved Path

You're liable to see a drawing that looks like a yin-yang sort of symbol. Sometimes the semicircles inside are of equal size; other times they're different. Either way, it's more important to know that when you're measuring the distance along the curved path, you use circumference.

EXAMPLE 1: LEVEL 3

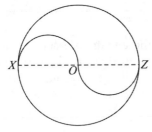

Note: figure not drawn to scale.

The area of the circle above is 100π, and point O is the center of the circle. If XO and OZ are semicircles, what is the distance along the curved path?

As usual, we're going to have find the radius of the big circle by "undoing" the area:

$$A = \pi r^2$$

$$100\pi = \pi r^2 \quad \leftarrow \pi\text{'s cancel}$$

$$100 = r^2$$

$$10 = r$$

Don't forget, that's the radius of the *big* circle. To find the circumferences of the smaller semicircles we have to split those radii in half:

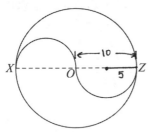

Each smaller circle has a radius of 5. Now, there are 2 ways of looking at this: like there are 2 equal-sized semicircles or like there's 1 whole small circle that's been split in half and shifted. What I'm saying is that you can solve for 1 whole circumference or 2 smaller half-circumferences and add.

$$\frac{1}{2} \cdot \frac{2\pi r}{1} + \frac{1}{2} \cdot \frac{2\pi r}{1} \qquad\qquad 2\pi r$$

$$\frac{1}{2} \cdot \frac{2\pi 5}{1} + \frac{1}{2} \cdot \frac{2\pi 5}{1} \leftarrow 2\text{'s cancel} \qquad \text{or} \qquad \frac{2\pi 5}{\boxed{10\pi}}$$

$$5\pi + 5\pi = \boxed{10\pi}$$

Needless to say, the second way is easier. Honestly, most students see it the first way, though, so I thought I'd show you both.

Polygons

The term polygon refers to any figure that has more than 2 sides; essentially, it refers to any 2-dimensional shape under the sun that's made of straight edges. Usually you'll work with polygons we've already talked about: triangles, squares, and rectangles. However, sometimes you'll come across a 5- or 6-sided polygon.

Interior Angles of a Polygon

To find the total degrees in a polygon on the SAT, there are 2 methods:

1) Remember the formula.

2) Use triangles to break up the figure.

If you're a formula fan, you can remember this: the total degrees in a figure $= 180(n-2)$, where n is the number of sides the figure has.

If you're not so keen on formulas, there's an ad hoc approach.

To use triangles to find the total degrees in any polygon, choose 1 vertex and get married to it (at least for the duration of the problem). Draw a line from that vertex to the first possible vertex you can, to create a triangle. Go *back* to that first vertex and draw another line to the very next possible vertex to create another triangle. Complete this process until you've created as many triangles that share a vertex as you can. Count up the triangles you've created, multiply by 180, and voilà, you have the sum of the interior angles.

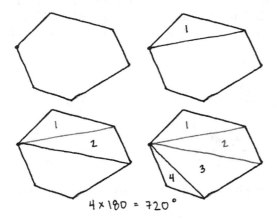

4 × 180 = 720°

Exterior Angles of a Polygon

Meanwhile, the exterior angles of a polygon are a little easier: they always add up to 360°. Labeling them can be a little tricky; the key is consistency. If you've got a figure like the hexagon above, start out by extending 1 of the sides beyond the figure. Next, work clockwise around the figure. This will keep you from extending angles twice off of the same side.

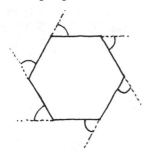

All of those exterior angles add up to 360°. No matter what shape you're dealing with, it's always true.

HOW THEY ASK THE QUESTIONS

EXAMPLE 1: LEVEL 2

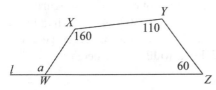

Note: figure not drawn to scale.

In the figure WXYZ, what is the value of angle *a*?

This should be quick and easy. We've got a 4-sided figure that's been placed on a line. Our first objective is simply to find the fourth angle. We could do that by adding up all the other angles and subtracting from 360° and going from there.

But what if we label that angle this way?

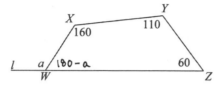

If we call the angle 180 − a, when we add, we'll have our answer in 1 step:

$$180 - a + 160 + 110 + 60 = 360$$
$$510 - a = 360$$
$$-a = -150$$
$$\boxed{a = 150}$$

The same problem could appear without any of the interior angles labeled, but with 1 key difference: the sides will be equilateral. If the sides of any polygon are equal, all of the interior angles are equal. You can just use the triangle trick to figure out how many angles are in the figure and then divide by how many sides there are.

Volume

WHAT YOU NEED TO KNOW

What is Volume?

Once a figure takes on a 3-dimensional form (rather than just lying flat on the page), it suddenly has a new attribute: volume. Volume is simply the amount of space that a 3-dimensional object occupies—it's the area the object would cover if you set it on a table times how tall it is. When we figure out how much water fills a fish tank, how much snow falls on an enclosed field, or the amount of space in a tin can, we're finding volume.

Although you can find the volume of both a cube and a "rectangular prism" (say, a brick) using the same formula, it can be helpful on the SAT to think of them as distinct from each other. Specifically, the volume of a rectangular prism can be found by multiplying its length by its width and its height:

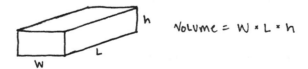

Again, the same is true for a cube. Still, the lengths of all sides of a cube are equal to each other; SAT questions are often easier to solve if you say the volume of a cube is side times side times side, or side cubed.

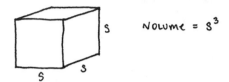

You will not need to know how to find the volume of a sphere (a ball) on the SAT, but you will need to find the volume of a cylinder. A cylinder is just a form like a tin can or a bucket. The easiest way to remember the volume of a cylinder is to imagine it sitting on the table in front of you: again, the volume of any form is just the area of the space it takes up on the table times its height.

Because a cylinder is round on the bottom, its volume is simply the area of a circle times its height:

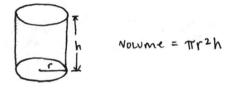

Surface Area

Surface area is a bit of a hybrid of volume and area. It can easily be described as the exact amount of wrapping paper you'd need to cover a present. The most common surface areas you'll work with on the SAT are the surface areas of a cube, a rectangular prism, and a triangular prism.

Surface Area of a Cube

A cube is just like a die or a tissue box—totally square, everything equal. You can get the surface area of a cube by finding the area of 1 side of the cube and multiplying by 6. (Makes sense: all dice have 6 sides, so all cubes have 6 sides.)

The formula, then, is 6 sides squared.

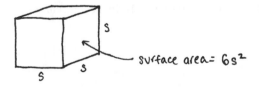

Surface Area of a Rectangular Prism

Finding the surface area of a rectangular prism is a little more tedious. First, *rectangular prism* just refers to anything shaped like a brick, or a stick of butter, or the trailer of a truck. Now, because these will have different lengths, heights, and widths, you'll need to calculate the areas of the different faces separately and then add.

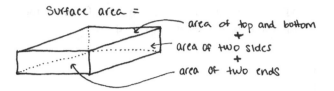

Surface Area of a Cylinder

This is composed of 3 elements: the lid of the tin can, the bottom of the tin can, and the rectangle that wraps around them to create the sides of the can. First, you'll need to find the surface areas of the 2 ends (which will be equal to each other, so you only need to find 1 of them). Second, you'll need to find the circumference of those circles to calculate the length of the rectangular piece.

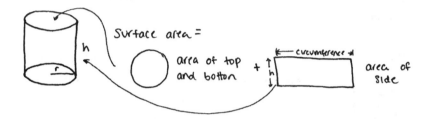

HOW THEY ASK THE QUESTIONS

Understanding Cylinders and Their Volumes

EXAMPLE 1: LEVEL 2

Wendy has a cylindrical bucket filled to the brim with motor oil. Her bucket measures 16 inches in diameter and 12 inches in height. If she pours the motor oil into a pan with diameter 24 inches, to what height will the oil fill the pan?

We're going to need to find the volume of the oil that she has first. Remember, the volume of a cylinder is how much space it takes up on the table times how tall it is. Be careful though! If the bucket measures 16 inches in diameter, *the radius is 8.*

$$V = \pi r^2 h$$
$$V = \pi \, 8^2 \cdot 12$$
$$V = \pi \cdot 64 \cdot 12$$
$$V = 768\pi$$

Notice that I didn't multiply the 768 by 3.14? It's rarely necessary on the SAT anyway, but I've left it in my answer specifically because I know I'm going to put that volume back into the formula to solve for the height of the oil in the new pan.

Now, Wendy is going to pour 768π cubic inches of oil into a pan with a diameter of 24 inches, which means it has *a radius of 12* inches. If I plug those numbers into the formula I should easily get the height of the oil in the pan.

$$V = \pi r^2 h$$
$$768\pi = \pi \cdot 12^2 \cdot h \quad \Leftarrow \pi\text{'s cancel}$$
$$768 = 144h$$
$$\boxed{5\frac{1}{3}" = h}$$

EXAMPLE 2: LEVEL 4

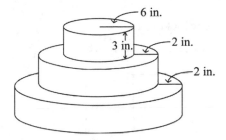

Note: figure not drawn to scale.

Lee builds a three-tiered wedding cake made of cylindrical layers. The top later has a radius of 6 inches and a height of 3 inches. The next two layers' heights remain the same and their radii increase by two inches successively. What is the total volume of the cake?

It makes sense to label this figure and work through the layers individually. Rather than write "+2" on each layer, I'm going to add and label them 8 and 10.

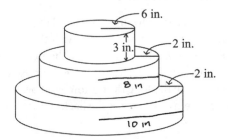

We're going to use the formula for the volume of a cylinder for each layer and add them up.

Layer one

$N = \pi r^2 h$

$N = \pi \cdot 6^2 \cdot 3$

$N = 36 \cdot 3 \cdot \pi$

$N = 108\pi$

Layer two

$N = \pi r^2 h$

$N = \pi \cdot 8^2 \cdot 3$

$N = 64 \cdot 3 \cdot \pi$

$N = 192\pi$

Layer three

$N = \pi r^2 h$

$N = \pi \cdot 10^2 \cdot 3$

$N = 100 \cdot 3 \cdot \pi$

$N = 300\pi$

$108\pi + 192\pi + 300\pi = \boxed{600\pi}$

Understanding Volume of Cubes and Rectangular Prisms

EXAMPLE 1: LEVEL 3

How many cubic erasers with edge length 3 cm can fill a packing container with dimensions 36 cm by 54 cm by 24 cm?

Let's draw a quick sketch of what we're looking at:

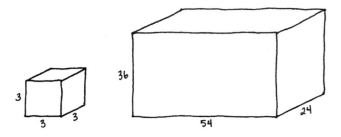

There are 2 schools of thought here: some students like to find the volume of an eraser and the volume of the box and divide to see how many erasers fit inside the box. Let's do that first.

$3 \times 3 \times 3 = 27\ cm^3$ $36 \times 54 \times 24 = 46,656\ cm^3$

divide: $46,656 \div 27 = \boxed{1728\ erasers}$

I do problems like this a little differently; I actually divide first and then multiply my answer. What I mean is that I bypass the volume stage with the eraser and instead mark up my drawing. For example, because I know the height of the box is 36, I know that 12 (3 cm) erasers will stack up in there. Because it's 54 cm long, I know that 18 (3 cm) erasers will fit along the bottom, and because it's 24 cm deep, that it'll take me 8 (3 cm) erasers to reach the back of the box.

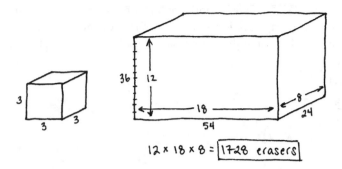

$12 \times 18 \times 8 = \boxed{1728 \ \text{erasers}}$

Then I multiply. Whichever method is easier for you is fine with me. The numbers in a real SAT problem will usually be a bit smaller than those chosen here, so you may find that you can do the problem easily without resorting to your calculator.

Understanding Surface Area

EXAMPLE 1: LEVEL 3

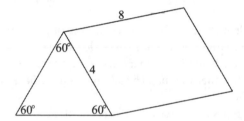

What is the surface area of the triangular prism shown above?

We're looking at a whole form here, with 2 triangles and rectangular sides. The surface area will be found by finding the area of the 2 triangles and adding them to the areas of the 3 rectangles. Finding the area of the rectangles should be pretty easy; they're labeled 4 by 8. 4 × 8 = 32, so each rectangle has an area of 32.

Determining the areas of the triangles is a little bit trickier. Because we need a height and base for the triangle, I'm going to go ahead and drop an *altitude* (a line from the top vertex of the triangle down to the base that's perpendicular to the base) and label the angles.

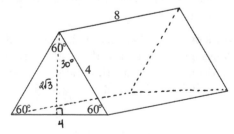

There it is—a 30-60-90 triangle. If we know the hypotenuse is length 4, we know the height is $2\sqrt{3}$. (If you're not sure how I got that, review the special triangle rules in the triangle section.) The base of the equilateral triangle is 4.

The formula for the area of the triangle is $A = \frac{1}{2} \times b \times h$, so we plug in:

$$A = \frac{1}{2} \cdot b \cdot h$$

$$A = \frac{1}{2} \cdot \frac{4}{1} \cdot \frac{2\sqrt{3}}{1}$$

$$A = \frac{8\sqrt{3}}{2} \quad \rightarrow \quad A = 4\sqrt{3}$$

To find the surface area, we add the areas of our 2 triangles and our 3 rectangles:

$$2\left(4\sqrt{3}\right) + 3\left(32\right) = \boxed{8\sqrt{3} + 96} \leftarrow \text{surface area}$$

Recipe Problems

WHAT YOU NEED TO KNOW

A "recipe problem" (my own little nickname) is a particular type of geometry problem that will usually ask you to find the area of a shape that's not a regular geometric form (meaning the shape won't be a square, triangle, circle, and so on). Instead, you'll need to piece together the shape by adding a square here or subtracting a circle there—like that.

Here are some samples of the types of figures I'm talking about:

Now, the complication in these types of problems is twofold:

1) You have to know how to piece together that particular shape—you can't do the problem successfully if you can't figure out what geometric forms contribute to the form you're looking for.

2) You have to be able to keep track of all of the smaller math problems that contribute to building the larger problem. Even if the math takes only 3 steps, it can get very tricky very quickly, particularly because so many of these problems involve fractions and our old friend π.

The best way to attack these problems is to plan ahead—to write a *recipe* for forming the shape before you begin doing any math.

For example, say you were asked to find the area of the shaded portion of this figure:

It should be clear that the process here is to find the area of that square and then subtract the area of the triangle, as though we had used a triangular cookie-cutter. Without worrying at all about the measurements, I want your first step to be writing down the recipe over in the corner of your workspace:

Area ☐
− Area △

I know, it seems simple, and for this particular problem it may seem a little overboard. However, as soon as the difficulty level in these problems picks up, you'll be glad you had the recipe.

The idea is that you find the chunk of information for each part of the recipe and then add and subtract them according to the directions you wrote for yourself at the outset.

You'll find that these forms are often most easily described as a basic geometric form with something removed. The problems are more easily solved this way, rather than trying to measure the shaded area itself (sometimes students try to break it up into multiple pieces, which can backfire big-time).

HOW THEY ASK THE QUESTIONS

EXAMPLE 1: LEVEL 3

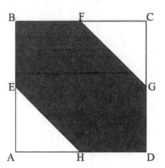

In the figure above, points E, F, G, and H are the midpoints of the sides of square ABCD. Side AB has length 4. What is the area of the shaded region?

I would describe the figure above as a square that has had 2 triangles cut off of it. In some problems it may be important to notice that those 2 triangles are *right isosceles triangles*; however, that doesn't come into play here.

Let's quickly jot down that recipe and then get to work labeling.

Area ⬜

−area △

−area ◿

Because we know E, F, G, and H are midpoints, we can label the sides of those triangles 2.

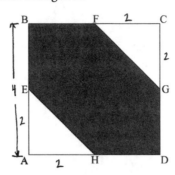

Now we fill in the bits of our recipe:

Area ⬜ $= s^2$ ➡ $4^2 =$ <u>16</u>

Area △ $= \frac{1}{2} \cdot b \cdot h$

$\qquad = \frac{1}{2} \cdot 2 \cdot 2$ ← cancel 2s

$\qquad =$ <u>2</u> ← also Area ◿

So your recipe would look like this:

Area ⬜ ⟿ 16

− Area △ ⟿ 2

− Area ◿ ⟿ 2

$\boxed{12}$

And we find the area of the shaded region is $\boxed{12}$.

EXAMPLE 2: LEVEL 3

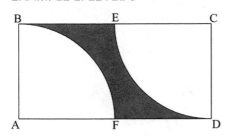

In rectangle ABDE, $\overline{BC}$ is length 4 and arcs ED and BF are centered around points A and C. What is the area of the shaded region?

Again, we need to look at this as a whole that has had parts removed. In this case we've got a rectangle that has had 2 quarter circles removed. Write the recipe and then label the drawing:

Area ▭

− area ◗

− area ◖

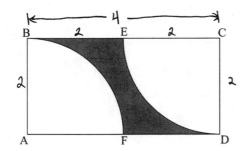

$$\text{Area } \rule{16pt}{9pt} = l \times w = 2 \times 4 = \underline{8}$$

$$\text{Area } \text{◗} = \frac{1}{4} \cdot \pi \cdot r^2 = \frac{2^2\pi}{4} = \underline{\pi}$$

$$\text{Area } \text{◖} = \frac{1}{4} \cdot \pi \cdot r^2 = \frac{2^2\pi}{4} = \underline{\pi}$$

So the recipe is

Area ▭ ⇝ 8

− area ◗ ⇝ π

− area ◖ ⇝ π

$$\boxed{8 - 2\pi}$$

$$\text{or } 2(4 - \pi)$$

EXAMPLE 3: LEVEL 4

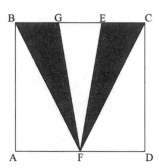

Square ABCD has sides of length 6. Point F is the midpoint of $\overline{AD}$ and the lengths of $\overline{BG}$ and $\overline{EC}$ are each 2. What is the area of the shaded region?

This time the shape isn't subtractive; we can simply find the areas of the 2 shaded triangles. The recipe is pretty simple: Area shaded triangle plus area shaded triangle. Most students would find the areas of the 2 upright right triangles and try to work from there. However, this is where those old triangle rules come into play. If we turn this drawing upside down we'll see 2 spiked triangles just like those we talked about in the triangle lesson:

> In the most difficult questions each individual element of the drawing will have its own dimension to add or subtract in the recipe.

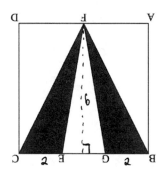

Here we can just find the areas of the 2 triangles and add them together:

$$A \triangledown + A \triangledown =$$

$$\frac{1}{2} \cdot b \cdot h + \frac{1}{2} \cdot b \cdot h$$

$$\frac{1}{2} \cdot 2 \cdot 6 + \frac{1}{2} \cdot 2 \cdot 6 \quad \leftarrow 2\text{'s cancel}$$

$$6 + 6 = \boxed{12}$$

Remember that geometry problems are all about the rules—knowing them and progressively labeling figures using them to solve problems. When a student isn't consistently successful on geometry problems it's usually because 1) they don't have every rule memorized, or 2) they have overlooked a piece of information given in English or geometry shorthand and therefore can't completely label the drawing. If you find yourself stuck, make sure you haven't missed an important piece of information that was given. Don't go into the test without fully memorizing the geometry rules. You'll thank yourself afterward.

data analysis, statistics, and probability

In this chapter we'll explore the odds and ends that round out the math concepts that appear on the SAT. Some of these concepts, such as pie charts, were likely introduced to you early on. The other topics we'll talk about are usually incorporated into other high school math courses as enrichment material.

Feel free to skip through and look only at the sample questions for easier concepts if you'd like. Remember, this material is here to ensure you have a grasp on everything you need to know, from the simplest pictograph to the most difficult probability problem. We're almost finished, so let's get going.

Mean, Median, and Mode

Mean (The Classic Average)

When you add up your test scores in your science class to figure out your grade, you're finding the *mean*, or the *arithmetic mean*. This is what we're finding whenever we total up what we've got and divide by how many we have. The *mean* is what we're really talking about when we say "find the average."

Averages are a hot topic on the SAT. Because of that, whenever you come across an *average* or *mean* problem, I want you to set it up the same way every time:

$$\frac{\underline{\quad} + \underline{\quad} + \underline{\quad}}{\text{\# of things added}} = \text{average}$$

In many of the problems you'll see that actually writing out that format and the slots or boxes you need will help you a great deal.

Median

When data is listed consecutively (smallest to largest or vice versa; it makes no difference), the median is the *middle* value on the list. When the list has an odd number of terms, this works out perfectly: just put them in order and pick the middle value. When the list has an even number of terms, the median is the mean (the average) of the 2 middle terms.

$$2, 4, \boxed{7}, 46, 82$$

or

$$2, 3, \boxed{7, 46}, 47, 82$$

$$\text{median} = \frac{7+46}{2}$$

Mode

The *mode* is the most frequently appearing term in a list of data. It is used to talk about the most commonly recurring score or level or whatever that the data describes. Truthfully, because it's not so easy to manipulate (and not too difficult to understand), mode does not often appear on the SAT.

HOW THEY ASK THE QUESTIONS

Understanding and Using Mean

EXAMPLE 1: LEVEL 2
If the average of n and $4n$ is 7, what is the value of n?

In this type of problem we plug in what we've been given and solve. The denominator is 2 because there are 2 terms. Simple:

$$\frac{n + 4n}{2} = 7$$

$$n + 4n = 14$$

$$5n = 14$$

$$\boxed{n = \frac{14}{5}}$$

EXAMPLE 2: LEVEL 2
If the average of 4, 6, 8, 8, 4, and n is equal to n, what is the value of n?

This is just supposed to freak you out by including the n on both sides of the equation. Don't think about it; set it up and *do it.*

$$\frac{4+6+8+8+4+n}{6} = n$$

$$\frac{30+n}{6} = n$$

$$30 + n = 6n$$

$$30 = 5n$$

$$\boxed{6 = n}$$

EXAMPLE 3: LEVEL 3

If the average of a and b is 10 and the average of a, b, and c is 14, what is the value of c?

It's fairly common for an SAT problem to require that you solve for the value of an expression rather than a specific variable. If we write down what we've been given, taking it chunk by chunk, we write out 2 distinct equations, $\frac{a+b}{2} = 10$ and $\frac{a+b+c}{3} = 14$. What we'll do, because we're looking for c, is solve for $a + b$ and plug it into the other equation so that we're left with only c.

$$\frac{a+b}{2} = 10 \qquad \frac{a+b+c}{3} = 14$$

$$a+b = \boxed{20} \qquad a+b+c = 42$$

$$20 + c = 42$$

$$\boxed{c = 22}$$

This same problem would be made more difficult by simply saying that the average of a and b is j rather than 10. Why? More variables are more intimidating. In that case you'd solve for c "in terms of j."

EXAMPLE 4: LEVEL 4

Five items are being packed in a crate for shipping. Each of the item's weights are measured in whole pounds. If the average weight of the items is 17 pounds, what is the heaviest that a single item could be?

Let's set this up right off the bat. We're loading 5 items into a crate and their average weight is 17. We don't know anything about their individual weights, so we start with this:

$$\frac{\_ + \_ + \_ + \_ + \_}{5} = 17$$

The best way to start here is to turn this into a simple addition problem, as we're more comfortable working with those. We'll do that by multiplying 17 by 5:

$$\_ + \_ + \_ + \_ + \_ = 85$$

Now for some quick thinking: in this problem we're looking for the *heaviest* that a particular item could be. To make that a reality we need everything else to be *the lightest* it could be. As there are no restrictions on weights other than that they need to be measured in whole pounds, I'm going to say that every other item in the box weighs 1 pound.

$$1 + 1 + 1 + 1 + x = 85$$
$$4 + x = 85$$
$$\boxed{x = 81}$$

So the heaviest an item could be is 81 pounds. This problem would be made more difficult by putting parameters on the weights, meaning that the problem might say that each item must weigh a different amount. In that case, in order to keep everything as low as it's allowed to be per the rules in the problem, you'd assign the weights as 1 pound, 2 pounds, 3 pounds, and so on.

EXAMPLE 5: LEVEL 3

If the average (arithmetic mean) age of 26 students is *y* years, in terms of *y*, what is the sum of all the students' ages, in years?

Plug what you've been given into the average formula; don't give it much thought, because overthinking would be a great way to screw up. As you as can see, we can just multiply and solve for the sum:

$$\frac{sum}{\#} = avg$$

$$\frac{sum}{26} = y$$

$$sum = 26y$$

EXAMPLE 6: LEVEL 4

The average (arithmetic mean) length of the sailboats in a fleet with *a* number of boats is 18 feet and the average length of the sailboats in a fleet with *b* number of boats is 24 feet. If the average length of the boats in both fleets is 21, what is the value of *a − b*?

We have no idea how many boats are in each fleet; rather than messing around on your calculator trying to figure this out (which I admit you could do), I'd like you to simply plug values into the average formula and work it out. I really want you to steer clear of doing too much messing around because it's more than likely that on the real SAT you will run out of time if you're inefficient.

So we need to plug info into $\frac{sum}{number}$ = average. What is most important to understand in this question is that if we know the average length of all the boats in fleet *a* is 18, it doesn't matter if 1 of them is 17 feet and the other is 19; we can treat them all as if they were 18 feet. We can represent their total length with 18*a*. The same goes for fleet *b*: if their average is 24, we can represent them using 24*b*. Now we need to plug in the number of boats we have; if there are *a* in the first fleet and *b* in the second, that means the total number of boats is *a* + *b*. The average is given right in the problem, 21.

$$\underset{\uparrow}{\frac{18a + 24b}{a + b}} = 21 \leftarrow \text{average weight}$$

total weight

total boats

Now we solve, using algebra to make sure our problem has *a* − *b* on its own side and a value on the other.

$$\frac{18a + 24b}{a+b} = 21$$

$$18a + 24b = 21(a+b)$$

$$18a + 24b = 21a + 21b$$

$$18a + 3b = 21a$$

$$3b = 3a$$

$$0 = 3a - 3b$$

$$0 = 3(a - b)$$

$$\boxed{0 = a - b}$$

EXAMPLE 7: LEVEL 3

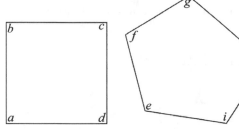

What is the average of *a, b, c, d, e, f, g, h,* and *i?*

Before thinking, what we're looking to find is this:

$$\frac{a + b + c + d + e + f + g + h + i}{9} = avg$$

Granted, we can't be completely sure what the individual value of *a* is (even though it looks an awful lot like a 90° angle). However, we know what *a* + *b* + *c* + *d* must equal—since they're interior angles of a 4-sided figure, they must add up to 360°. Same goes for *e, f, g, h,* and *i*. We don't know what they equal, but we know they're in a 5-sided figure so they have to add up to 540°.

Suddenly we have something we can solve:

> To learn more about finding the interior angles in a polygon, check out page 268.

$$\frac{360 + 540}{9} = avg$$

$$\frac{900}{9} = avg$$

$$\boxed{100° = avg}$$

EXAMPLE 8: LEVEL 4

Luke is skipping rocks on a lake and decides to record the number of skips he is able to accomplish on each throw. The following chart shows his throws and skips. If Luke throws one more rock, how many times must the rock skip to make the average equal to 2?

# throws	# skips
1	2
2	3
3	3
4	2
5	1

It would make the most sense to find out what the average is *now* so we can figure out what we have to do to it to make the average equal 2.

I'm going to total up skips by multiplying each number of skips by how many times each happened. For the total number of throws I just, well, add up the throws:

$$\frac{1(2) + 2(3) + 3(3) + 4(2) + 5(1)}{15} = avg$$

$$\frac{30}{15} = avg$$

$$2 = avg$$

Let's stop here for a second. It seems that our average is *already* 2. That's enough to confuse any student and have him select 0 as his answer. However, Luke is going to throw "one more rock" . . . which means that the new number of throws is going to change from 15 to 16:

$$\frac{1(2) + 2(3) + 3(3) + 4(2) + 5(1) + 1(s)}{16} = 2$$

Now, could we have just written this equation in the first place? Yes. Would you have likely written 15 throws instead of 16? Yes. That's why I took the long route.

So that *s* buried in the equation represents how many times the stone has to skip on a single throw (the new throw) to make the average equal 2. We solve:

$$\frac{30 + s}{16} = 2$$

$$30 + s = 32$$

$$\boxed{s = 2}$$

Understanding and Using Median

Median questions are all about manipulating or adding new numbers to a list and knowing which numbers affect the median. These can feel a little like trick questions because the entire question is based on the concept that a particular number has to be the middle number—like, it's so simple it can be scary.

EXAMPLE 1: LEVEL 2
In a set of 11 consecutive integers, the median is 37. What is the least of these integers?

I really like to visualize these problems; *seeing* what's happening on the number line makes these so much easier.

$$\longleftarrow \underline{\quad 37 \quad} \longrightarrow$$
$$| \; | \; | \; | \; | \quad \uparrow \quad | \; | \; | \; | \; |$$

So, if I have 11 consecutive integers and the middle integer is 37, that means that I have 5 numbers on either side of the 37. That being the case, the least number on my list must be 37 minus 5:

$$37 - 5 = x$$

$$\boxed{32 = x}$$

EXAMPLE 2: LEVEL 4
A list of numbers is created by drawing ping-pong balls out of a lottery machine. After the 8th ball is drawn, the list is as follows: 24, 75, 82, 56, 19, 99, 45, 46. If after the 9th ball is drawn, the median is 56, what is the lowest possible number that could be written on the 9th ball?

Whenever you're dealing with a given list of numbers in a median question and they're not already in ascending order, it's going to be in your best interest to put them into order. Let's do that first:

$$19, \; 24, \; 45, \; 46, \; \boxed{56}, \; 75, \; 82, \; 99$$

I took the liberty of circling the 56 in the list so that we can really focus in on it as the median of the final list. If we're going to keep that 56 in the middle of the list, we can't add any more numbers to the left side of the list; we need to have 4 numbers on the left side and 4 on the right. So we need to get as close as we can to 56 without going below it. But there's a trick; most people would say: "Oh, OK! We'll put a 57 in there and be fine!" And it's true, 57 *works*, but 57 isn't the answer.

In fact, we can add another 56 to the list:

. . . and 56 is still the median. So the thing to remember is this: it's OK to repeat numbers already in a list, unless the problem specifically stipulates that every number on the list must be different.

Charts and Graphs

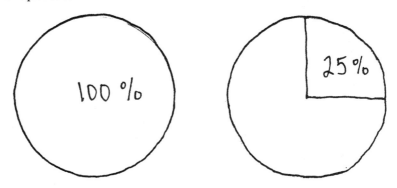

WHAT YOU NEED TO KNOW

Here we're going to take a look at the different types of graphical representations of data that you may encounter on the SAT.

Circle Graphs

Circle graphs are a visual way to express the relationships we talked about in the introduction to percentages (for a refresher, check out page 135). Rather than using a circle's 360 degrees, circle graphs allot different pieces of the "pie" to data based on percentages. A whole circle will equal 100%; $\frac{1}{4}$ of the circle will equal 25%.

Line Graphs

Line graphs are generally used to track trends. Although they are not always perfectly linear, they work very much like a $y = mx + b$ equation you'd see in algebra. Each point on the line represents a pair of related data: say, speed at a particular time, weight at a particular age, or earnings compared to years of experience.

Sometimes line graphs are drawn exactly from the data they represent. Other times, the lines are *lines of best fit*, created to represent a general trend shown by the data. Rather than plotting every piece of data, a line of best fit represents what you would expect that data to reveal in a similar experiment.

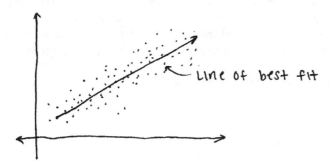

Bar Graphs and Pictographs

Bar graphs and pictographs really do the same thing—they represent measurements or quantities at specific times or in certain circumstances. These are the graphs that show how many cars a factory produces each year or the sales of account executives on an annual basis. When you're reading these charts, the most important things you'll want to pay attention to are these:

o The dates they represent: do the bars show the measurement at the beginning of the year, January 1, or the end of the year, December 31?

o What each of the pictures in the pictograph represents: if the symbol is an apple, does it represent a bushel of apples or 1,000 apples or 10 apples?

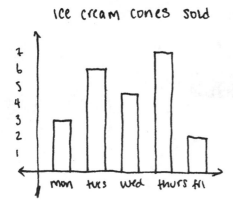

Scatterplots

Scatterplot graphs provide 2 pieces of information and depict the data pair's specific relationship to each other. They are often used to represent the data for each individual participant in timed trials. Whereas a line graph is used to show trends, scatterplots give specifics: a mouse ate 3 pieces of cheese on the first trial and 5 pieces of cheese on the second trial; a student jogs 5 miles on Monday and 8 miles on Tuesday; Jack scores a 75 and a 92 on 2 different math tests.

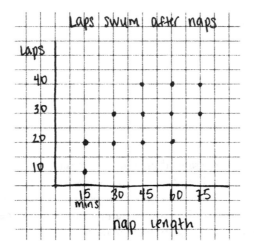

HOW THEY ASK THE QUESTIONS

Understanding and Using Circle Graphs

EXAMPLE 1: LEVEL 2

Eighth Grader's Favorite Beverages

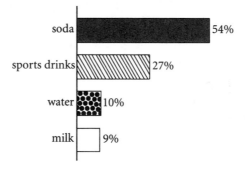

The bar graph above shows the beverage preferences of eighth graders. Which of the following circle graphs represents the same information?

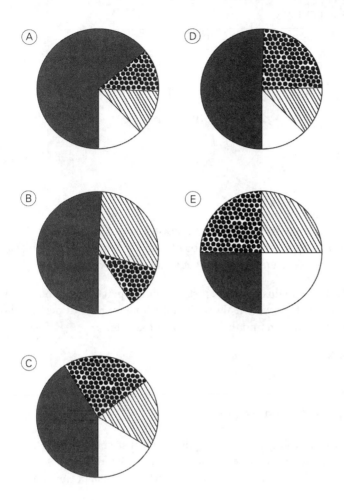

In this type of problem you'll want to zero in on a particular chunk (usually the biggest) and compare it to what you see in the graphs. Then you can work from there. For example, the biggest chunk we have here is 54%; it's the shaded gray, and it should be just over half of the circle. From that fact alone we can eliminate C and E because they're less than a half and D because it's exactly half.

Now we zero in on A and B. The next largest piece we have is 27%: that's a just a tad larger than a quarter of the circle. In choice A those 3 small slices seem to be about the same size, but in choice B the striped slice is around a quarter and the other 2 are far smaller. We have to go with B.

EXAMPLE 2: LEVEL 3

Ages of People in Movie Complex

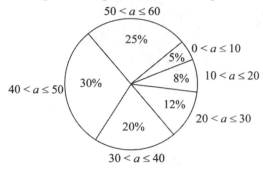

The graph above represents the ages of moviegoers on a single day. If the number of people between the ages of 50 and 60 is 3,250, how many people at the theater were 20 years of age and younger?

There are 2 ways to do this problem. Just like with all percentage problems, if we're given the percentage, we can always find the total number of people who went to the theater and then find the part we're looking for.

$$\frac{25}{100} = \frac{3250}{x}$$

$$25x = 325000$$

$$x = 13,000 \leftarrow \text{total people}$$

The trick in this problem, either way, is to not just choose the 8% slice; because we're looking for everyone 20 and under, that includes the $0 < a \leq 10$ *and* the $10 < a \leq 20$ slices. That's 8% plus 5%, which is 13% of the total:

$$\frac{13}{100} = \frac{x}{13000}$$

$$169000 = 100x$$

$$\boxed{1690 = x}$$

Or you can set up a proportion of percentage to part, like this:

$$\frac{25}{3250} = \frac{13}{x}$$

$$25x = 42250$$

$$\boxed{x = 1690}$$

Understanding and Using Line Graphs

EXAMPLE 1: LEVEL 2

Smith's Savings Account

The figure above represents the amount of money in the Smiths' savings account over the course of 25 years. What value is closest to the increase per year between 1990 and 2005?

(A) $2,500.00
(B) $3,333.33
(C) $5,000.00
(D) $6,666.66
(E) $8,000.00

That "per year" is asking for the increase. All we need to do is figure out how many years we're dealing with, how much the account went up, and just divide. From 1990 to 2005 is 15 years (you can subtract if you're unsure). Now, looking at the graph, it seems that in 1990 the Smiths had $10,000 saved and by 2005 they had $60,000. That's an increase of $50,000 (again, subtract if you're not sure).

Now we divide $50,000 by 15 years:

$50,000 ÷ 15 = $3333.33

Understanding and Using Bar Graphs

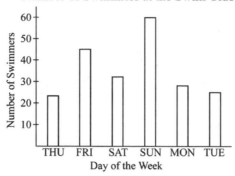

Number of Swimmers at the Swim Club

Between which two days on the graph above was the change in attendance the greatest?

(A) Thursday and Friday
(B) Friday and Saturday
(C) Saturday and Sunday
(D) Sunday and Monday
(E) Monday and Tuesday

OK, this should be really simple. Just don't get tripped up: a big *decrease* in attendance is just as much a *change* as a big *increase* in attendance. Since you'll naturally look for an increase, don't overlook the decrease here.

I always find it helpful to draw lines from the labels on the graphs over to the different bars so that I can really see and measure:

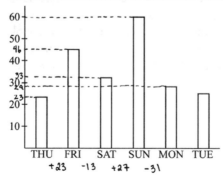

Number of Swimmers at the Swim Club

It seems that the greatest change was, in fact, a decrease. The change from Sunday to Monday was a difference of 31 people.

The most important thing about bar graphs is to stop and *read the key* and *read the text*. Make sure you know what each bar represents (if they're shaded differently, they likely represent different things). If the bars represent entire years, be sure you know if the bar represents a period from January 1 of that year or from December 31. It can make all the difference! If you know your way around a bar graph, you should be in good shape.

Understanding and Using Pictographs

EXAMPLE 1: LEVEL 2

In the pictograph below, each 🍎 represents 10,000 bushels of apples. What is the difference between the number of bushels shipped in September and the number of bushels shipped in November?

Bushels of Apples Shipped

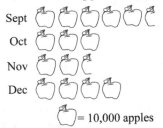

Sept

Oct

Nov

Dec

🍎 = 10,000 apples

Don't start multiplying! Let's look at a direct comparison between September and November. Rather than solving for the total value of each row, let's just solve for the *difference*. We can see that there are 3 extra apples in September's row, so we multiply by 10,000 to get our answer.

$$3 \times 10,000 = \boxed{30,000 \text{ bushels}}$$

Understanding and Using Scatterplots

EXAMPLE 2: LEVEL 2

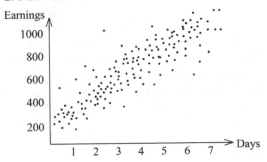

Which of the following functions most accurately represents the data shown above?

(A) $e(d) = 200$

(B) $e(d) = 0.8d + 200$

(C) $e(d) = 2d + 400$

(D) $e(d) = 600$

(E) $e(d) = 200d$

I'm going to draw a line of best fit right through that graph so we can see what we're dealing with.

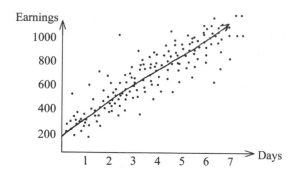

Now, we could do a full analysis of each of our answer choices, but we don't really have to. We know we need a function that has a *y*-intercept around 200 and isn't flat. The only answer that we have that's remotely like that is B: the *y*-intercept is 200 and the *d* value (which is acting like *x* on my graph) is being multiplied by a value a little less than 1, which would give us a slope just a little flatter than 45°. Answer B is the only option that's remotely possible.

Probability

WHAT YOU NEED TO KNOW

When we're talking probability we're talking odds. What are the odds your parents will send you to Saint Tropez for the summer so you can go yachting with P. Diddy/Puff Daddy/Sean Combs? One in a billion, I'd imagine.

That's probability—and a fraction.

The probability that you'll be enjoying the Mediterranean with Diddy in June is 1/1,000,000,000. The 1 in that fraction represents your success: trip to Saint Tropez; the 1,000,000,000 represents all your other possible outcomes (including babysitting your kid sister, interning at a law office, bagging groceries, researching science at a local university, watching reruns of *Gilligan's Island* or *The O.C.*, and the other 999,999,995 things you could be doing).

So, put simply, probability is always represented by the same fraction:

$$\frac{\text{\# of successful outcomes}}{\text{\# of all possible outcomes}}$$

An important thing to be aware of is that probability fractions are always expressed in their most reduced form. For example, if we have a bag of 3 red handkerchiefs, 2 yellow handkerchiefs, and 1 blue handkerchief, the probability that we will pull out the blue handkerchief if we randomly reached into the bag is $\frac{1}{6}$ (1 blue over 6 options).

However, the probability of pulling out a yellow handkerchief is $\frac{2}{6}$ (2 yellows over 6 options), which fraction rules say we must reduce to $\frac{1}{3}$. You can think about that $\frac{1}{3}$ as though it says "1 out of every 3 handkerchiefs in the bag is yellow." Likewise, the probability of picking a red handkerchief is $\frac{3}{6}$; this we reduce to $\frac{1}{2}$.

Now, the key here is that in the same scenario with the same number of handkerchiefs in the bag every time, the probabilities of pulling out a different color handkerchief could each have a different denominator, in this case 6, 3, or 2. So? So the denominator of a probability fraction is not always the exact total number of handkerchiefs in the bag. Instead, a probability fraction talks about the relationship of the numerator to a proportional part of the total, a lot like other ratios and proportions.

And & Or: The Probability of Two Independent Events

The probability of 2 independent events happening is calculated 2 different ways; it depends on whether we want the probability that they both happen or the probability that either of them happens.

To calculate the probability that event 1 *and* event 2 happen, we *multiply* their probabilities.

this AND that happens?

MULTIPLY.

To calculate the probability that event 1 *or* event 2 happens, we *add* their probabilities.

this OR that happens?

ADD.

If you think about it, this makes sense: the probability that 2 different things both will happen is usually a lot lower than the probability that just 1 or the other will happen. You'd likely feel much more comfortable betting that if a pair of dice is rolled, 1 of them will show a 3 than betting that both will show a 3. The math agrees with you.

What If It Doesn't Happen?

The probability that something does not happen is just 1 minus the probability that it does happen.

Replacement

Sometimes probabilities of multiple events are calculated "without replacement." That means that if you're pulling handkerchiefs out of a bag, every time you pull a handkerchief out you don't "replace" it—that is, you don't put it back in the bag. So if you start out with a bag of 6 handkerchiefs, your first probability will be $\frac{x}{6}$, but on the next pull your next probability will be $\frac{y}{5}$. Another pull and your probability will be $\frac{z}{4}$, and so on.

HOW THEY ASK THE QUESTIONS

Straight-Up Probability Calculations

Most probability problems focus on simply finding the probability that something will or will not happen. More advanced versions of these problems give you the probability of a particular outcome or several outcomes and then ask about the total number of scarves in the bag or fruit in the bowl.

EXAMPLE 1: LEVEL 2

If there are 3 cans of lemon-scented wood polish in a case of 12 cans, what is the probability that someone would randomly select a can that *is not* lemon-scented?

If there are 12 cans and 3 of them are lemon, we subtract and find that 9 cans are other scents. The probability of selecting a can of polish with a scent other than lemon is $\frac{9}{12}$. Don't forget to reduce the fraction, though!

$$\frac{9}{12} \rightarrow \boxed{\frac{3}{4}}$$

EXAMPLE 2: LEVEL 3

A complete cycle on a washing machine includes a 5-minute presoak, a 20-minute wash, and 5 minutes of spinning. If a washing machine is opened at a random time during a complete cycle, what is the probability that the machine will not be in the wash phase?

The first step here should be to find the total number of minutes in the cycle—that will give us our total number of outcomes (when opening the machine during any particular minute in the cycle). Adding 5 minutes and 20 minutes and 5 minutes gives us a 30-minute cycle. Now, because we want to know the probability of the machine being opened on any cycle other than the wash cycle, we can do 1 of 2 things: we can calculate the probability that it *will* be opened on the wash cycle and subtract from 1, or we can add up the total time of the other cycles and put the result over 30. Because we're dealing with only 3 different elements here, I would most likely just add the 5 minutes and 5 minutes, get the 10, put that over 30, and reduce:

$$\frac{5+5}{30} = \frac{10}{30} = \boxed{\frac{1}{3}}$$

Problems like this will be made more difficult on the SAT by putting some times in minutes and other measurements in hours. This can also be done with other measurements (inches and feet, centimeters and meters, and so on). It's imperative that you put all your units into the same measurement before calculating probability or else your answer will invariably be incorrect.

EXAMPLE 3: LEVEL 3

The probability of choosing a piece of green sea glass from a jar is $\frac{1}{6}$. The probability of choosing a piece of blue sea glass from the same jar is $\frac{1}{4}$. Which of the following could be the total number of pieces of sea glass in the jar?

(A) 8
(B) 12
(C) 16
(D) 20
(E) 26

Because probability is related to basic fractions, you may be inclined to simply multiply the 4 and 6 together to find that there could be 24 pieces of sea glass in the jar. This is not incorrect, but it's also not an answer choice. Because the green glass and the blue glass come in groups of 6 and 4, respectively, we definitely need a common multiple of 4 and 6. In this case our answer choice happens to be the least common multiple, 12.

Geometric Probability

These problems use the area of different spaces to calculate the probability of touching a randomly selected area (for example, *what is the probability of hitting the target?* or *what is the probability that the egg will land in the basket?*).

EXAMPLE 1: LEVEL 3

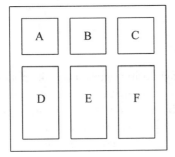

In a beanbag toss at a school fair, students try to toss beanbags through different sized slots on a board. A student wins if he or she is able to throw a beanbag through slot A. Losing slots B and C are the same size as slot A. Three other losing slots, D, E, and F, are each twice the size of slot A. Not including the edges and solid board, what is the probability of throwing a bean bag through the winning slot A?

To calculate probability, we need to find a way of assessing the total area of open slots (all the places that this student could throw a beanbag into). Because the problem asks only about slots, we discard the rest of the playing board. We haven't been given information about the individual areas of each of the slots, but we do have information about them as they relate to each other. If slot A is

1 unit, slots B and C must be 1 unit each, as well. That's 3 units so far. If slots D, E, and F are each twice the size of A, they must be worth 2 units each. If we add up all the slots we'll find that we have 9 units of area, no matter how big or small they may actually be. Because probability is defined as success over possible outcomes, the probability of throwing a beanbag through slot A (1 unit) is $\frac{1}{9}$.

Options, Arrangements, Permutations, and Combinations

WHAT YOU NEED TO KNOW

Options

Options in math are just choices or opportunities. We're usually interested in counting up how many options we have no matter how the problem is set up. Basic option problems appear early in the test and ask about combos of given things. For example

- T-shirts come in 4 sizes and 3 different colors. How many different T-shirt size and color combinations can we come up with?

- Some kid has 2 pairs of pants, 3 shirts, and 2 pairs of shoes. How many different outfits can he create?

When we want every single selection possible, we simply find the product of what's available to us. Right. Just multiply

- 4 sizes × 3 colors = 12 different possible T-shirts
- 2 pants × 3 shirts × 2 shoes = 12 different outfits

Arrangements and Permutations

These problems test your knowlege of when choosing swimming, biking, and diving is different from choosing diving, biking, and swimming. Arrangements and permutations are technically different, but I solve them the same way— with slots for all my options. Truth be told, I've never actually used the formulas for either problem type; I'm always afraid I'm going to screw up the formulas because I'm not so great with math when I'm just plugging numbers into something I don't *understand*. So here's what I do.

Arrangements are all about putting people or things in specific places or assigning them roles or jobs. We "arrange" when we assign actors to parts or create a seating chart in a classroom; the number of different ways we can arrange those things is the point of an arrangement problem.

You'll always want to start these problems with the number of "slots" you'll be filling. In the following problem we'll arrange 4 dogs and 4 doghouses. Rather than just multiplying 4 × 4, we actually have to put the dogs in the houses. Each dog gets his own house, so we draw a slot for each. (Bear with me.)

Before anyone is assigned, we have 4 dogs available for house #1. So we decide to put Astro into the first house.

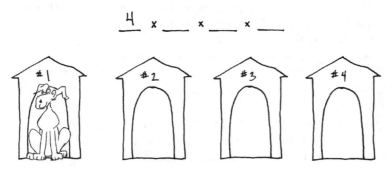

After we do that, there are only 3 dogs left to take over house #2. Once we put Baron into house #2, there are only 2 dogs available to live in house #3. We give Luna house #3, so Daisy, by default, takes house #4.

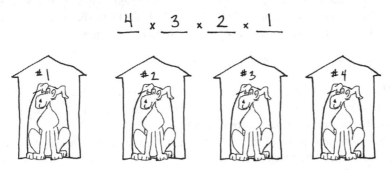

Arrangements track that process by calculating the available options at each stage of the assignments: 4 dogs × 3 dogs × 2 dogs × 1 dog = 24 possible arrangements.

Permutations are really just arrangement problems that give you more dogs than you have houses for (or more of whatever you're arranging than you have room for). All you can do is house the dogs you have. Say we have 8 dogs and 4 houses. To start, we have 8 dogs available for house #1. After we assign a dog to house #1, we have 7 dogs available for house #2. Another dog takes house #2 and we're down to 6 dogs that need houses. Following that pattern our slots will read $8 \times 7 \times 6 \times 5$. Once the houses (the slots on our paper) are full, we have to stop. That's it. Even so, there are 1,680 ways we can arrange those 8 dogs in those 4 houses.

No matter what happens, always draw out your slots first and go from there.

Combinations

These problems test your knowledge of when choosing swimming, biking, and diving is *not* different from choosing diving, biking, and swimming.

Combinations are actually a little worse than permutations. Rather than just arranging things into slots, which really focuses on individual placement, we create teams or committees. The thing about teams is that we're interested in the *group*, not where each individual is standing. That means I need to use math that makes sure that the group "Johnson, Grace, and Ryan" isn't counted again as "Grace, Johnson, and Ryan."

In other words, in the dog problem we just looked at, Astro, Baron, and Luna would have been a different arrangement (because we know which house each of them has) than Baron, Astro, and Luna. In combination problems we're just pulling 3 dogs into a group, so it doesn't matter what order they're standing in.

Basically, the same 3 things equals the same group. Can't count the group twice. Got it?

So what to do we do? Well, I'll admit that I like to draw a diagram for myself to figure this out rather than use the formula. I know. That's bad. Math teachers nationwide will probably freak out when I admit that, but like I said, I'm not so hot with memorizing, and I promised I'd tell you what I tell my own students.

Even worse, it may be a little more time consuming than the formula, but I usually have time to figure it out.

OK, let's say we're going to create a team of 3 student representatives out of a class of 6. Let's also call the students A, B, C, D, E, and F to spare ourselves any confusion. First, I'll write out the options that include student A:

abc   abd   abe   abf   acd   ace   acf   ade   adf   aef

Now, if you look carefully at my pattern, you'll see I wrote A and B choices, A and C and their remaining choices, A and D and their remaining choices, and so on. It was very organized. It took about 15 seconds.

OK, now that A is out of the way, let's make sure we have all the options that include student B that we didn't already list:

bcd   bce   bcf   bde   bdf   bef

Because I already listed B's options that included A, I didn't have to write them again.

Continuing the process, I include student C in places I hadn't already. The list gets much shorter.

cde   cdf   cef

Then the remaining D options:

def

Last step: count 'em up. There are 20 possible teams of 3 people when we choose from 6.

HOW THEY ASK THE QUESTIONS

Option Problems

These problems test whether you can correctly count up the number of combinations of colors, stones, carpeting and so on.

> **EXAMPLE 1: LEVEL 2**
> Mr. Smith is choosing among 4 paint colors and 3 carpet colors. How many different color combinations of paint and carpet are possible?

This is simple multiplication! Do not write down a giant list of combinations! Check it out: $4 \times 3 = \boxed{12}$. You're done.

Arrangement Problems

In these problems you'll be asked how many different ways you can line up these dachshunds, digits, or delegates.

> **EXAMPLE 1: LEVEL 3**
> How many 3-digit integers can be created using 4, 5, and 6 if each digit is used only once?

Asking you to arrange digits rather than delegates or dogs—that is, to think about arranging 4's and 5's—can be confusing, because you reflexively use these entities to count. However, we're going to put down our 3 slots and fill them in like any basic arrangement:

___ x ___ x ___

Before we write down any digits, how many choices do we have for the first slot? 3. Put that in the first slot.

_3_ x ___ x ___

Now that we've used up 1 of our digits, how many options do we have for that second slot? 2. Put that in the second slot.

_3_ x _2_ x ___

Now that we've arranged 2 of our 3 digits, how many are left to go in the last slot? Whichever digit we haven't used yet: 1. That goes in the last slot:

$$\underline{\quad3\quad} \times \underline{\quad2\quad} \times \underline{\quad1\quad}$$

Now multiply: $3 \times 2 \times 1 = \boxed{6}$. There are 6 ways those 3 digits can be arranged to create a 3-digit integer.

EXAMPLE 2: LEVEL 3

How many 4-digit integers can be created if the first digit must be a 2 and the last digit must be either a 3, a 5, or a 7?

Before we do anything, let's jot down our slots so we can see what we're working with:

$$\underline{\quad\quad} \times \underline{\quad\quad} \times \underline{\quad\quad} \times \underline{\quad\quad}$$

Now we'll just work through the list: if the first digit must be a 2, how many *options* do we have for the first slot? Just 1. We put that 1 in the first slot:

$$\underline{\quad1\quad} \times \underline{\quad\quad} \times \underline{\quad\quad} \times \underline{\quad\quad}$$

The second slot can be any digit under the sun. How many digits are available? *Not 9!!* This was in our very first integer lesson—there are 10 digits from 0 through 9. Put 10 in the second slot:

$$\underline{\quad1\quad} \times \underline{\quad10\quad} \times \underline{\quad\quad} \times \underline{\quad\quad}$$

The third slot also can be any digit, so this slot gets a 10 too.

$$\underline{\quad1\quad} \times \underline{\quad10\quad} \times \underline{\quad10\quad} \times \underline{\quad\quad}$$

The final stipulation is that the last digit may be only a 3, a 5, or a 7—that's a total of 3 options. The 3 goes in the last slot:

$$\underline{\quad1\quad} \times \underline{\quad10\quad} \times \underline{\quad10\quad} \times \underline{\quad3\quad}$$

Multiply: $1 \times 10 \times 10 \times 3 = \boxed{300}$. There are 300 4-digit integers that satisfy those limits.

EXAMPLE 3: LEVEL 4

If four playing cards—the kings of hearts, clubs, diamonds, and spades—are to be laid out next to each other, how many different ways can the cards be arranged if the king of diamonds is never to be on either end?

There are a few ways to do problems like this, but I always do them the same way, so I'll show you my method. Many students have other ways of handling a problem like this, and if you've got a foolproof accurate method, super.

Because I'm arranging 4 cards, I'll put down my 4 slots:

$$\underline{\quad\quad} \times \underline{\quad\quad} \times \underline{\quad\quad} \times \underline{\quad\quad}$$

I have limitations on where that king of diamonds can go, so I'm going to first arrange around him as though he is already placed in the slot second from the left:

___ × _◇_ × ___ × ___

Now, with the king of diamonds already placed, I can simply arrange the other 3 cards around him:

_3_ × _◇_ × _2_ × _1_

. . . and multiply: 3 × 2 × 1 = 6. If the king of diamonds is in the second slot, there are 6 ways the other cards can be arranged around him.

Now I assign the king of diamonds to the third slot:

___ × ___ × _◇_ × ___

. . . and arrange around him:

_3_ × _2_ × _◇_ × _1_

Then, again, I multiply: 3 × 2 × 1 = 6. There are 6 ways the cards can be arranged when the king of diamonds is in the third slot.

If I total up all my "suboptions," 6 + 6 = ⏭12⏮, I find that there are 12 ways the playing cards can be arranged.

Sequences: Patterns, Arithmetic Sequences, and Geometric Sequences

WHAT YOU NEED TO KNOW

Before we get into more mathematical sequences, let's talk about patterns. Pattern problems sometimes use numbers and sometimes use rows of different dingbats. Either way, the sequence is always going to make up the pattern, which is always going to repeat itself over and over. The trick is to figure out exactly how many numbers or dingbats appear in a single cycle of the pattern before it repeats itself. You'll usually do this by completing the pattern according to the given directions.

Invariably, the test maker doesn't ask you to find the third digit or dingbat in the sequence. Too easy! You usually have to find the 52nd term or the 74th term or something equally difficult—and potentially time consuming if you were to write the whole thing out. Fortunately, you don't have to write the whole thing out. Instead, we're going to take a shortcut, get all old school, and use long division to find whatever term we need.

Say we're asked to find the 62nd term of the sequence AQMEAQME—we can see the basic loop is 4 terms long. All we do is divide 62 by 4. We don't want to use a calculator for this because we really need the remainder, which calculators don't provide.

$$\begin{array}{r} 15 \\ 4\overline{\smash{\big)}62} \\ -4 \\ \hline 22 \\ -20 \\ \hline 2 \end{array} \text{R}\boxed{2}$$

how many times
the pattern repeats

\# of terms in → the loop

how many extra terms into the loop the complete sequence goes

Now, what that division problem tells us is that when we get to the 62nd term the basic loop of 4 will have repeated itself 15 times with a remainder of 2. The remainder gives us all the info—the loop repeats 15 times with *2 extra*. All we do is go to the beginning of our pattern, count 2 over, and voilà! We have our answer: Q.

Other pattern questions are simpler (because they have to be), as they require that you actually solve for the fifth or sixth term. Sometimes you just need to find that term; other times you use the term you've found to find some other information, like the value of a variable embedded within it (we'll discuss this more in the examples of How They Ask the Questions).

Arithmetic Sequences

An arithmetic sequence is just a sequence created by starting with some term and then adding the same number to the preceding term over and over and over. For example, you can start with 5 and then add 4: 5, 9, 13, 17, 21, 25, 29, ... It's actually a good idea to recognize the formula for finding "the *n*th" term of an arithmetic sequence:

$$\text{term } n = \text{first term} + (n-1)\, d$$

where d is the number added each time

If I wanted to find the 7th term in that sequence, I'd write

$$\begin{aligned} \text{the 7}^{th} \text{ term} &= 5 + (7-1)4 \\ &= 5 + 6 \cdot 4 \\ &= 5 + 24 \\ &= 29 \end{aligned}$$

Geometric Sequences

Rather than add the same term over and over to form a sequence, geometric sequences multiply by the same term. Forget that they're called "geometric"; they're just repeated multiplication. For example, if we start with 5 and multiply by 4, we have this sequence:

5, 20, 80, 320, 1280, 5120 ....

Now, because we're exponent experts, we know that an exponent is the tool we need to multiply the same thing over and over and over. So yes, there is an exponent in this formula, but don't let it scare you.

$$\text{term } n = \text{first term} \times (d)^{n-1}$$

where d is the number by which each term is being multiplied.

Let's use that sequence that starts with 5 and multiplies by 4 and find its 7th term:

$$7^{\text{th}} \text{ term} = 5 \times (4)^{7-1}$$
$$= 5 \times 4^6$$
$$= 5 \times 4096$$
$$= \boxed{20,480}$$

HOW THEY ASK THE QUESTIONS

Build-It-Yourself Sequences

In these sequence problems, you actually need to write out the work to find the answer. They're formula-free.

EXAMPLE 1: LEVEL 1

180, 60, 20 . . .

A sequence begins as shown above. If each term is $\frac{1}{3}$ of the preceding term, what is the sixth term of the sequence?

There are no fancy sequence rules to use here; we're just going to keep finding $\frac{1}{3}$ of the preceding term until we find the sixth. The thing is, because our next term, made from $20 \times \frac{1}{3}$, is already a fraction, I'm just going to keep multiplying the denominator of each term by 3 and then reduce at the end (if I have to).

$$180, \ 60, \ 20, \ \frac{20}{3}, \ \frac{20}{6}, \ \boxed{\frac{20}{9}}$$

Turns out that $\frac{20}{9}$ is already reduced, so we're in good shape.

You'll see this problem over and over; you'll be given the start of a sequence and then be told the operation to use to arrive at the next term. Sometimes it's just adding; sometimes you multiply, then add something. Sometimes they ask you to find the nth term; other times it's the first term that's odd or a fraction or negative. The problems are all basically the same: they define the process and you do it.

EXAMPLE 2: LEVEL 2
The first term of a sequence is *e*. Each term thereafter is 4 times the preceding term. The sum of the first 4 terms is 1,615. What is the value of *e*?

So, it's scarier now because there are variables involved. Really though, we just want to write out the first 4 terms of the sequence in terms of *e*: *e*, 4*e*, 16*e*, 64*e*—then add them all up and set them equal to 1,615. Piece of cake.

$$e + 4e + 16e + 64e = 1615$$
$$85e = 1615$$
$$\boxed{e = 19}$$

Finding the Bazillionth Term in a Repeating Sequence

Everyone knows this classic "tricky" problem. If you know what you're doing, you're in great shape; if you don't, forget it. Who has time to write out 103— or however many your asked for—terms?

EXAMPLE 1: LEVEL 3

7, 12, −12 . . .

The sequence above is formed by starting with 7, adding 5 to the previous term to create each even-numbered term, and multiplying the previous term by −1 to create each odd-numbered term. What is the 87th term in the sequence?

First, an "even-numbered term" refers to the second, fourth, sixth (and so on) terms in the sequence. That's often a point of confusion. Now, obviously we're not going to write out that pattern to the 87th term; it would eat valuable minutes.

Instead, first we need to find the full pattern. Let's start filling in the sequence. We're starting at an even-numbered term, so we add 5 to the previous term . . .

7, 12, −12 , −7

Now, multiply −7 by −1 . . .

7, 12, −12 , −7

Now add 5 . . .

7, 12, −12 , −7 , 7 , 12

Multiply by −1 (and so on)

7, 12, −12 , −7 , 7 , 12 , −12 , −7 , 7 , 12 , −12

OK, at this point we should be able to see the repetition in the pattern. Our pattern repeats itself every 4 terms:

$\left[7, 12, -12 , -7 \right]$ 7, 12, −12 , −7 , 7 , 12 , −12

In other words, once those 4 terms are written out, we go back to the beginning and start writing out the pattern again, over and over and over.

The number of terms in the pattern is the key to the problem. Instead of writing out the pattern up to 87 terms, we're going to use old-school long division to get our answer. We're going to divide the 87 terms by 4, the number of terms in the pattern.

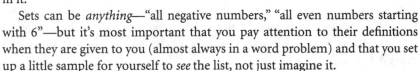

See how I left the remainder? That's the trick. What that division problem tells us is that a pattern of 4 terms will have to be written down in its entirety 21 times *plus* an extra 3 terms to get 87.

All we do is start at the beginning of the pattern, count over 3, and the third term will be the 87th term. In this case, it's -12.

Sets: Elements, Union, and Intersection

WHAT YOU NEED TO KNOW

A set is a just a group of numbers listed between curly brackets that are given a name like Set S or Set B. They can be named anything. Sets can be composed of seemingly random numbers, like "Set S contains the numbers 5, 7, 8, 14, 16," which is written {5, 7, 8, 14, 16}. Or the set could be defined as "Set B contains all real numbers," which you'd write as {R}, because *every* number is included in it.

Sets can be *anything*—"all negative numbers," "all even numbers starting with 6"—but it's most important that you pay attention to their definitions when they are given to you (almost always in a word problem) and that you set up a little sample for yourself to *see* the list, not just imagine it.

Each member of a set, every number on the list, is called an *element*.

Union and Intersection

The *union* of 2 sets is basically just what it sounds like: a new set that includes every element of both original sets—you're just slamming the 2 sets together, basically, but you need to list each element only once. (That means if 4 is in both sets, write it only once in your union set.)

The *intersection* of 2 sets is also a new set—a new list of numbers that includes only the common elements in both sets. Again, each element is written down only *once*.

HOW THEY ASK THE QUESTIONS

Sets questions are relatively easy, provided you know the rules. In fact, generally, sets questions either are extremely easy or appear at the very end of a math section. There are 2 typical types of set problems: those in which the set is described in words and those in which the set is written out, by saying something like "Set M = {1, 2, 3}." The difficulty level is ratcheted up simply by putting in an easily overlooked detail.

EXAMPLE 1: LEVEL 2
If set E = {2, 4, 6, 8, 10, 12} and set T = {2, 3, 4, 5, 6, 7, 9, 10}, how many members do sets E and T have in common?

This is really just a matter of counting how many members match: they each have a 2, they each have a 4, they each have a 6, and they each have a 10. That's it—they have 4 common members. (Just don't count everything twice and say that there are 8. . . .)

EXAMPLE 2: LEVEL 3
If B is the set of all integers that can be written in the form $6x + 4$, where x is an integer, which of the following is in set B?

(A) 18
(B) 24
(C) 33
(D) 44
(E) 52

This question is saying, in English: we've got a set B, and in order to be a number in that set, you've got be the result when someone multiplies something by 6 and then adds 4. For example, let's look at answer A, 18. Is it true, if we set up the equation $18 = 6x + 4$, that the x value will be an integer? If so, it's in set B. Let's see:

$$18 = 6x + 4$$
$$14 = 6x$$
$$\frac{14}{6} = x$$
$$\frac{7}{3} = x \leftarrow \text{not an integer, so it's not in set B}$$

Keep working through these, testing them all in the same way. When you get to answer E, you'll have it:

$$52 = 6x + 4$$
$$48 = 6x$$
$$\boxed{8 = x} \text{ integer } \checkmark$$

Visualizing Forms, Paths, and Symmetry

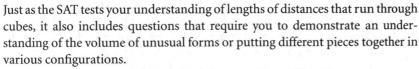

Visualizing Forms

Just as the SAT tests your understanding of lengths of distances that run through cubes, it also includes questions that require you to demonstrate an understanding of the volume of unusual forms or putting different pieces together in various configurations.

This may mean recognizing what a box would look like if it were cut on its seams and flattened out. When flattened, this box

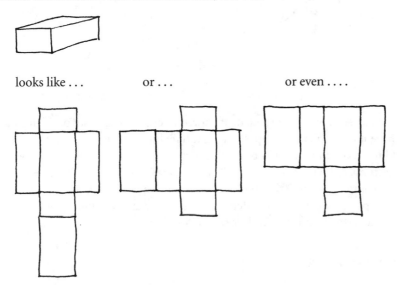

looks like . . .   or . . .   or even . . . .

Or visualizing forms may mean identifying how many different lines can be pulled *through* an unusual form, like a giant diamond.

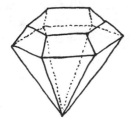

For example, here are some of the lines that can connect vertices in that diamond:

There is a particular kind of learning aptitude required to solve these problems; students who are very visually oriented usually find such problems to be less challenging.

The big tip would be to decide on an anchoring point in the drawing off of which you base all of your conclusions. For example, I imagined, in that box illustration, what the base of the box looked like (a rectangle already lying flat on the floor) and then added each piece around it as I unfolded the box in my head. And to place those vertical strings inside the diamond, I focused on the top facet and worked my way clockwise around the vertices.

In fact, there are more connections within that diamond:

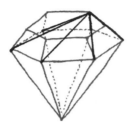

The pattern could be repeated, anchored at each vertex. The problem may be made more difficult by stipulating that only lines that go *through* the figure (not lines that would lie in a plane/facet) count. Or perhaps they would want connections *only* along planes. The SAT rules make up half the challenge.

Make sure you know that the *vertex* is the place where 2 *lines* intersect. An *edge* is a place where 2 *planes* intersect (they're basically the lines that are connecting a vertex to another in the original form).

This anchoring strategy can be used to connect vertices in complex figures, too.

Paths on a Grid

For some reason, measuring the lengths of the paths on a grid and the number of possible paths between 2 points on a grid seem to pop up on the SAT. Grid problems are pretty simple—just *stay on the grid*. The trick is to keep track of how many paths you've counted from the starting point to another point; again, that's all about anchoring yourself and counting systematically—including 1 square at a time—when necessary. We'll see a problem that covers this in the examples of How They Ask The Questions.

Symmetry

Symmetry is, well, the state of being symmetrical. Forms are symmetrical when they can be folded in half on top of themselves and all of the points on 1 side will line up perfectly with all the points on the other side. Take the letter H, for example. An H is symmetrical:

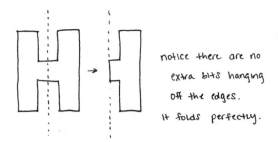

notice there are no
extra bits hanging
off the edges.
It folds perfectly.

Understanding and Using Visualization

EXAMPLE 1: LEVEL 3
Which of the following forms can be created using puzzle pieces A, B, or C?

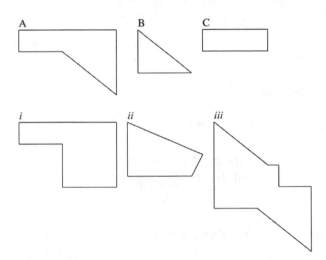

For each of the figures you'll want to identify an anchor piece and see if you can add other pieces around it to form the final shape. For example, in figure *i*, you can probably see shape A in there. It will be easiest to actually draw in the anchor shape you can immediately identify and go from there. Your page should look something like this when you're done:

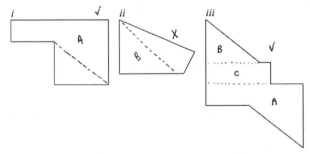

So the choice that includes answers *i* and *iii* is correct.

Grids

EXAMPLE 1: LEVEL 1

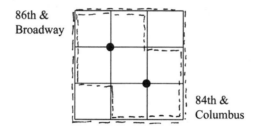

86th &
Broadway

84th &
Columbus

Jenn wants to walk from 86th Street and Broadway to 84th Street and Columbus, shown on the map. Two intersections are closed between these points, as indicated by the dots on the map. How many routes can Jenn take to 84th and Columbus?

Just eliminate, step by step by step. This is really just a question of organization.

86th &
Broadway

84th &
Columbus

When your grid is symmetrical like this, I recommend exhausting all of your options on 1 side of the grid and then multiplying by 2. It's so easy to lose count, even on small problems. So $2 \times 2 = \boxed{4 \text{ routes}}$.

Understanding and Using Symmetry

EXAMPLE 1: LEVEL 3

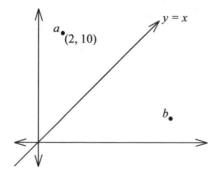

In the figure above, points a and b are symmetrical about the line $y = x$. What are the coordinates of point b?

This question is designed using $y = x$ for a reason. "Symmetrical about the line $y = x$" tells us that they're both equidistant from that line. Conveniently, $y = x$ happens to split that first quadrant right up the middle, too.

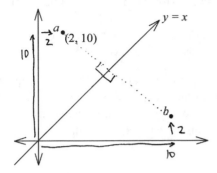

So the coordinates for point b are $\boxed{(10, 2)}$.

Organizing Schedules, Times, and Time Zones

WHAT YOU NEED TO KNOW

There's not much to this, really. It's more a matter of making sure you're clear on how time zones work, and hours and minutes—basics.

Schedules and Times

So here it is, short and sweet: because an hour has 60 minutes, you'll see questions about hours in fractional form (for example, $1\frac{1}{2}$-hour games, $\frac{3}{4}$-hour bike trips, $\frac{4}{5}$ hourly naps). Tricky. Just make sure to keep your conversions proportional to 60 minutes. Let's see how many minutes long a $\frac{4}{5}$-hour nap is.

$$\frac{4}{5} = \frac{x}{60}$$

$$5x = 240$$

$$x = 48 \leftarrow 4/5 \text{ of an hour is } 48 \text{ minutes}$$

Time Zones

You'll probably find that it's easiest to keep track of time zones by writing out a list of corresponding times. I know, many people, particularly the well-traveled, can do this in their heads. However, drawing up a little sketch of parallel times can be helpful.

EXAMPLE 1: LEVEL 4

Jane flies from Cairo to Rio de Janeiro; Cairo's time is always 4 hours later than Rio's. Jane's flight takes off at 9 PM and arrives in Rio at 3 AM Leo takes the returning flight from Rio to Cairo. If Leo's flight leaves one hour after Jane's flight arrives, what time will he arrive in Cairo?

Believe me, I know the following chart looks tedious, but it's also very quick to make and can prevent mistakes that often happen when students add and subtract times. Frankly, if you don't need to fill in extra info (there is extra info in there), don't feel like you have to. It's just easy to *see*, that's all.

```
Rio            Cairo

5  pm          9  pm  ← jane takes off
6              10
7              11
8              12 am
9              1
10             2
11             3
12 am          4
1              5
2              6
3              7   ← jane arrives
4              8   ← leo departs
               9
               10
               11
               12 pm
               1
               2
               3
               4
               5
               6   ← leo arrives
```

What I did here was just make a list of times next to each other, starting at 9 PM Cairo time and running Rio time next to it. Because we're given Jane's trip schedule in both time zones, I found that if she arrives at 3 AM Rio time, it's 7 AM in Cairo (which you could also find by adding).

So Leo's plane takes off an hour later (at 4 AM Rio time), which is 8 AM Cairo time. We can see from the chart that Jane's flight was 10 hours long, so this means that Leo's flight will be 10 hours long, as well. We add those 10 hours to 8 AM and find he has a 6 PM arrival time.

EXAMPLE 2: LEVEL 3

A typical day at Camp Summer includes meals, activities, classes, and free time. Each meal is 40 minutes, each activity is $1\frac{1}{2}$ hours, each class is 2 hours, and free time blocks are 1 hour long. What time does the first meal of the day begin?

Slot	Begin	End
Meal		
Class		
Free time		
Meal		
Activity		
Class		
Meal		
Free time		
Activity		7:30 PM

This is as tedious as they come; if you see a problem like this, skip it and come back to it, particularly if you're someone who has a tough time finishing sections. This thing will eat at least a minute or more.

Also, as you work backward, fill in only 1 column, because 1 thing begins as another ends:

Slot	Begin	End
Meal	8:30 am	
Class	9:10 am	
Free time	11:10 am	
Meal	12:10 pm	
Activity	12:50 pm	
Class	2:20 pm	
Meal	4:20 pm	
Free time	5:00 pm	
Activity	6:00 pm	7:30 PM

So we can see that the first meal of the day begins at 8:30 AM.

Logic

WHAT YOU NEED TO KNOW

The logic questions on the SAT are very simple—you won't need to be creating charts and eliminating and guessing as if you were taking the LSAT to get into law school. These are very basic "get a couple of facts and draw a conclusion" questions. In fact, there's not much strategy here.

EXAMPLE 1: LEVEL 3

If all trees over 12 feet tall on the Smiths' property must be spruce trees, which of the following must be true?

(A)   No tree on the Smiths' property over 12 feet tall is a pine tree.

(B)   There is 1 spruce tree under 12 feet tall on the Smiths' property.

(C)   Every tree on the Smiths' property is a spruce tree.

(D)   All trees not on the Smiths' property are under 12 feet tall.

(E)   All trees over 12 feet tall must be on the Smiths' property.

It makes the most sense to me to systematically eliminate answer choices that can't possibly be correct. Let's look through the answer choices:

(A)   No tree on the Smiths' property over 12 feet tall is a pine tree.

That's true, because *every* tree *over* 12 feet on the Smiths' property *must be* a spruce.

(B)   There is 1 spruce tree under twelve feet tall on the Smiths' property.

No, there are *no* spruce trees under 12 feet tall on the Smiths' property.

(C)   Every tree on the Smiths' property is a spruce tree.

No, it didn't say that they didn't have shorter trees, just that the shorter trees aren't spruces.

(D)   All trees not on the Smiths' property are under 12 feet tall.

No again. We don't know anything about any of the other trees worldwide.

(E)   All trees over 12 feet tall must be on the Smiths' property.

No. Think about that. That would mean every tall tree on Earth is at the Smiths' house. Forget it.

Just eliminate 1 by 1 and be sure you stop and think about what each statement is saying. Sometimes creating a really exaggerated explanation (like "every tree on Earth") can help you clarify what you're talking about. So here the answer is A.

EXAMPLE 2: LEVEL 3

All numbers that are divisible by both 3 and 5 are divisible by 10.

Which of the following numbers disproves the statement above?

(A)   15
(B)   20
(C)   30
(D)   35
(E)   60

First, you can *only* use answer choices that are divisible by 3 and 5—that's the stipulation. The answer choice *must be* divisible by 3 and 5 *and* must not be divisible by 10. Right off the bat that eliminates B, 20, and D, 35. Now, both C, 30, and E, 60, are divisible by 3 and 5, but they're both also divisible by 10. Only A, 15, is a multiple of both 3 and 5 *and* is not divisible by 10, so that's our answer.

You could consider data analysis problems to be the enrichment problems on the test—it often feels like the test has been peppered with them just to change gears and keep you one your toes. You'll likely only see 3 or 4 of these types of problems on any given test, as the skills they test are so varied and difficult to define. Again, these problems are often deceptively simple, so be disciplined and keep your energy up while you work on them. These are all about attitude; make sure you've got a good one!

NEXT STEPS

So, by this point you've pored over the Critical Reading strategies, learned esoteric grammar rules, and reviewed how to write a solid essay. You've spent hours discovering new ways to attack algebra word problems and relearned the Pythagorean Theorem. Now what?

Now it's time to practice. First, you should pick up a free copy of the most recent sample SAT in your guidance counselor's office. You can also find a copy of it on The College Board's website, www.collegeboard.com. The sample SAT includes an answer key, so you can check your responses and calculate your score. Use the sample test as a way to diagnose which parts of the test are still giving you trouble, and review the relevant lessons in this book to brush up. I also recommend completing as many of the sample tests in The College Board's book *The Official SAT Study Guide* as you can; there's no better source of sample material than the company that produces the test.

It makes sense to practice writing essays under timed conditions. Consider writing a couple of essays and sharing them with your English teacher, if that's not already part of your curriculum.

Also, maintain your vocabulary! Make a conscious effort to continually build your personal word bank by reading daily and creating flash cards.

Finally, keep learning and building skills and strategies. You can check out my website, www.elizabethonline.com, for even more information about the SAT, obscure problem styles, solutions to tricky questions in *The Official SAT Study Guide*, and other resources. You can also reach me—and a network of other great tutors—through my website.

That's it! Remember what I told you at the very beginning of this book: What's most important is that you believe you can do well on this test. Deep breath. You can do it.

INDEX

Page numbers in italics indicate a representation.